D1570998

Advanced Computer System Design

Advanced Computer System Design

Edited by

George W. Zobrist
University of Missouri at Rolla

Kallol Bagchi
Florida Atlantic University at Boca Raton

and

Kishor Trivedi
Duke University
Durham, North Carolina

Gordon and Breach Science Publishers

Australia   Canada   China   France   Germany   India   Japan   Luxembourg
Malaysia   The Netherlands   Russia   Singapore   Switzerland

Copyright © 1998 OPA (Overseas Publishers Association) N.V. Published by license under the Gordon and Breach Science Publishers imprint.

Amsteldijk 166
1st Floor
1079 LH Amsterdam
The Netherlands

British Library Cataloguing in Publication Data

Advanced computer system design
   1. System design
   I. Zobrist, George W. (George Winston), 1934- II. Bagchi,
   Kallol III. Trivedi, Kishor Shridharbhai
   004.2'1

   ISBN 90-5699-634-7

This book is dedicated to
all the people
who helped make it a success

CONTENTS

EDITORS' PREFACE

Performance modeling and simulation have been used extensively in computer and communication system design for some time. This book makes the argument that this topic has become a central issue in computer science and engineering research and should be considered seriously. Its object is to lead researchers, practitioners and students involved in this discipline. Distinctive in many ways, it provides tutorials and surveys on important topics, relates new research results that should be of interest to all working in the field and covers a broad area in the process. Each chapter presents background, describes and analyzes important work in the field and provides direction to the reader on future work and further readings. The volume can be used as a reference book by all associated with computer science and engineering. Our hope is that this set of carefully selected papers will be of interest to all computer scientists and engineers.

This book deals primarily with systems and applications as related to advanced computer system design. A previously published accompanying volume, *Advanced Computer Performance Modeling and Simulation* (Gordon and Breach, 1998), describes theory, tools and techniques of advanced computer system design.

The book begins with a chapter on performance modeling of a multi-threaded processor spectrum. This chapter presents particularly simple forms of DT and CT models of multithreaded processor systems. These models are validated against previously published results; corresponding analytic models for the general case of multithreaded are presented and used to explore and assess performance potential of multithreading. The conclusion reached is that the single thread performance can be significantly boosted with a second thread, under almost all input conditions of interest.

Chapters 2–5 deal with various aspects of performance prediction. The second chapter discusses an approach based on an extended task graph model of a parallel system. Task precedence constraints in synchronization are explicitly modeled by an acyclic graph whose nodes represent tasks and management communication between tasks. The modeling approach for programs and architectures in detail are described and compared to other approaches developed for the same purposes. There are also details of the analytical technique as implemented in ES, which was evaluated using both simulation and real systems.

Chapter 3 covers performance modeling through functional algorithm simulation. A fundamental problem in parallel processing is to identify sources of performance, degradation and parallel applications, both quantitatively and qualitatively. A functional algorithm simulation is presented that is an approximate simulation scheme enabling one to model and study parallel executions of much larger problem sizes and more processors than those reported so far in a workstation environment. It also allows collection of detailed information characterizing parallel executions on various message passing architectures.

The fourth chapter highlights Networks of Workstations (NOW), since they have become important distributed platforms for large-scale scientific computations. In practice, a NOW system is heterogeneous in timesharing. Two classes of methods have been used for parallel computing performance studies: experimental methods that employ simulation tools, and analytical models that provide relatively quick estimates of performance but often lack sufficient accuracy due to unrealistic assumptions. This chapter presents a prediction method in its implementation for parallel computing on heterogeneous NOW, where analytical models, experimental techniques and software are integrated. Important static and dynamic execution data are prepared for simulation and performance analyses.

Trace transformation as a tool for incremental simulation of parallel program execution on NOW is covered in the next chapter (chapter 5). The performance of program execution on NOW is dictated by various and complex interactions of the hardware, communication library, systems software and applications. The need for tools that give quick and reasonably accurate estimates for effected changes in the institutional environment on application performance is more important now than ever before, due to the growing number of parallel applications and diverse execution environments. The incremental trace transformation technique discussed here simply provides a convenient means of gauging the impact of changes in the execution environment for one instance of the problem size and number of processing nodes.

Chapters 6–8 deal with performance data and evaluation for various machine architectures. Chapter 6 details cache-only memory architecture and discusses the mean value analysis model and modifications adopted to analyze hierarchical 3-level COMA systems with different configurations. It concludes with optimal configurations of COMA systems analyzed for a variety of parameter settings.

Use of private cache memories in multiprocessors with common memory introduces the data coherence problem (chapter 7). This is a useful and flexible model to implement analytically solvable queueing networks for evaluating the system using different workloads—using a lower computational time than required with simulation techniques.

The eighth chapter describes the development of a data parallel simulation system, together with the creation of a new parallel programming language—

Parallaxis. This language is machine independent among SIMD systems. The author believes this approach has significant advantages in parallel programming of complex tasks and especially in teaching parallel concepts.

Chapters 9 and 10 deal with theoretical concepts related to real-time systems design and best-case analysis of systems with global spares. Chapter 9 discusses the performance model derivation from the systems design description and shows that this task can be automated. In chapter 10, basically tutorial in nature, the case analysis of systems with global spares is analyzed. A global spare is a module that can replace any failed module in the system performing an equivalent function. Analysis has led to an efficient algorithm with which to numerically evaluate such systems in the best case.

Markov Renewal Theory as applied to performability evaluation is handled in chapter 11. Performability measures provide better insight into the behavior of fault-tolerant systems. Performability analysis of real systems with nondeterministic components and/or environmental characteristics results in stochastic modeling problems. Several techniques for solving these problems for transient and steady-state measures were proposed and later combined under the framework of Markov reward models. This chapter introduces basic terminology associated with the theory, including concepts and distinction between semi-Markov process and Markov regenerative process. Basic solution techniques for stochastic process with embedded Markov renewal sequences are presented, and examples are offered to illustrate the methodology associated with the semi-Markov and Markov regenerative processes.

The next chapter covers modeling and distributed system simulation techniques for synthetic training environments (chapter 12). Synthetic training environments can be used to teach people to function within complex systems without the real world limitations of safety, costs, training areas or personnel. Successful application of a simulation training tool is ModSAF, built by Loral Advanced Distributed Simulation. It is a distributed interactive simulation used for military training and combat doctrine development.

The evaluation of the performance of a computer concept/technology in the real world is needed for future system design. The final chapter details the modeling of the adoption and diffusion of CASE. For some time, CASE has created controversies regarding its success as an information technology tool. The author illustrates, on the basis of empirical data, that CASE has not emerged as successfully as was assumed in the computer and information industrial arena. He shows how the adoption and diffusion of CASE can be modeled with S-curve based models.

ACKNOWLEDGMENTS

Dr. Carey Williamson of the University of Saskatchewan in Canada and Prof. Jason Lin of National Chiao Tung University in Taiwan deserve special mention for providing help with L^{A}T$_E$X script, which many authors used in preparing final versions of their chapters. We are indebted to Dr. Ana Pont of Universidad Politecnica de Valencia in Spain for lending others her Microsoft Word script for this purpose.

Many authors provided feedback for improving the structure of the book. Thanks are due to all of them. We are grateful to the reviewers, editorial board members and all the contributors, who deserve a great deal more than acknowledgment. Without their help, patience and cooperation, this book would not have been possible. We are indebted to Tara Lynch and Frank Cerra for their help in various stages of the book.

CONTRIBUTORS

Douglas M. Blough, Department of Electrical and Computer Engineering, University of California, Irvine, California 92717 USA email: blough@ece.uci.edu

David B. Cavitt, Department of Computer Science, Old Dominion University, Norfolk, Virginia 23529-0162 USA email: cavitt@cs.odu.edu

William Price Dawkins, ViaSat, Inc., 2290 Cosmos Court, Carlsbad, California 92009-1595 USA email: bdawkins@viasat.cam

Marios D. Dikaiakos, Department of Computer Science, University of Cyprus, Kallipoleos 75, POB 537, 1678 Nicosia, Cyprus email: mdd@turing.cs.ucy.ac.cy http://zeus.cc.ucy.ac.cy/ucy/cs/mdd/

Pradeep K. Dubey, IBM T. J. Watson Research Center, J1-P05, 30 Saw Mill River Road, Hawthorne, New York 10532 USA email: pradeep@watson.ibm.com

Ricardo Messias Fricks, Center for Advanced Computing and Communication, Department of Electrical and Computing Engineering, Duke University, Durham, North Carolina 27708-0291 USA email: fricks@ee.duke.edu

José A. Gil, Departamento de Ingenieria de Sistemas, Computadores y Automatica, Universidad Politecnica de Valencia, Camino de Vera s/n, 46022 Valencia, Spain email: jagil@aii.upv.es

Ting-Li Hu, Department of Electrical Engineering, The University of Akron, Akron, Ohio 44325-3904 USA

Arvind Krishna, IBM T. J. Watson Research Center, J1-P05, 30 Saw Mill River Road, Hawthorne, New York 10532 USA

Albert Llamosí, Departamento d'Enginyeria Informatica, Universitat Rovira i Virgili, Calle de 1''Escorxador s/n, 43003 Tarragona, Spain email: allamosi@etse.urv.es

Kurt J. Maly, Department of Computer Science, Old Dominion University, Norfolk, Virginia 23592 USA email: maly@cs.odu.edu

C. Michael Overstreet, Department of Computer Science, Old Dominion University, Norfolk, Virginia 23592 USA

Ana Pont, Departamento de Ingenieria de Sistemas, Computadores y Automatica, Universidad Politecnica de Valencia, Camino de Vera s/n, 46022 Valencia, Spain email: apont@aii.upv.es

Ramon Puigjaner, Faculty of Computer Science, Universitat de les Illes Balears, Campus Universitari, Cra. de Valldemossa km 7.5, 07071 Palma de Mallorca, Spain email: putxi@ps.uib.es

Antonio Puliafito, Istituto di Informaticae Telecomunicazioni, University of Catania, Viale Andrea Doria 6, 95125 Catania, Italy email: ap@iit.unicet.it

Anne Rogers, Department of Computer Science, Princeton University, Princeton, New Jersey 08544 USA

Sekhar R. Sarukkai, Future Systems Department, HP Labs, 1501 Page Mill Road, MS 3U6, Palo Alto, California 94304-1126 USA email: sekhar@cello.hpl.hp.com

Fadi N. Sibai, Intel Corporation, 2200 Mission College Boulevard, Santa Clara, California 95052-8119 USA email: sibai@uakron.edu

James B. Sinclair, Department of Electrical and Computer Engineering, MS 366, Rice University, Houston, Texas 77251-1892 USA email: bs@rice.edu

Yongsheng Song, High Performance Computing and Software Laboratory, University of Texas at San Antonio, Texas 78249 USA

Mark S. Squillante, IBM T. J. Watson Research Center, J1-P05, 30 Saw Mill River Road, Hawthorne, New York 10532 USA

Kenneth Steiglitz, Department of Computer Science, Princeton University, Princeton, New Jersey 08544 USA

Miklós Telek, Department of Telecommunications, Technical University of Budapest, Sztoczek u. 2 1111, Budapest, Hungary email: telek@hit.bme.hu

Meng-Lai Yin, Hughes Aircraft Company, 1801 Hughes Drive, Fullerton, California 92633-2100 USA

Xiaodong Zhang, High Performance Computing and Software Laboratory, University of Texas at San Antonio, San Antonio, Texas 78249 USA email: zhang@ringer.cs.utsa.edu

Editorial Board

Thomas Bräunl, Universitat Stuttgart IPVR, Bretwiesenstrasse 20–22, D-70565 Stuttgart, Germany email: braunl@informatik.uni-stuttgart.de http://URL.informatik.unistuttgart.de/ipvr/bv/braunl

Jean Walrand, Department of EECS, Cory Hall, University of California, Berkeley, California, 94720-1770 USA http://www.eecs.berkeley.edu/~wlr

Editors

Kallol Bagchi, Department of DIS/Business, Florida Atlantic University, Boca Raton, Florida 33431 USA email: kbag@fauvms.acc.fau.edu

Kishor Trivedi, Center for Advanced Computing and Communication, Department of Electrical and Computing Engineering, Duke University, Durham, North Carolina 27708-0291 USA email: kst@ee.duke.edu

George W. Zobrist, Department of Computer Science, University of Missouri–Rolla, 1870 Miner Circle, Rolla, Missouri 65409-0350 USA email: zobrist@umr.edu

CHAPTER 1

Performance Modeling of a Multithreaded Processor Spectrum

P.K. Dubey, A. Krishna, M.S. Squillante

1.1. INTRODUCTION

Processor performance has been increasing at the rate of approximately 50% per year, while memory access times have been only improving 5–10% a year. As a result, the latency of cache misses in terms of processor cycles is increasing rapidly. Moreover, cache miss latencies are becoming a larger fraction of overall processor performance due to the increase in the instruction and data bandwidths required to support higher degrees of instruction-level parallelism. The current trend towards deeper pipelines, also known as *superpipelines* (capable, in principle, of providing higher clock rates), is leading to more frequent long interlock delays. Processor utilization suffers due to cycles during which a processor stage sits idle, waiting for its operands. These operand request delays arise out of instances such as interlocks in pipelined processors due to inter-stage dependencies, and remote memory accesses due to cache misses.

There are two alternatives available to deal with operand request delays such as those due to cache misses and pipeline interlocks. One approach is to *reduce* these delays and hence their performance impact.

The authors are with the IBM Research Division, T. J. Watson Research Center, Yorktown Heights, NY 10598 and can be reached via e-mail at {pradeep,krishna,mss}@watson.ibm.com

1

Strategies such as branch prediction, second-level caches, and prefetching of data and instructions have been used to reduce the average cache miss and branch related delays. An alternative approach is to hide or *tolerate* these delays. This is normally done by switching the execution to a sequence of instructions that are data-and-control-independent of the previous instruction sequence which is blocked due to the cache miss, or a pipeline interlock. In other words, the processor utilization is enhanced by sharing it with multiple independent instruction *threads*. In principle, this concept is similar to that of multiprogramming and time-sharing, where disk I/O or keyboard latencies were tolerated by sharing the resources among multiple programs or multiple users, respectively. This concept was extended by Flynn and Podvin[1] to a *shared resource multiprocessor* architecture proposal in which several skeleton processors share the common ALU pipeline resource. This form of multithreading where a certain resource is shared in time by multiple threads can be termed a *temporal* form of multithreading. An alternate form of multithreading simultaneously executes the independent threads on separate resources to further exploit the parallelism. This alternate form of multithreading can be termed *spatial*[2] multithreading. The models presented here deal solely with the temporally multithreaded architectures, and the word multithreading is used only in the specific context of temporal multithreading.

Several temporally multithreaded architectures have been proposed. Byrd and Holliday[3] provide a recent survey of such architectures. Threads for these architectures are generated statically or dynamically. These threads come from a wide variety of sources. At the coarsest level, threads may represent independent tasks or processes that run together in a certain application environment, whereas at finer levels, threads can be derived from concurrently executable sections of a certain program. Multithreaded machines maintain hardware contexts of several independent instruction threads. The execution control switches between these threads either on every instruction[1,4-8] or every cache miss[9,10] or every remote memory[11,12] reference. Roughly speaking, such architectures can be subdivided into two categories on the basis of the nature of the *trigger* event, the event that causes a context switch. Architectures in the first category switch threads on every operation that causes a delay, including short data and control interlock delays. The machines in this category can be referred to as *small latency* multithreaded machines. On the other hand, architectures in the second category are characterized by the switching of processor control among independent threads only on remote memory references, whose delays are typically much longer than those experienced in small latency machines. In fact, large cache-miss delays on the order of hundreds of processor cycles are not uncommon[10] for processors that are part of a large-scale multiprocessor system. The machines in this category can be referred to as *large latency* multithreaded machines.

The class of small latency multithreaded architectures typically have multiple distinct sources of delay (such as instruction dependency, branch delay and multi-cycle execution), each with distinct probabilities and distinct corresponding durations, and negligible delays for switching from one thread to another. The machines in the large latency category, however, can often afford to incur some context-switch overhead. We also make the observation that large latency architectures often incur network delays when responding to a context-switching event, e.g., a cache miss leading to a remote memory[10] access, and hence the latency can have its own architecture-dependent probability distribution.

The primary objective of this chapter is to develop analytic models for a spectrum of multithreaded architectures, ranging from small latency to large latency machines. We formulate discrete-time (DT) and continuous-time (CT) analytic models for this complete multithreading spectrum. Specifically, we present a DT model of small latency machines that allows a bounded general distribution for interlock delays, and a DT model of the full spectrum that addresses the state space explosion problems of this small latency model by assuming a geometric delay distribution. In addition, we present a CT model of the multithreaded processor spectrum that supports phase-type distributions for the model parameters, a distributional assumption that is motivated by their important mathematical properties and by the fact that any real distribution can in principle be represented arbitrarily close by a phase-type distribution. We derive an exact solution for each of these models that can be efficiently computed, yielding closed-form expressions for many model instances.

We are not aware of any previously published work on such general analytic models of the complete spectrum of multithreaded processors. McCrackin[6] presents simulation-based performance estimates for a small latency machine under various parameter distributions, but our methods provide performance statistics in a significantly more efficient manner without any loss of accuracy. A few analytic models of large latency multithreaded machines have also appeared[13,14] in the research literature. Unlike these studies, however, our models support general parameter distributions that make it possible to efficiently compute accurate results for the wide variety of multithreaded system environments without imposing any practical restrictions on the modeling analysis. This is especially important for multithreaded systems because of the architecture-dependent nature of the distribution of operand request delays, as previously noted.

In Section 1.2 we present a particularly simple form of our DT and CT models of multithreaded processor systems, and we validate these models against previously published results. Section 1.3 then provides the corresponding analytic models for the general case of multithreading. In Section 1.4 we use our models to explore and assess the performance potential of multithreading given the current state of processor technology. The final section presents our concluding remarks.

1.2. MODELS AND ANALYSIS

We consider a spectrum of multithreaded processor architectures that switch execution among N identical instruction threads. Each thread alternates between (waiting for and) receiving service at the processor and waiting for outstanding operand requests to be satisfied. Hereafter we use the term *miss* to generally refer to operand requests that cause delays, independent of the cause. The thread service times at the processor including the associated context-switch are given by $\{ S_\ell ; \ell \geq 1 \}$. When the number of *ready* threads $N_r \geq 1$, S_ℓ denotes the time between the $\ell - 1^{\text{st}}$ and ℓ^{th} occurrences of a miss, whereas when N_r becomes 0, S_ℓ denotes the time between the subsequent completion of an outstanding miss and the ℓth miss. The miss processing times are given by $\{ M_\ell ; \ell \geq 1 \}$, where M_ℓ denotes the time to satisfy the ℓth miss. Threads are executed at the processor serially, whereas misses are assumed to be processed in parallel. The times $\{ M_\ell ; \ell \geq 1 \}$ and $\{ S_\ell ; \ell \geq 1 \}$ are assumed to form two independent sequences of i.i.d. $\mathbb{R}^+$-valued r.v.s with distribution functions (d.f.s) $\mathbf{A}(\cdot)$ and $\mathbf{B}(\cdot)$, respectively. Let L be the average delay for satisfying misses, let R be the average processing time between misses, and let C be the average context-switching overhead. $\mathbf{A}(\cdot)$ and $\mathbf{B}(\cdot)$ therefore have means $L < \infty$ and $C + R < \infty$, respectively. We also define $\lambda \equiv 1/L$, $\mu_C \equiv 1/C$ and $\mu_R \equiv 1/R$.

This general multithreaded system is modeled by various DT and CT Markov chains (MC). To elucidate the basic structure of our models, in the remainder of this section we present a mathematical analysis of the models for the case where there is negligible overhead in terms of lost cycles for switching from one thread to another, i.e., $C = 0$. The corresponding DT and CT modeling analyses are developed in turn, which yield closed-form solutions for many instances of the models. We end this section by validating our analytic models. As addressed in Section 1.3, the inclusion of non-zero context-switch overhead follows naturally from the analysis that is presented below.

1.2.1. Discrete-Time Process

We model the system as a DTMC[15,16] $\{X_n, n \geq 0\}$ defined over a finite state space Ω. To simplify the model definition, our attention here is restricted to $\mathbf{B} \equiv \text{geom}(\mu_R)$. This geometric assumption implies that in any clock cycle a thread suffers a miss with probability (w.p.) μ_R. We consider two different assumptions for the miss delays, namely a bounded general d.f. and a geometric d.f..

1.2.1.1. General Miss Delays

The miss delay is bounded by $K - 1$ cycles[17] and has a d.f. defined by the probability vector $(b_1, b_2, \ldots, b_{K-1})$, $L = \sum_{j=1}^{K-1} j b_j$, where b_j is the probability that a miss delay consists of j cycles. The state of this system for the current cycle n, before any scheduling, can be represented by the vector $Y = (y_0, y_1, \ldots, y_{K-1})$ where $y_0 = N_r$, and y_j is 1 if there is a blocked thread that has waited $j - 1$ cycles since its last instruction was scheduled, $1 \leq j < K$, and is 0 otherwise. Since only one of the ready threads is scheduled in every cycle, there can be at most one thread that has waited exactly $j > 0$ cycles since its last scheduling, and hence $\sum_{j=0}^{K-1} y_j = N$. The number of states with exactly m non-zero components y_j, $1 \leq j < K$, is given by $\binom{K-1}{m}$, and thus when $N < K$ the size of the state space is given by $D = \sum_{j=0}^{N} \binom{K-1}{j}$. When $N \geq K$, D is same as that for $N = K - 1$ and is given by 2^{K-1}. The state $(0, y_1, y_2, \ldots, y_{K-1})$ is not possible when $N \geq K$, which implies that $N_r > 0$ always and the system is fully utilized.

Let $Y_0, Y_1, \ldots, Y_{D-1}$ be a lexicographical ordering of the system states. We define

$$\pi(Y_i) \equiv \lim_{n \to \infty} \Pr[X_n = Y_i], \quad 0 \leq i < D, \tag{1}$$

and
$$\boldsymbol{\pi} = [\pi(Y_0), \pi(Y_1), \ldots, \pi(Y_{D-1})]. \tag{2}$$

The limiting probability vector $\boldsymbol{\pi}$ is the stationary distribution for $\{X_n, n \geq 0\}$. Assuming this DTMC to be irreducible and ergodic, its stationary distribution is obtained by solving the global balance equations (GBEs)

$$\boldsymbol{\pi} = \boldsymbol{\pi P} \tag{3}$$

together with
$$\boldsymbol{\pi} \mathbf{e} = 1, \tag{4}$$

where $\mathbf{P}$ is the transition probability matrix for the MC and $\mathbf{e}$ is a column vector of all ones.

The first step in solving the GBEs is to compute the entries of $\mathbf{P}$. To do so, we construct an intermediate state $\bar{Y} = (\bar{y}_0, \bar{y}_1, \ldots, \bar{y}_K)$ for the system immediately after the thread scheduling phase of cycle n, given that the system was in state $Y = (y_0, y_1, \ldots, y_{K-1})$ prior to the scheduling operation. The elements of $\bar{Y}$ can be obtained from Y as

$$\bar{y}_j = \begin{cases} \min(y_{j-1}, 1), & 1 \leq j \leq K, \\ \\ \max(y_0 - 1, 0), & j = 0, \end{cases} \tag{5}$$

where $\sum_{j=0}^{K} \bar{y}_j = N$. Note that $\bar{y}_K = 1$ implies that a thread has waited $K-1$ cycles since its last scheduling, and thus will become ready in the next cycle. Moreover, $\bar{y}_0 = N_r$ and some or all of the remaining $N - N_r$ threads can become ready at the end of the current cycle.

Let $Z = (z_0, z_1, \ldots, z_{K-1})$ represent the state of the system at the start of cycle $n+1$, where the components of Z are defined analogous to those of Y above. The probability of a transition from state Y in cycle n to state Z in the next cycle $n+1$ is given by

$$P(Y, Z) = \left(\binom{\bar{y}_1}{z_1} (\mu_R)^{z_1} (1 - \mu_R)^{\bar{y}_1 - z_1} \right) \prod_{j=2}^{k} \binom{\bar{y}_j}{z_j} q_{j-1}^{\bar{y}_j - z_j} (1 - q_{j-1})^{z_j}, \tag{6}$$

where $\binom{\bar{y}_j}{z_j} = 0$ if $z_j > \bar{y}_j$, and q_j is the probability that a miss requires j cycles to be processed given that it has already taken $j - 1$ cycles. The value of q_j can be computed from the miss delay d.f. as

$$q_j = \frac{b_j}{1 - \sum_{i=1}^{j-1} b_i}, \quad 1 \leq j < K. \tag{7}$$

Once the state transition matrix $\mathbf{P}$ is constructed from Eq. (6), the invariant probability vector $\boldsymbol{\pi}$ is obtained by solving Eqs. (3) and (4) using standard numerical methods. The $\boldsymbol{\pi}$ vector can then be used to compute the processor utilization U as

$$U = 1 - \sum_{Y:y_0=0} \pi(Y) \tag{8}$$

where the summation is over all states with no ready thread.

1.2.1.2. Geometric Miss Delays

The above model can be used to efficiently obtain performance statistics for bounded general miss delay d.f.s, allowing multiple distinct miss delays. However, for systems with a maximum miss delay greater than 15, the size of the state space becomes too large for an efficient solution. We therefore consider in this section our system model under the assumptions $\mathbf{A} \equiv \mathrm{geom}(\lambda)$ and $\mathbf{B} \equiv \mathrm{geom}(\mu_R)$. This yields a significant reduction in the state space size and allows us to derive a recursive expression to solve Eqs. (3) and (4), which imposes no practical restrictions on the model size. More general d.f.s are considered in Section 1.2.2, although similar techniques could be applied to the DT model considered here since there are no important mathematical differences between the corresponding theorems for DTMC.

The states of the MC can be defined by the number of ready threads N_r, as opposed to the detailed state vector of the previous section. An executing thread becomes *blocked* w.p. μ_R. We use Y_r to denote the system state with $N_r = r$, $0 \leq r \leq N$, and thus $\Omega = \{Y_0, Y_1, Y_2, \ldots, Y_r, \ldots, Y_{N-1}, Y_N\}$. Eqs. (1) – (4) continue to hold with $D = N + 1$.

Let $P(Y_j, Y_k)$ denote the (j, k) element of $\mathbf{P}$, and consider a system state Y_r with $r < N$. The next step is to compute the probability of entering this state from other valid system states. When $r \leq N - 1$, state Y_r can be entered from state Y_{r+1} if the running thread becomes blocked, which occurs w.p. μ_R, and if none of the $N - r - 1$ blocked threads become ready. N_r would therefore be reduced by one. Note that since there can be no more than one active thread, the value of N_r in cycle n cannot be reduced by more than one in the next cycle $n + 1$. In other words, state Y_r cannot be entered from state Y_j, $j > r + 1$. We then have

$$P(Y_{r+1}, Y_r) = \Pr\left[\,X_{n+1} = Y_r \mid X_n = Y_{r+1}\,\right] = \mu_R\, B(N - r - 1, 0), \tag{9}$$

for $n \geq 0$, $0 \leq r < N$, where $B(k, l)$ refers to the probability that l of the k blocked threads become ready. This probability can be expressed as

$$B(k, l) = \begin{cases} \binom{k}{l} (\lambda)^l (1 - \lambda)^{k-l}, & l \leq k, \\ \\ 0, & l > k. \end{cases} \qquad (10)$$

State Y_r can also be entered from any state Y_j, $0 \leq j \leq r < N$. In particular, the system moves from state Y_0 to state Y_r if r of the blocked threads become ready, the probability of which is given by

$$P(Y_0, Y_r) = B(N, r). \qquad (11)$$

When $j > 0$, two possibilities exist. If the executing thread becomes blocked and $r - j + 1$ of the $N - j$ blocked threads become ready, then the system would enter state Y_r, an event that occurs w.p. $\mu_R B(N-j, r-j+1)$, $0 < j \leq r$. On the other hand, if the thread continues to execute and $r - j$ of the $N - j$ blocked threads become ready, then the system would enter state Y_r, an event that occurs w.p. $(1 - \mu_R) B(N - j, r - j)$, $0 < j \leq r$. Hence, for $0 < j \leq r < N$,

$$P(Y_j, Y_r) = \mu_R B(N - j, r - j + 1) + (1 - \mu_R)B(N - j, r - j). \qquad (12)$$

Combining Eqs. (9) – (12), we obtain the invariant probability for Y_r as

$$\pi(Y_r) = \pi(Y_{r+1})\mu_R B(N - r - 1, 0) + \sum_{j=1}^{r} \pi(Y_j)\mu_R B(N - j, r - j + 1)$$

$$+ \sum_{j=1}^{r} \pi(Y_j)(1 - \mu_R)B(N - j, r - j) + \pi(Y_0)B(N, r).$$

Rewriting this recursive formula to express $\pi(Y_{r+1})$ in terms of $\pi(Y_0)$, $\pi(Y_1)$, …, $\pi(Y_r)$ yields

$$\pi(Y_{r+1})\mu_R B(N - r - 1, 0) = \pi(Y_r) - \pi(Y_0)B(N, r) -$$

$$\sum_{j=1}^{r} \pi(Y_j)(1 - \mu_R)B(N - j, r - j) -$$

$$\sum_{j=1}^{r} \pi(Y_j)\mu_R B(N - j, r - j + 1). \qquad (13)$$

Starting with $r = 0$, Eq. (13) can be used to successively compute the probabilities $\pi(Y_1)$, $\pi(Y_2)$, $\pi(Y_3)$, ..., $\pi(Y_N)$ in terms of $\pi(Y_0)$, and $\boldsymbol{\pi}$ is uniquely determined by Eq. (4). This invariant probability vector then can be used to compute the processor utilization U as

$$U = 1 - \pi(Y_0). \tag{14}$$

1.2.2. Continuous-Time Process

We also model the multithreaded system as a CTMC[15,16] $\{X(t), t \geq 0\}$ defined over a finite state space Ω. To simplify the model definition, we restrict our attention here to phase-type[18,19] (PH) d.f.s for the model parameters. The use of PH d.f.s is motivated by their important mathematical properties and the fact that any d.f. on $\mathbb{R}^+$ can in principle be represented arbitrarily close by a PH d.f.. We therefore have a general queueing theoretic formulation that can be used to provide an accurate modeling analysis of real multithreaded systems.

Consider the MC defined on the states $\{1, 2, \ldots, n_A, n_A + 1\}$ with the infinitesimal generator matrix

$$\mathcal{Q}_A = \begin{bmatrix} \mathcal{S}_A & \underline{S}_A \\ \mathbf{0} & 0 \end{bmatrix}, \tag{15}$$

where $\mathcal{S}_A$ is an $n_A \times n_A$ matrix, $\underline{S}_A$ is a column vector of order n_A, the states $1, 2, \ldots, n_A$ are transient, the state $n_A + 1$ is absorbing, and $\mathcal{S}_A \mathbf{e} + \underline{S}_A = \mathbf{0}$. Let $(\underline{\alpha}, 0)$ be the initial probability vector for $\mathcal{Q}_A$. The d.f. of the time until absorption in this MC then defines a PH d.f. with parameters $(\underline{\alpha}, \mathcal{S}_A)$. We assume $\mathbf{A} \equiv \mathrm{PH}(\underline{\alpha}, \mathcal{S}_A)$ with $L = -\underline{\alpha} \mathcal{S}_A^{-1} \mathbf{e}$. A $\mathrm{PH}(\underline{\beta}, \mathcal{S}_B)$ d.f. of order n_B is analogously constructed for processor service times with $R = -\underline{\beta} \mathcal{S}_B^{-1} \mathbf{e}$.

The states of the MC are given by $(i, j_1, \ldots j_{n_A}, k)$ where $i \in \{0, \ldots, N\}$ denotes the value of N_r, $j_\ell \in \{0, \ldots, N - i\}$, $1 \leq \ell \leq n_A$, denotes the number of blocked threads whose outstanding miss delay is in phase ℓ, and $k \in \{1, \ldots, n_B\}$ denotes the phase of the next miss. Since the value of $N - i$ represents the number of blocked threads, $\sum_{\ell=1}^{n_A} j_\ell = N - i$.

We define

$$\pi(i, j_1, \ldots, j_{n_A}, k) \equiv \lim_{t \to \infty} \Pr\left[X(t) = (i, j_1, \ldots, j_{n_A}, k)\right], \tag{16}$$

for $0 \leq i \leq N$, $\sum_{\ell=1}^{n_A} j_\ell = N - i$, $1 \leq k \leq n_B$, and

$$Z_i \equiv \left\{ (j_1, \ldots, j_{n_A}, k) \,\middle|\, \sum_{\ell=1}^{n_A} j_\ell = N - i,\ 1 \leq k \leq n_B \right\}, \tag{17}$$

for $0 \le i \le N$. Let $x_{i,z} \in Z_i$, $0 \le z < D_i \equiv \|Z_i\|$, $0 \le i \le N$, be a lexicographical ordering of the elements of Z_i, and let $D \equiv \sum_{i=0}^{N} D_i$. Hence, $\Omega = \{(0, x_{0,0}), \ldots, (0, x_{0,D_0-1}), (1, x_{1,0}), \ldots, (1, x_{1,D_1-1}), \ldots, (N, x_{N,0}), \ldots, (N, x_{N,D_N-1})\}$. Using this we define

$$\boldsymbol{\pi} \equiv [\, \boldsymbol{\pi}_0, \ldots, \boldsymbol{\pi}_N \,] \tag{18}$$

where

$$\boldsymbol{\pi}_i \equiv (\, \pi(i, x_{i,0}), \; \pi(i, x_{i,1}), \; \ldots, \; \pi(i, x_{i,D_i-1}) \,), \quad 0 \le i \le N. \tag{19}$$

The limiting probability vector $\boldsymbol{\pi}$ is the stationary distribution for $\{X(t), t \ge 0\}$. Assuming this CTMC to be irreducible and ergodic, its stationary distribution is obtained by solving the GBEs

$$\boldsymbol{\pi} \mathbf{Q} = \mathbf{0} \tag{20}$$

together with

$$\boldsymbol{\pi} \mathbf{e} = 1, \tag{21}$$

where $\mathbf{Q}$ is the infinitesimal generator matrix for the MC and e is the column vector of all ones.

The invariant probability vector $\boldsymbol{\pi}$ can be obtained in a number of ways. We first consider the simple model instance with $\mathbf{A} \equiv \exp(\lambda)$ and $\mathbf{B} \equiv \exp(\mu_R)$, which is equivalent to an $M/M/1//N$ queueing system. The solution of Eqs. (20) and (21) in this case is easily shown[20] to be

$$\boldsymbol{\pi}_i = \boldsymbol{\pi}_0 \left(\frac{R}{L}\right)^i \frac{N!}{(N-i)!}, \quad 1 \le i \le N, \tag{22}$$

and

$$\boldsymbol{\pi}_0 = \left[\sum_{i=0}^{N} \left(\frac{R}{L}\right)^i \frac{N!}{(N-i)!} \right]^{-1}. \tag{23}$$

We next consider the case where $\mathbf{A} \equiv \exp(\lambda)$ and $\mathbf{B} \equiv \mathrm{PH}(\underline{\beta}, \mathcal{S}_B)$. The generator matrix $\mathbf{Q}$ for this system, arranged in the same order as the elements of $\boldsymbol{\pi}$, has a structure given by

$$\mathbf{Q} = \begin{bmatrix} -N\lambda & N\lambda\underline{\beta} & \cdots & 0 & 0 \\ \underline{S}_B & \mathcal{S}_B - (N-1)\lambda\mathbf{I} & \cdots & & \\ 0 & \underline{S}_B\underline{\beta} & \cdots & \vdots & \vdots \\ 0 & 0 & \cdots & \vdots & \vdots \\ \vdots & \vdots & \ddots & & \\ & & \cdots & \mathcal{S}_B - \lambda\mathbf{I} & \lambda\mathbf{I} \\ 0 & 0 & \cdots & \underline{S}_B\underline{\beta} & \mathcal{S}_B \end{bmatrix}, \tag{24}$$

where $\mathbf{I}$ denotes the $n_B \times n_B$ identity matrix. Recall that $\underline{S}_B$ and $\underline{\beta}$ have dimension $n_B \times 1$ and $1 \times n_B$, respectively, and thus $\underline{S}_B\underline{\beta} = [b_{i,j}]$ where $b_{i,j} \equiv \underline{S}_{Bi}\,\underline{\beta}_{\,j}, 1 \le i,j \le n_B$.

The GBEs for this queueing system can be expressed as

$$-N\lambda\,\boldsymbol{\pi}_0 \,+\, \boldsymbol{\pi}_1\underline{S}_B \;=\; 0, \tag{25}$$

$$N\lambda\,\boldsymbol{\pi}_0\underline{\beta} \,+\, \boldsymbol{\pi}_1(\mathcal{S}_B - (N-1)\lambda\mathbf{I}) \,+\, \boldsymbol{\pi}_2\underline{S}_B\underline{\beta} \;=\; 0, \tag{26}$$

$$(N-i+1)\lambda\,\boldsymbol{\pi}_{i-1}\mathbf{I} \,+\, \boldsymbol{\pi}_i(\mathcal{S}_B - (N-i)\lambda\mathbf{I}) \,+\, \boldsymbol{\pi}_{i+1}\underline{S}_B\underline{\beta} \;=\; 0, \tag{27}$$

for $2 \le i \le N-1$, and

$$\lambda\,\boldsymbol{\pi}_{N-1}\mathbf{I} \,+\, \boldsymbol{\pi}_N\mathcal{S}_B \;=\; 0. \tag{28}$$

We multiply Eqs. (26) – (28) on the right by $\mathbf{e}$, and upon simplifying we obtain

$$\boldsymbol{\pi}_{i+1}\underline{S}_B \;=\; (N-i)\lambda\,\boldsymbol{\pi}_i\,\mathbf{e}, \quad 1 \le i \le N-1. \tag{29}$$

We then multiply this eq. on the right by $\underline{\beta}$, and substituting the results into Eqs. (26) and (27) yields

$$N\lambda\,\boldsymbol{\pi}_0\underline{\beta} \;=\; \boldsymbol{\pi}_1\big((N-1)\lambda\mathbf{I} - (N-1)\lambda\mathbf{e}\underline{\beta} - \mathcal{S}_B\big) \tag{30}$$

and

$$(N-i+1)\lambda\,\boldsymbol{\pi}_{i-1}\mathbf{I} \;=\; \boldsymbol{\pi}_i\big((N-i)\lambda\mathbf{I} - (N-i)\lambda\mathbf{e}\underline{\beta} - \mathcal{S}_B\big), \tag{31}$$

for $2 \le i \le N$. Let $\tilde{R}(i) \equiv (N-i)\lambda\mathbf{I} - (N-i)\lambda\mathbf{e}\underline{\beta} - \mathcal{S}_B, 1 \le i \le N$. Substituting this into Eqs. (30) and (31) and simplifying, we obtain

$$\boldsymbol{\pi}_1 \;=\; N\lambda\,\boldsymbol{\pi}_0\underline{\beta}\,\tilde{R}(1)^{-1} \tag{32}$$

and

$$\boldsymbol{\pi}_i \;=\; (N-i+1)\lambda\,\boldsymbol{\pi}_{i-1}\,\tilde{R}(i)^{-1}, \quad 2 \le i \le N. \tag{33}$$

One can easily show that $\tilde{R}(i)$ is nonsingular, and thus $\tilde{R}(i)^{-1}$ exists, $1 \le i \le N$. The solution of the GBEs is therefore given by

$$\boldsymbol{\pi}_i \;=\; \frac{N!\lambda^i}{(N-i)!}\,\boldsymbol{\pi}_0\underline{\beta}\,\prod_{k=1}^{i}\tilde{R}(k)^{-1}, \quad 1 \le i \le N. \tag{34}$$

Substituting (34) into (21) then yields the expression

$$\boldsymbol{\pi}_0 \;=\; \left[\sum_{i=0}^{N}\frac{N!\lambda^i}{(N-i)!}\,\underline{\beta}\,\prod_{k=1}^{i}\tilde{R}(k)^{-1}\,\mathbf{e}\right]^{-1}. \tag{35}$$

We next consider the case where $\mathbf{A}$ is a general d.f. and $\mathbf{B} \equiv \exp(\mu_R)$. Under these parameter assumptions, our model is equivalent to a well-known closed queueing network that consists of N identical customers and two service centers, the first of which has a single FCFS server with exponential service whereas the second has N servers and general service demands. One can easily show[19,21] that this queueing network model has a product-form solution in which certain invariant probabilities depend only upon the service means at the two service centers, and not on the detailed form of the d.f. $\mathbf{A}$. In particular, the vector $\boldsymbol{\pi}$ is insensitive to $\mathbf{A}$, and thus is the same as that for the $M/M/1//N$ queue given in Eqs. (22) and (23).

In all other instances of the CTMC $\{X(t), t \geq 0\}$, the exact elements of its generator $\mathbf{Q}$ depend upon the specific PH d.f.s chosen, but in each case the matrix $\mathbf{Q}$ can be constructed in a form similar in *structure* to that given in Eq. (24). The corresponding stationary distribution can then be determined by solving Eqs. (20) and (21) using standard numerical methods. For very large models in which the costs of these methods prove to be expensive, one can exploit special features[18] of the d.f.s $\mathbf{A}(\cdot)$ and $\mathbf{B}(\cdot)$ to obtain algorithmic simplifications that considerably reduce the computation costs.

Once the invariant vector $\boldsymbol{\pi}$ is obtained, it can be used to compute the processor utilization U as

$$U = 1 - \boldsymbol{\pi}_0 \mathbf{e}. \tag{36}$$

1.2.3. Validation

A multithreaded processor architecture is considered by McCrackin[6] in which multiple threads share a deep pipeline in an interleaved fashion. Both the data dependency and control interlocks are prevented by enforcing a sufficiently large inter-instruction dispatch delay on each individual thread. The sharing of the pipeline resource by multiple threads significantly improves the utilization of the pipeline. Four instruction dispatching mechanisms are proposed: *Fixed Delay, Known Delay, Enforced Delay with Fixed Minimum*, and *Modified Fixed Delay*. The Fixed Delay mechanism enforces the worst-case interlock delay after every instruction, yielding pipeline utilization that is a linear function of N and hence is easily predictable. However, the utilization in the other three cases is a non-linear function of N. McCrackin performed detailed simulations of the multithreaded system under each of these dispatching mechanisms and various interlock delay d.f.s, and reported[6] the corresponding pipeline utilization results.

We validated our analytic models against the detailed results presented[6] by McCrackin. In particular, we constructed DT and CT interlock delay d.f.s that match those studied by McCrackin. The processor utilization measures of the corresponding models were then obtained via the analysis of Sections 1.2.1.1 and 1.2.2, respectively. Our DT and CT processor utilization results are indistinguishable from all of those reported[6] by McCrackin. We refer the interested reader to an earlier paper[22] for more details.

We also compared the results of the DT model in Section 1.2.1.2 and the $M/M/1//N$ model instance of Section 1.2.2 with those provided[6] by McCrackin, where the d.f. means were appropriately set to those used by McCrackin. The worst-case discrepancies due to these simple approximations are 11% and 15% for the two cases considered, with the majority of the measures matching more closely. While such inaccuracies may not be tolerable for single-pipeline CPI predictions in a small latency[6] multithreaded pipelined processor, they may be acceptable in a large latency[10,13] multithreaded multiprocessor environment. We also constructed DT and CT models for the latter environment and validated them against the results of Saavedra[13] et al. Some of these validations can be found in an earlier[23] paper. Note that the results presented in Section 1.4 (Table 1) are for different model parameters than the results presented[23] there.

1.3. CONTEXT-SWITCH OVERHEADS

The previous section presents our DT and CT models for a spectrum of multithreaded processor architectures under the assumption that $C = 0$. Although appropriate for a number of multithreaded machines, such as those capable of switching contexts every cycle[6–8] at the cost of additional hardware, this assumption was primarily made to elucidate the basic structure of our models, and the inclusion of non-zero context-switch overheads follows quite naturally from the previous formulations.

1.3.1. Discrete-Time Process

We continue to model the system as a DTMC $\{X_n, n \geq 0\}$ defined over a finite state space Ω. The system can be in one of two types of states, depending on whether or not a context-switch is taking place. As in Section 1.2.1.2, we use Y_r to denote the *non-context-switch (NCS)* system state with $N_r = r$, $0 \leq r \leq N$, and we use $\widehat{Y}_r$ to denote the *context-switch (CS)* system state with $N_r = r$, one thread being context-switched, and the remaining $N - r - 1$ threads being blocked, $0 \leq r \leq N - 1$. The set of valid system states is thus given by $\Omega = \{Y_0, \widehat{Y}_0, \ldots, Y_{N-1}, \widehat{Y}_{N-1}, Y_N\}$. One of the ready threads is always active in each *NCS* state Y_r, $r > 0$.

We assume $\mathbf{A} \equiv \mathrm{geom}(\lambda)$ and $\mathbf{B} \equiv (\mathrm{geom}(\mu_C) * \mathrm{geom}(\mu_R))$, where $*$ is the convolution operator. This implies that one of the $r > 0$ ready threads enters the *NCS* state Y_r after a miss w.p. μ_C, and that this active thread subsequently enters the *CS* state $\widehat{Y}_r$ w.p. μ_R.

The next step is to compute the probability of entering the *NCS* state Y_r from other valid system states, for which there are 3 possibilities. When $r \leq N - 1$, state Y_r can be entered from the *CS* state $\widehat{Y}_j$ if the context-switching thread becomes blocked (w.p. μ_C), and $r - j$ of the $N - j - 1$ blocked threads become ready. Hence,

$$P(\widehat{Y}_j, Y_r) = \mu_C \, B(N - j - 1, r - j), \ 0 \leq j \leq r \leq N - 1. \quad (37)$$

The system moves to state Y_r from the state Y_j, $1 \leq j \leq r$, when the executing thread remains active (w.p. $1 - \mu_R$) and $r - j$ of the $N - j$ blocked threads become ready. This can be expressed as

$$P(Y_j, Y_r) = (1 - \mu_R) \, B(N - j, r - j), \ 1 \leq j \leq r. \quad (38)$$

Finally, state Y_r can be entered from Y_0 if r of the N blocked threads become ready, which yields

$$P(Y_0, Y_r) = B(N, r). \quad (39)$$

Eqs. (37) – (39) can be combined to compute the invariant probability for Y_r as

$$\pi(Y_r) = \sum_{j=0}^{r<N} \mu_C \pi(\widehat{Y}_j) B(N - j - 1, r - j) +$$

$$\sum_{j=1}^{r} (1 - \mu_R) \pi(Y_j) B(N - j, r - j) + \pi(Y_0) B(N, r).$$

Rewriting this recursive formula to obtain $\pi(\widehat{Y}_r)$, $0 \leq r \leq N-1$, in terms of $\pi(\widehat{Y}_j)$, $j \leq r - 1$, and $\pi(Y_j)$, $j \leq r$, we obtain

$$\pi(\widehat{Y}_r) \mu_C B(N - r - 1, 0) = \pi(Y_r) - \sum_{j=0}^{r-1} \mu_C \pi(\widehat{Y}_j) B(N - j - 1, r - j) -$$

$$\sum_{j=1}^{r}(1 - \mu_R)\pi(Y_j)B(N - j, r - j) -$$

$$\pi(Y_0)\, B(N, r). \tag{40}$$

We now consider transitions into the *CS* state $\widehat{Y}_r$, $0 \le r < N$, for which there are 2 cases. State $\widehat{Y}_r$ can be entered from the state $\widehat{Y}_j$, $0 \le j \le r$, if the system continues to stay in the *CS* state (w.p. $1 - \mu_C$), and $r - j$ of the $N - j - 1$ blocked threads become ready. This yields

$$P(\widehat{Y}_j, \widehat{Y}_r) = (1 - \mu_C)\, B(N - j - 1, r - j), \ 0 \le j \le r. \tag{41}$$

The system moves to state $\widehat{Y}_r$ from the state Y_j, $1 \le j \le r + 1$, when the active thread enters the *CS* state (w.p. μ_R) and $r - j + 1$ of the $N - j$ blocked threads become ready. Hence,

$$P(Y_j, \widehat{Y}_r) = \mu_R\, B(N - j, r - j + 1), \ 1 \le j \le r + 1. \tag{42}$$

Combining Eqs. (41) and (42), we obtain

$$\pi(\widehat{Y}_r) = \sum_{j=0}^{r}(1 - \mu_C)\pi(\widehat{Y}_j)B(N - j - 1, r - j) +$$

$$\sum_{j=1}^{r+1}\mu_R\pi(Y_j)B(N - j, r - j + 1).$$

Rewriting this recursive formula to express $\pi(Y_{r+1})$ in terms of $\pi(\widehat{Y}_j)$ and $\pi(Y_j)$, $j \le r$, yields

$$\pi(Y_{r+1})\mu_R B(N - r - 1, 0) = \pi(\widehat{Y}_r) - \sum_{j=1}^{r}\mu_R\pi(Y_j)B(N - j, r - j + 1) -$$

$$\sum_{j=0}^{r}(1 - \mu_C)\pi(\widehat{Y}_j)B(N - j - 1, r - j). \tag{43}$$

Eq. (40) expresses $\pi(\widehat{Y}_0)$ in terms of $\pi(Y_0)$. Given $\pi(Y_0)$ and $\pi(\widehat{Y}_0)$, Eq. (43) can be used to compute $\pi(Y_1)$ in terms of $\pi(Y_0)$. Then applications of Eqs. (40) and (43) yield $\pi(\widehat{Y}_1)$ and $\pi(Y_2)$, respectively. Thus, all of the stationary probabilities for both *CS* and *NCS* system states, can be successively computed in terms of $\pi(Y_0)$. Finally, Eq. (4) uniquely determines the invariant probability vector $\boldsymbol{\pi}$. The processor utilization is then given by

$$U = \sum_{j=1}^{N}\pi(Y_j). \tag{44}$$

1.3.2. Continuous-Time Process

We continue to model the system as a CTMC $\{X(t), t \geq 0\}$ defined over a finite state space Ω. As in Section 1.2.2, we assume that each of the model parameters has a PH d.f., and thus $\mathbf{A} \equiv \mathrm{PH}(\underline{\alpha}, \mathcal{S}_A)$ and $\mathbf{B} \equiv (\mathrm{PH}(\underline{\gamma}, \mathcal{S}_C) * \mathrm{PH}(\underline{\beta}, \mathcal{S}_B))$ where $C = -\underline{\gamma}\mathcal{S}_C^{-1}\mathbf{e}$. The convolution of $\mathrm{PH}(\underline{\gamma}, \mathcal{S}_C)$ and $\mathrm{PH}(\underline{\beta}, \tilde{\mathcal{S}}_B)$ yields a PH d.f. with parameters $([\underline{\gamma}, 0], \mathcal{S}_B')$ where

$$
\mathcal{S}_B' = \begin{bmatrix} \mathcal{S}_C & \mathcal{S}_C\underline{\beta} \\ 0 & \mathcal{S}_B \end{bmatrix} \tag{45}
$$

(see reference[18] for a proof) and $C + R = -[\underline{\gamma}, 0]\mathcal{S}_B'^{-1}\mathbf{e}$.

The model solution is then obtained exactly as described in Section 1.2.2, with the exception that $\mathbf{B} \equiv \mathrm{PH}([\underline{\gamma}, 0], \mathcal{S}_B')$. In this case, however, Eq. (36) provides an upper bound on processor utilization because it represents the total proportion of time that the processor is busy, including the cycles spent context switching among threads. Since context switching is strictly overhead, and thus not an effective use of processor cycles, this factor must be excluded from the processor utilization estimate.

One effective approach is to simply exclude the invariant probabilities of all non-idle states that represent context switching in the calculation of Eq. (36). In particular, the processor utilization can be computed by

$$
U = \sum_{i=1}^{N} \boldsymbol{\pi}_i \, \nu_i, \tag{46}
$$

where the nth element of the binary vector ν_i is 1 if the corresponding state reflects the execution of a thread, and is 0 otherwise, $0 \leq n < D_i$, $1 \leq i \leq N$. Another possibility is to use a mean-value approach to estimate the fraction of busy time that reflects useful processor cycles, which yields

$$
U = (1 - \boldsymbol{\pi}_0\mathbf{e}) \frac{R}{C + R}. \tag{47}
$$

We note that any other causes of wasted processor cycles, e.g., thread[14] management, can be excluded via either of the above methods to obtain an accurate estimate of effective processor utilization.

As a specific example, we consider the simple model instance with $\mathbf{A} \equiv \exp(\lambda)$ and $\mathbf{B} \equiv \mathrm{GE}_2(\mu_C, \mu_R)$, which is equivalent to an $M/\mathrm{GE}_2/1//N$ queueing system where GE_2 denotes a two-stage generalized Erlang[24] d.f. The generator matrix $\mathbf{Q}$ is described by Eq. (24) with $\underline{\beta} = [1 \ \ 0]$,

$$\mathcal{S}_B = \begin{bmatrix} -\mu_C & \mu_C \\ 0 & -\mu_R \end{bmatrix} \text{ and } \underline{S}_B = \begin{bmatrix} 0 \\ \mu_R \end{bmatrix}. \text{ The model solution is given by}$$

Eqs. (34) and (35), where $\tilde{R}(i)^{-1}$ can be expressed as

$$\tilde{R}(i)^{-1} = \begin{bmatrix} \frac{(N-i)\lambda+\mu_R}{\mu_R\mu_C} & \frac{1}{\mu_R} \\ \frac{(N-i)\lambda}{\mu_R\mu_C} & \frac{1}{\mu_R} \end{bmatrix}, \quad 1 \le i \le N. \tag{48}$$

The processor utilization is then obtained via Eqs. (35), (48) and (46) with $\nu_i = [0 \;\; 1]$, $1 \le i \le N$, noting that this is identical to the result obtained from Eq. (47).

1.4. RESULTS

In this section, our analytic models are used to obtain several important results for evaluating the performance potential of multithreading with current and (near) future microprocessor technology, as well as the modeling of such multithreaded systems. We first demonstrate the importance of accurate model parameter d.f.s as these factors can have a significant impact on multithreading performance. We then quantitatively evaluate the potential performance benefits of multithreaded systems.

A particularly important aspect of our modeling approach is that parameter d.f.s can be matched to real measurement data to obtain an accurate and realistic performance analysis of multithreaded systems. In a recent study[25] of a specific multithreaded system, it is shown that the d.f. of inter-operand-request times tends to be highly variable, exhibiting a coefficient of variation greater than 1, most often around 2 and as large as 3. Furthermore, unpredictable network delays in the memory access path of large-latency multithreaded systems[10] suggest (relatively) highly variable inter-operand-request times. Both of these are in contrast to the assumptions of previous[13] modeling studies, where the context-switch delay is assumed to be deterministic and the times between remote references are assumed to be geometric. To consider the impact of large interrequest variability and the importance of capturing these effects in the multithreaded system model, our first set of results compares the performance measures obtained from our model under $\exp(1/(C + R(N)))$ and $H_2(1/(C + R(N)))$ interrequest times with those presented[13] earlier. The monotonically nonincreasing function

$$R(N) = \begin{cases} R(1)N^{-0.57}, & if\ N \le \lfloor R(1)^{1/0.57} \rfloor, \\ 1, & if\ N > \lfloor R(1)^{1/0.57} \rfloor, \end{cases} \tag{49}$$

is used for the mean time between remote memory requests, where $R(1) = R$, to be consistent with the earlier[13] study. We also assume an $\exp(1/L)$ remote memory latency (as opposed to the deterministic assumption[13]) because these latencies tend to be variable in practice[10,14] due to network delays. In Table 1 we restate the earlier results[13] ($SCvE$) together with the corresponding results from our model (DKS), where the $M/M/1//N$ case (EX) is obtained from Eq. (23) and the $M/H_2/1//N$ case (HY) is obtained from (35), both together with Eq. (47).

Parameters			Max Utilization		Number of Threads Needed to Achieve:					
					Max Util		0.5 (Max Util)		0.75 (Max Util)	
L	C	R	DKS EX/HY	SCvE	DKS EX/HY	SCvE	DKS EX/HY	SCvE	DKS EX/HY	SCvE
32	0	16	1.0/1.0	0.993	-/-	16	2/2	2	6/7	6
32	0	32	1.0/1.0	0.991	-/-	8	1/1	1	2/3	3
32	0	64	1.0/1.0	0.993	-/-	5	1/1	1	1/1	2
32	1	16	0.780/0.757	0.803	12/14	10	1/1	2	4/4	4
32	1	32	0.900/0.887	0.908	8/10	7	1/1	1	2/2	2
32	1	64	0.956/0.951	0.959	6/7	5	1/1	1	1/1	1
32	4	16	0.550/0.524	0.594	6/7	5	1/1	1	2/2	2
32	4	32	0.738/0.715	0.759	5/6	5	1/1	1	2/2	2
32	4	64	0.867/0.853	0.864	4/5	4	1/1	1	1/1	1
32	16	16	0.312/0.298	0.348	3/3	3	1/1	1	1/1	1
32	16	32	0.487/0.470	0.528	3/3	2	1/1	1	1/1	1
32	16	64	0.666/0.653	0.705	2/3	2	1/1	1	1/1	1
64	0	16	1.0/1.0	0.990	-/-	33	7/7	7	18/20	17
64	0	32	1.0/1.0	0.991	-/-	17	2/2	3	6/7	6
64	0	64	1.0/1.0	0.990	-/-	8	1/1	1	2/3	3
64	1	16	0.701/0.677	0.727	25/29	21	3/3	4	8/9	9
64	1	32	0.863/0.845	0.874	15/19	13	2/2	2	4/5	4
64	1	64	0.944/0.935	0.946	9/12	2	1/1	1	2/2	2
64	4	16	0.465/0.442	0.507	12/13	10	2/1	2	4/4	4
64	4	32	0.672/0.646	0.702	9/10	8	1/1	1	3/3	3
64	4	64	0.832/0.814	0.846	6/8	6	1/1	1	2/2	2
64	16	16	0.257/0.243	0.301	5/5	4	1/1	1	2/1	1
64	16	32	0.426/0.404	0.472	4/5	4	1/1	1	1/1	1
64	16	64	0.618/0.596	0.657	4/4	3	1/1	1	1/1	1
128	0	16	1.0/1.0	0.991	-/-	61	27/28	26	71/73	40
128	0	32	1.0/1.0	0.991	-/-	45	7/7	7	18/20	17
128	0	64	1.0/1.0	0.990	-/-	17	2/2	3	6/7	6
128	1	16	0.594/0.575	0.706	59/65	42	9/8	13	22/22	29
128	1	32	0.801/0.781	0.815	33/40	30	4/4	5	11/12	11
128	1	64	0.920/0.908	0.924	18/23	16	2/2	2	5/5	5
128	4	16	0.373/0.355	0.406	24/26	21	3/3	4	8/8	10
128	4	32	0.585/0.560	0.615	17/20	15	2/2	3	6/6	6
128	4	64	0.780/0.757	0.797	12/14	10	1/1	2	4/4	4
128	16	16	0.204/0.192	0.236	8/9	7	1/1	1	3/3	4
128	16	32	0.354/0.334	0.396	7/8	6	1/1	1	2/2	3
128	16	64	0.550/0.524	0.589	6/7	6	1/1	1	2/2	2

TABLE 1: Performance Impact of Parameter Distributions

We first observe that the interrequest time d.f. can have a significant impact on the maximum utilization achievable with multithreaded processors for $C > 0$. In particular, increasing the variance of interrequest times decreases the maximum processor utilization and increases the number of threads required to achieve this (smaller) utilization. The maximum observed reduction in processor utilization is 24%, with an average of 10%. This results from the fact that a greater percentage of the interrequest times are very small, which in turn causes the processor to spend more time waiting for one of the N threads to become ready. Moreover, a larger number of threads are needed to keep the processor as busy as possible due to the greater percentage of blocked threads. Note that when $C = 0$, there are no disadvantages to multithreading (the cache miss ratio, given by the inverse of Eq. (49), does increase with N, but there is no penalty for this increase with $C = 0$) and thus $U \to 1$ in the limit as $N \to \infty$ for finite L and R, as reflected in the results of our model.

Our next set of results assesses the current commercial processor technology as it relates to multithreading. The gap between processor and memory cycle times is on the rise. This implies that, for a fixed runlength, the ratio of memory latency (L) to run-length (R) is increasing. On the other hand, new compiler techniques of aggressive instruction/data prefetching and memory consistency models (which allow loads to be percolated ahead of non-conflicting stores) are enabling the compiler to reduce cache-misses, and thus increase R. Therefore, the ratio L/R may not rise as quickly as L. For uniprocessor benchmarks with relatively large working sets, such as scientific and transaction processing benchmarks with respect to L1 cache misses, typical run-lengths may be as small as 10-20 cycles, whereas those based on memory accesses[26] can be 50-100 cycles. A similar range of run-lengths have also been reported[10] for multiprocessor traces of scientific benchmarks. While typical L2 access latencies are in the 10-20 cycles range, memory access times are expected to grow from 50 to 100-200 cycles.

The context-switch overhead (C) for large-latency machines cannot be null due to the significant amount of required state saving and restoration. If the context is being switched to a thread that has very little sharing of state with the current state (e.g., switch to a different process thread), most of the current machine state consisting of architected registers, etc. must be saved and the new state restored. However, with techniques such as multiple on-chip register banks, the context-switch may simply imply switching to an alternate bank. The latter is a more hardware-intensive solution but can be quite feasible for machines with only a few threads. Since most of the current commercial processors are only beginning to include multithreading support, the level of support would mostly be restricted to 2–4 threads. The context switch overhead (C) in such a case may be within 1–4 cycles.

The cache-interference factor used in Eq. (49) is 0.57, which was chosen to be consistent with earlier[13] results. Although this value may seem high, it helps to restrict the reported performance advantage of multithreading to conservative levels. Using our CT model, and keeping the above scenario in mind, a set of experiments were performed and the corresponding results are plotted in Figs. 1–3. The context-switch overhead is assumed to be 1, 2 and 4 cycles in Figs. 1, 2 and 3, respectively. The L/R ratio is varied from 1 to 1.5 to 2.0, with run-lengths of 16, 32, 64 and 128.

Several observations can be made from these results. The single-thread utilization can be significantly increased by adding a second thread, even with $C = 4$ and $L/R = 2$, almost irrespective of the actual run-length. Moreover, if $C \leq 2$, a set of around 5 threads would be sufficient for doubling the single-thread utilization even for $R = 16$, with $L/R = 2$.

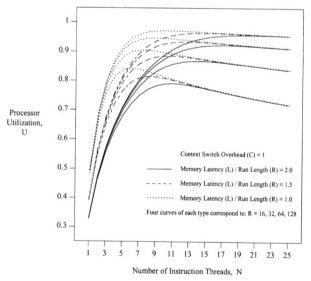

FIGURE 1: Processor Utilization as a Function of N for a Cache Interference Factor of 0.57.

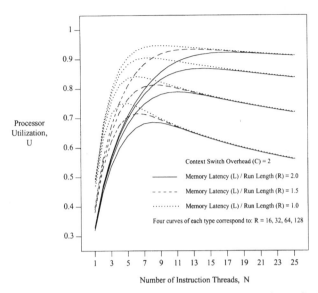

FIGURE 2: Processor Utilization as a Function of N for a Cache Interference Factor of 0.57.

Approximately 3 to 5 threads would be sufficient to significantly improve the single-thread utilization for larger run-lengths. If C increases to 4 cycles, single-thread performance cannot be doubled for $R = 16$ and $L/R > 1$. In other words, for multithreaded machines attempting to tolerate L2 access latencies, where such small run-lengths may be quite typical, limiting C to approximately 2 cycles would be quite crucial to realizing a good increase in performance, under the assumptions in Figs. 1–3. As N continues to increase, the effects of cache interference dominate and the performance starts to degrade, as expected. The performance in this region is almost completely determined by C and R, and is independent of L. More specifically, the performance here is determined by the ratio R/C. This is clearly shown in Figs. 1–3, as the curves corresponding to different values of the L/R ratio, yet a common R/C, merge.

1.5. CONCLUSION

In this chapter, we have presented a comprehensive analytic framework
to quantitatively evaluate the performance potential of a wide spectrum
of multithreaded machines, ranging from those that are aimed at hid-
ing small latencies and are capable of switching threads every cycle with
negligible context-switch overheads, to those that switch threads only on
long inter-instruction latencies and have significant context-switch overhead. We formulated general models of this multithreading spectrum,
and we derived an exact solution for these models. Our approach makes
it possible to efficiently compute accurate results for the wide variety
of multithreaded system environments without imposing any practical
restrictions on the modeling analysis. This was verified by a comparison
of the outputs of various instances of our models against previously published simulation and modeling results under similar input conditions.

Our models were then used to assess the performance potential of multithreading with current processor technology. The results show that the
context switching overhead greatly influences the machine performance.

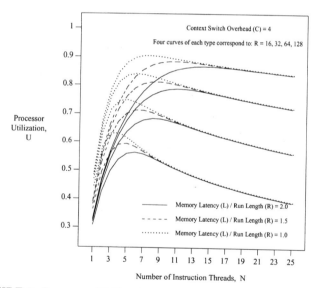

FIGURE 3: Processor Utilization as a Function of N for a Cache Interference Factor of 0.57.

Both the maximum throughput and the number of threads required to achieve this maximum are sensitive to the context switch overhead, as is evident from the results in Section 1.4. Specifically, even though one might be tempted to ignore the switching overhead when it is only a small fraction (1-5%) of the average memory latency or run length, our results show that it can disproportionately effect the machine performance.

The single-thread performance can be significantly boosted with a second thread, under almost all input conditions of interest. If the context-switch overhead does not exceed two cycles, a set of around five threads is enough for doubling the single-thread performance even for small run-lengths, high cache-miss latencies, and quite high cache-interference. For multithreaded machines designed to hide L2 access latencies (implying small run-lengths), limiting the context-switch overhead to around two cycles is crucial to achieve a good performance boost.

REFERENCES

1. M. J. FLYNN and A. PODVIN, "Shared Resource Multiprocessing," IEEE Computer, **5**, pp. 20-28 (Mar./Apr. 1972).

2. P. DUBEY, K. O'BRIEN, K. M. O'BRIEN and C. BARTON, "Single-Program Speculative Multithreading (SPSM) Architecture: Compiler-assisted Fine-Grained Multithreading," Proc. PACT '95 Parallel Architecture and Compilation Techniques Conference, June 1995, pp. 109-121.

3. G. T. BYRD and M. A. HOLLIDAY, "Multithreaded Processor Architectures," IEEE Spectrum, **32**, 8, pp. 38-46 (Aug 1995).
 This paper is a recent survey of several temporally multithreaded architectures.

4. R. H. HALSTEAD JR. and F. FUJITA, "MASA: A Multithreaded Architecture for Parallel Symbolic Computing," Proc. of the 15th Annual Int. Symp. on Comp. Arch., Honolulu, Hawaii, June 1988, pp. 443-451.

5. H. HIRATA, K. KIMURA, S. NAGAMINE, Y. MOCHIZUKI, A. NISHI-MURA, Y. NAKASE and T. NISHIZAWA, "An Elementary Processor Architecture with Simultaneous Instruction Issuing from Multiple Threads," Proc. of the 19th Annual Int. Symp. on Comp. Arch., Gold Coast, Australia, May 1992, pp. 136-145.

6. D. C. MCCRACKIN, "Eliminating Interlocks in Deeply Pipelined Processors by Delay Enforced Multistreaming," IEEE Trans. on Computers, **40**,

10, pp. 1125-1132 (Oct. 1991).
This paper proposes a small latency multithreaded processor architecture and includes simulation-based performance estimates.

7. B. J. SMITH, "A Pipelined, Shared Resource MIMD Computer," Proc. of the 1978 International Conference on Parallel Processing, 1978, pp. 6-8.

8. M. R. THISTLE and B. J. SMITH, "A Processor Architecture for Horizon," Supercomputing '88, Florida, Oct. 1988, pp. 35-40.

9. K. KURIHARA, D. CHAIKEN and A. AGARWAL, "Latency Tolerance Through Multithreading in Large Scale Multiprocessors," Proc. of the Second International Symposium on Shared Memory Multiprocessing, Tokyo, Japan, April 1991, pp. 91-101.

10. W. WEBER and A. GUPTA, "Exploring the Benefits of Multiple Hardware Contexts in a Multiprocessor Architectures: Preliminary Results," Proc. of the 16th Annual Int. Symposium on Computer Architecture, Jerusalem, Israel, June 1989, pp. 273-280.
This paper presents simulation-based performance estimates for a large latency multithreaded machine.

11. A. AGARWAL, B.-H. LIM, D. KRANZ and J. KUBIATOWICZ, "APRIL: A Processor Architecture for Multiprocessing," Proc. of the 17th Annual International Symposium on Computer Architecture, May 1990, pp. 104-114.

12. T. E. MANKOVICH, V. POPESCU and H. SULLIVAN, "CHoPP Principles of Operation," Proc. of the Second International Conference on Supercomputing, May 1987, Vol. 1, pp. 2-10.

13. R. H. SAAVEDRA-BARRERA, R. H. CUELLER and T. VON EICKEN, "Analysis of Multithreaded Architectures for Parallel Computing," SPAA '90, Second Annual ACM Symposium on Parallel Algorithms and Architectures, Crete, Greece, July, 1990, pp. 169-178.
This paper presents a discrete-time model for large latency multithreaded machines with deterministic remote memory access latency and geometric inter-operand-request times.

14. A. AGARWAL, "Performance Tradeoffs in Multithreaded Processors," IEEE Trans. on Parallel and Distributed Systems, **3**, 5, pp. 525-539 (Sep. 1992).
This paper presents a deterministic (and exponential) model for large latency multithreaded machines, which includes the effects of cache interference and network contention.

15. S. KARLIN and H. M. TAYLOR, A First Course in Stochastic Processes,

Second Edition, Academic Press, 1975.

16. S. M. ROSS, Stochastic Processes, John Wiley and Sons, New York, 1983.

17. P. DUBEY, A. KRISHNA AND M. FLYNN, "Analytical Modeling of Multithreaded Pipeline Performance," Proc. of the 27th Hawaii International Conference on System Sciences, Hawaii, Jan 1994, pp. 361-367.

18. M. F. NEUTS, Matrix-Geometric Solutions in Stochastic Models: An Algorithmic Approach, The Johns Hopkins University Press, 1981.

19. J. WALRAND, An Introduction to Queueing Networks, Prentice Hall, 1988.

20. L. KLEINROCK, Queueing Systems Volume I: Theory, John Wiley and Sons, 1975.

21. S. S. LAVENBERG, Ed., Computer Performance Modeling Handbook, Academic Press, 1983.

22. P. DUBEY, A. KRISHNA AND M. S. SQUILLANTE, "Performance Modeling of a Multithreaded Processor Spectrum", Technical Report RC 19661, IBM Research Division, July 1994.

23. P. DUBEY, A. KRISHNA and M. S. SQUILLANTE, "Analytical Performance Modeling for a Spectrum of Multithreaded Processor Architectures", Proc. of the International Workshop on Modeling, Analysis and Simulation of Computer and Telecommunication Systems (MASCOTS'95), Durham, NC, Jan. 1995, pp. 110-122.

24. D. GROSS and C. HARRIS, Fundamentals of Queueing Theory, Second Edition, John Wiley and Sons, New York, 1985.

25. R. J. EICKEMEYER, R. E. JOHNSON, S. R. KUNKEL, M. S. SQUILLANTE, and S. LIU, "Evaluation of Multithreaded Uniprocessors for Commercial Application Environments," Proc. of the 23rd Annual International Symposium on Computer Architecture, May 1996.

26. J-H. TANG and K. SO, "Performance and Design Choices of Level-two Caches," Proc. of the 27th Hawaii International Conference on System Sciences, Hawaii, Jan. 1994, pp. 422-430.

CHAPTER 2

PERFORMANCE PREDICTION OF PARALLEL SYSTEMS

J.B. Sinclair and W.P. Dawkins

2.1. INTRODUCTION

Parallel processing is becoming increasingly important as the demand for computing power in many applications exceeds the capabilities of single processor systems. Even so, the difficulties in designing cost-effective parallel processing systems are apparent in the number of companies with multiprocessor products that have dropped out of this market in recent years. Building good parallel hardware is not sufficient; software at both the application and system levels must be carefully designed and tuned to provide good performance. Designers need accurate, efficient tools to evaluate the interaction of hardware and software as early in the design process as possible.

Analyzing the performance of a parallel program executing on a multiprocessor is challenging for a number of reasons. A parallel program is usually thought of as consisting of *tasks* which are allocated processors for their execution. Tasks communicate with one another to exchange data or to synchronize. Contention for processors and/or communication links may be difficult or impossible to predict exactly because of data-dependent task execution times and the effects of resource scheduling policies.

This chapter discusses an approach based on an extended task graph model of a parallel system. Task precedence constraints and synchro-

27

nization are explicitly modeled by an acyclic graph whose nodes represent tasks and edges represent communication between tasks. Each task has one or more associated resources that are required for its execution. To account for non-deterministic task execution times, the method computes task starting time *distributions* for each task, and an execution time distribution for the task graph as a whole. Scheduling decisions are in general probabilistic. Determining which of two (or more) contending tasks will be allocated a resource next will depend on the finish time distributions of their predecessor tasks. This approach has been implemented in a software package called ES (**E**vent **S**equencer)[1,2].

Markov chains[3], queueing networks[4,5], and timed Petri nets[6] or generalized stochastic Petri nets[7] are often used to study the performance of parallel systems, but all three methods have limitations. The probability distributions used in continuous time Markov chains and timed Petri nets must be exponential (or Coxian in the more generalized case). Also, as the size of the system being modeled increases, the time required to solve the model increases exponentially. Queueing networks restrict the scheduling disciplines and service time distributions that can be modeled, and are unable to model precedence constraints. Queuing networks and Markov chains are typically used to solve for steady-state behavior. This may be inappropriate when modeling a parallel system executing a particular application program where "steady-state" is not well-defined.

Simulation allows the system to be described at virtually any level of detail. Precedence constraints, scheduling policies, and other features that prove difficult to incorporate in analytic models can be dealt with easily. However, instruction-level simulations of uniprocessor systems may run one thousand times or more slower than the systems they model, and detailed simulations of parallel systems on uniprocessors would be still slower[8]. Furthermore, simulation models can take a long time to implement. Ideally, the designer would use analytical techniques to evaluate designs, and then use detailed simulations to study and improve the more promising ones.

Section 2.2 describes the modeling approach for programs and architectures in detail, and compares it to other approaches developed for the same purposes. Section 2.3 provides some details of the analytical technique as implemented in ES. ES was evaluated using both simulation and real systems, and the accuracy of its predictions is sig-

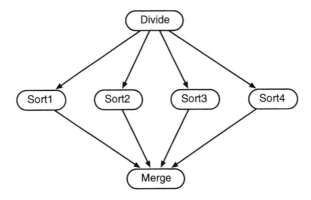

FIGURE 1.   Mergesort task graph

nificantly better than other techniques with which it can be compared.
The results of one such experiment, involving measurements obtained
from an Intel hypercube multiprocessor, are given in Section 2.4.

2.2. MODEL SPECIFICATION

Task graphs are often used to analyze parallel computing systems, but
do not incorporate information about the architecture of the system
directly. An *extended task graph* (ETG) is a combination of a task
graph representing the various tasks of a parallel algorithm and the
precedence constraints between these tasks, random variables representing the execution times of each of the tasks in the task graph, and
a description of the resources the tasks require for execution.

2.2.1 Extended Task Graphs

Many parallel algorithms consist of a set of tasks that can be represented by the nodes of a directed acyclic graph called a *task-graph*. Fig.
1 shows an example of a task graph for a parallel mergesort algorithm.
Here a task is the computation between two successive synchronization or interaction points of the parallel algorithm. Once started, a
task runs to completion without interruption. Interactions with other
tasks take place only at the beginning and end of a task[9]. The directed
edges in a task graph represent precedence constraints. For example,
the merge task in Fig. 1 may not begin execution until all of the sort

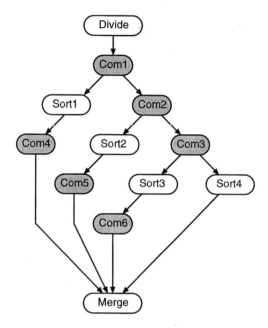

FIGURE 2.   Mergesort task graph with communications tasks added

tasks have completed. An edge (a, b) denotes that a (b) is a *predecessor* (*successor*) of b (a). A task with no predecessors is an *initial* task, and a task with no successors is a *final* task.

Each task in the graph has a random variable associated with it that represents the *task execution time*, the amount of service time the task requires on some resource. The execution time T_G of a task system with task graph G is a random variable for the time at which the last task finishes.

Tasks are not restricted to computation. The mergesort task graph of Fig. 1 can be extended to include explicit communications among computation tasks. The communications themselves are representing as communication tasks (the shaded nodes of Fig. 2. Note that sorting task Sort4 has no communication tasks associated with it; the assumption is that it executes on the same processor as the divide and merge tasks. Communications tasks may require processors, communication links, or other resources.

A number of analytical performance evaluation techniques use task graph models of parallel algorithms. Robinson[10] uses task graphs to predict bounds on the mean execution time of parallel algorithms in the absence of resource contention. Madala[9] improves on these bounds by using specific knowledge of the distributions of the task execution times at each level rather than just the means and standard deviations. Like Robinson, Madala ignores resource contention.

Thomasian and Bay[11] use a task graph to represent an algorithm and a queueing network to represent the resources in a system. They develop a Markov chain in which the states represent the tasks currently executing on the resources. The transition rates between states are the throughputs of the system resources in processing various combinations of tasks, and can be calculated using closed queuing network models. One limitation of this approach is that the Markov chain developed from a task graph with I tasks can have as many as $2^I - 1$ states. This means the number of closed queueing networks (one for each state) that must be solved can also grow exponentially.

Mak and Lundstrom[12] also use task graphs to represent algorithms and closed queueing networks to represent resources. However, they use an iterative approach that does not require the generation of Markov chains to solve their model. This makes the method computationally more efficient. Both of these approaches are limited by the use of product-form queueing network models. For example, no priority-based scheduling policies are allowed.

Sahner and Trivedi[13] assign Coxian distributed execution time random variables to each task, and perform a series of convolutions and multiplications of these distributions to determine the distribution of the execution time of the task graph. One major limitation is that they ignore resource contention.

All three of the above approaches require task graphs to be be *series-parallel* . The set of all series-parallel task graphs can be defined recursively by starting with a single node which represents the entire program and replacing a node with either a series or parallel combination of nodes[13]. Although many important classes of algorithms can be satisfied as series-parallel, others cannot. More importantly, extended task graphs have added edges which destroy the series-parallel nature of the original task graph. Fig. 3 illustrates this for the mergesort task graph of Fig. 2. The edges which have been added between communication tasks Com4 and Com5 and between Com5 and Com6 imply that these pairs of tasks require a common resource and that these tasks will

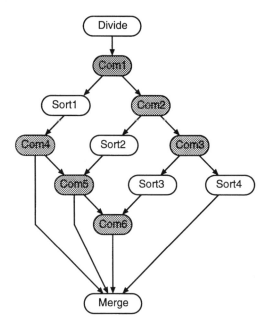

FIGURE 3. Mergesort task graph with resource-based constraints

be serialized as a result in the order Com4, Com5, and Com6. This is one of six possible orderings, and each ordering will correspond to a leaf node of the sequencing tree discussed in Sec. 2.3.

2.2.2 Resources

All hardware components of a parallel system are modeled by resources. A task must be given exclusive use of a resource for its execution. When two or more tasks are queued at the same resource, the scheduling policy associated with the resource determines which task will execute first. ES allows arbitrary non-preemptive scheduling policies to be included in the model.

2.2.3 Execution Time Distributions

The ETG approach, in common with a number of task graph analysis methods, in principle requires the ability to convolve density func-

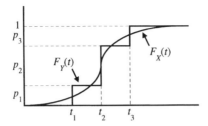

FIGURE 4.   A three-step distribution approximation

tions (when summing two independent random variables) and multiply distribution functions (to find the distribution of the maximum of independent random variables). Analyzing ETGs also involves computing probabilities of making various sequencing decisions when resource contention occurs. Efficiently performing these operations on arbitrary distributions is difficult. One way to deal with this problem is to approximate a distribution function by a member of a class of distribution functions for which these operations are greatly simplified.

One such class of approximations is those distribution functions consisting of n steps . Fig. 4 shows a 3-step distribution F_Y of a random variable Y, given by

$$F_Y(t) = p_1 u(t - t_1) + p_2 u(t - t_2) + p_3 u(t - t_3)$$

which approximates the distribution F_X of a random variable X. p_1, p_2, and p_3 are the probabilities that Y has value t_1, t_2, and t_3, respectively.

Step distributions offer several advantages. They are simple to represent, and it is trivial to convert a distribution to a density function or vice versa. Convolution of density functions and multiplication of distributions for this type of random variable are computationally efficient. Also, evaluating scheduling decision probabilities as required in the construction of the sequencing trees described in Section 2.3 is also simple.

Finding an appropriate n-step approximation for a distribution function can be done in several ways. In the present implementation of ES, approximations are based on *moment matching* . In pure moment matching, the first $2n$ moments m_0, m_1, ..., m_{2n-1} of the n-step approximation must match the first $2n$ moments of the distribution being approximated. ES currently uses 3-step approximations to match 4 moments. For the first four moments of the approximation F_Y in Fig. 4 to match the first four moments $m_0, \ldots, m_3$ of F_X, the following equations must hold.

$$
\begin{aligned}
m_0 &= p_1 + p_2 + p_3 = 1 \\
m_1 &= p_1 t_1 + p_2 t_2 + p_3 t_3 \\
m_2 &= p_1 t_1^2 + p_2 t_2^2 + p_3 t_3^2 \\
m_3 &= p_1 t_1^3 + p_2 t_2^3 + p_3 t_3^3
\end{aligned}
$$

The equations are constrained by $0 \leq p_1, p_2, p_3 \leq 1$ and $t_1 < t_2 < t_3$. Since there are six variables and only four equations, there are two degrees of freedom which can be used to satisfy additional constraints.

If the distribution of X were bounded with lower limit t_L and upper limit t_U, and the values of t_1 and t_3 were set equal to t_L and t_U, respectively, then not only would F_Y have the same first four moments as F_X but also the same upper and lower limits. This presupposes that values for p_1, p_2, p_3, and t_2 can be found that solve the above moment equations. ES uses a moment-matching method, described in [15], which finds the ranges of possible values for t_1 and t_3, allowing them to be set to arbitrary values within these ranges. In particular, t_1 and t_3 can always be set to t_L and t_U, respectively (when t_U exists).

2.3. SEQUENCING TREES

If all task execution times are deterministic, the resource scheduling policies will uniquely determine the times at which each task execution begins. However, non-deterministic execution times mean that the time at which a task begins to contend for its assigned resource is a random variable, and hence the contention at each resource and the order of task service is unpredictable.

One approach to dealing with this problem is to construct a *sequencing tree*. A sequencing tree represents the different orders of events that can occur during the execution of the task system due to *sequencing decisions* arising from resource contention and the non-deterministic finishing order of tasks. Sequencing decisions must be made when two or more tasks use the same resource and there is a non-zero probability that their executions overlap. Each possible outcome of a sequencing decision may change the sequence of subsequent events and thus affect execution time.

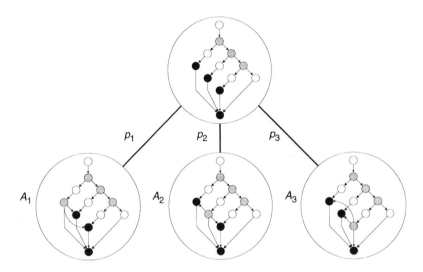

FIGURE 5.   Branching in a sequencing tree

Each node of the tree represents a state of the execution of a task system. State is defined as the condition of the tasks (unexecuted, executing, or completed), the condition of the individual resources (idle or running), and the tasks currently being service by each running resource. The directed edges in the sequencing tree represent the outcomes of sequencing decisions. Each *branching probability* p_i is the probability that a sequencing decision results in a particular outcome. A node's *path probability* is the product of all branch probabilities on the path from the root node to the node.

Fig. 5 shows a partially completed sequencing tree corresponding to the task system whose task graph is shown in Fig. 2. Assume that communication tasks Com4, Com5, and Com6 use the same communication link (e.g., a bus connecting all processors). The root node of the sequencing tree shows the state of the task system analysis at the point where the first sequencing decision must be made. The solid black nodes correspond to all the tasks whose start time distributions (and hence finish time distributions) have not been computed yet. If Com4, Com5, and Com6 did not share any resources, their start time distributions could be computed since the finish times of the sort tasks Sort1, Sort2, and Sort3 are known.

However, assuming that the finish time distributions of Sort1, Sort2, and Sort3 overlap, it is necessary to determine the probabilities p_1, p_2, and p_3 that Sort1, Sort2, and Sort3, respectively, finish first. A node is added as a child of the root node for each of these possible outcomes. The task graph associated with each new node adds edges representing contention-based serialization from the communication task which uses the bus first to the other two communication tasks.

The leaf nodes in the partially completed sequencing tree of Fig. 5 may not be leaf nodes in the final sequencing tree. For instance, the task graph corresponding to leaf node A_1 in Fig. 5 has two tasks (Com5 and Com6) that contend for the use of the bus. When the latest possible finish times of Sort2 and Sort3 are less than the latest finish time of Com4, the sequencing of Com5 and Com6 is determined by the scheduling policy associated with the bus. If this policy is deterministic (for example, based on fixed and distinct priorities for the processors), A_1 will be a leaf node in the final sequencing tree. Otherwise, a sequencing decision based on the finish time distributions of Com4, Sort2, and Sort3 as well as the scheduling policy for the bus must be made, and A_1 will not be a leaf node of the complete sequencing tree.

If the completed sequencing tree has n leaf nodes $A_1, \ldots, A_n$, and if leaf node A_i has path probability P_i and a task graph finish time distribution F_i, then the overall finish time distribution $F(t)$ for the task system is given by

$$F(t) = \sum_{i=1}^{n} P_i F_i(t)$$

One problem with this technique is that as the size of the task system model increases the number of nodes in the sequencing tree can grow exponentially. To curb this exponential growth, ES provides a heuristic for basing predictions on partial constructions of sequencing trees. The method allows a tradeoff between accuracy and efficiency. A terminal node of the sequencing tree represents a completed task system execution. When specifying a task system, the user may specify a *cumulative terminal node probability level* with or without a *terminal node limit*. ES will generate a sequencing tree until the sum of the path probabilities of the terminal nodes created exceeds the cumulative terminal node probability level, or the number of terminal nodes created exceeds the terminal node limit. When a new node of the sequencing tree are created, ES computes the probability that the node is the outcome of a sequencing decision. At each sequencing decision, ES expands the sequencing tree below the outcome nodes with higher probabilities first.

When the cumulative terminal node probability level or terminal node limit is reached, ES predicts the execution time of the task system based on the terminal nodes already created. For example, if the user specifies a cumulative terminal node probability level of 50%, a sequencing tree is constructed until the sum of the terminal node path probabilities exceeds 50%. The depth-first construction method attempts to make sure the higher probability sequences of events are represented in the predictions returned by ES. However, there is no guarantee that a terminal node not generated will have a node path probability less than that of each of the generated terminal nodes. ES also attempts to reduce the number of nodes in the sequencing tree by eliminating sequencing decisions that are not needed to resolve resource contention [1].

2.4. EXPERIMENTAL RESULTS

This section illustrates the accuracy of this approach by comparing the mean execution time of a mergesort algorithm implemented on an Intel iPSC/860 hypercube parallel computer to the mean estimated by ES. Fig. 1 shows the task graph of the mergesort algorithm analyzed. The mergesort algorithm operates in the following manner. For an n-processor system, the *divide* task partitions the unsorted data into n equal parts and sends the data over the interconnection network to the n *sort* tasks. There is one sort task assigned to each processor. Each sort task sorts its local data and sends the sorted data to the merge task. Fig. 1 does not show the tasks associated with communication. These include tasks associated with software overhead and tasks representing the actual transmission of data over physical links.

The distributions of the computation task execution times were obtained experimentally by running the mergesort on one processor of the iPSC/860. Other experiments were run to determine the software and hardware overheads of sending messages of various sizes on the iPSC/860. The software overheads generally were orders of magnitude larger than hardware overheads. Thus, messages traveling through intermediate nodes did not see a significant increase in transmission time. Consequently, we modeled the communication structure of the

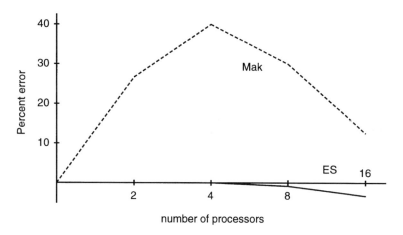

FIGURE 6.   Error for predicted mean execution time of mergesort

iPSC/860 as a fully connected network. The data taken from the message passing experiments and the single processor measurements were used in the ES task system models of the mergesort algorithm executing on larger systems.

The parallel program sorted 100,000 32-bit integers on an iPSC/860, using subcubes of up to sixteen processors. The average execution times were compared to estimates from ES. Fig. 6 shows the error between the ES estimates of the mean execution times to those measured on the iPSC/860. Multiple sorts of different sets of random data were performed on the iPSC/860, and the means of the task execution times and the total execution time were calculated with 99.9% confidence intervals for confidence interval widths less than 1% of the sample means. In this experiment, ES constructed complete sequencing trees to obtain the maximum accuracy.

Fig. 6 shows that the error of the ES estimate increased as the number of processors being modeled increased. The maximum error was 4.4% at sixteen processors. The increase in error was most likely due to an unmodeled increase in software overhead for handling larger numbers of messages simultaneously. Fig. 6 also shows estimates obtained using the Mak-Lundstrom approach. The Mak-Lundstrom predictions, which are based only on means and not on higher moments, are considerably less accurate than ES.

2.5. CONCLUSIONS

The combination of extended task graph models, sequencing trees, and simple distribution approximations as implemented in ES provides a powerful tool for the study of parallel systems, particularly those with coarse-grain parallelism. It is possible to analyze models of parallel systems that include precedence and synchronization constraints, arbitrary task execution time distributions, and resource contention with non-preemptive scheduling policies. The size of the sequencing tree can grow exponentially with the number of sequencing decisions that must be made, but this growth can be controlled by pruning less likely branches, without significant loss of accuracy.

REFERENCES

1. W.P. DAWKINS, *Analytical Performance Prediction of Parallel Systems* (Ph.D. Thesis, Rice University, 1993).

This thesis provides much more detail on the performance prediction technique described in this chapter.

2. W.P. DAWKINS and J.B. SINCLAIR, "ES: A Tool for Predicting the Performance of Parallel Systems," in *Proc. Int. Workshop on Modeling, Analysis, and Simulation of Computer and Telecommunication Systems* (1994), 164–168.

Details of a modeling tool (ES) based on sequencing trees, including a description of the input language.

3. W.J. STEWART, "A Comparison of Numerical Techniques in Markov Modeling," *CACM*, **21**, 144–152 (1978).

A good survey of five approaches to obtaining the stationary probability vector of a continuous time Markov model, including the reasons for accuracy problems with some of the methods.

4. F. BASKETT, K.M. CHANDY, R.R. MUNTZ and F.G. PALA-CIOS, "Open, Closed and Mixed Networks of Queues with Different Classes of Customers," *JACM*, **22**, 248–260 (1975).

The classic paper characterizing queueing networks with product-form solutions based on the queueing disciplines and service time distributions of the individual queues.

5. E.D. LAZOWSKA, J. ZAHORJAN, G.S. GRAHAM and K.C. SEV-CIK, *Quantitative System Performance* (Englewood Cliffs, NJ, Prentice-Hall, 1984).

This book focuses on the use of operational analysis to solve models of computer systems. It provides several good examples of approximate solution techniques for models which are not product form.

6. M.A. HOLLIDAY and M.K. VERNON, "A Generalized Timed Petri Net Model for Performance Analysis," *IEEE Trans. Software Engineering*, **SE-13**, 1297–1310 (1987).

Parallel system performance modeling based on a generalization of Timed Petri Nets which has capabilities not in other Petri net-based models.

7. M.A. MARSAN, G. BALBO, and G. CONTE, *Performance Models of Multiprocessor Systems* (Cambridge, MA, MIT Press, 1986).

An excellent survey of several important techniques in the analysis of parallel computer systems. Chapter 4 provides a brief but good introduction to Petri nets and some of the more interesting extensions.

8. R.G. COVINGTON, S. DWARKADAS, J.R. JUMP, J.B. SIN-CLAIR and S. MADALA, "Efficient Simulation of Parallel Computer Systems," *Int. J. Computer Simulation*, **1**, 31–58 (1991).

The Rice Parallel Processing Testbed uses execution-driven simulation to obtain performance information about multiprocessors executing parallel programs. The paper compare the accuracy of its estimates with measurements obtained from real multiprocessors.

9. S. MADALA, *Performance of Synchronous Parallel Algorithms with Regular Structures*, (Ph.D. Thesis, Rice University, 1988).

An example of the use of extreme-value theory to obtain both non-parametric and distribution-dependent estimates of the expected execution time of a task graph representing a parallel program.

10. J.T. ROBINSON, "Some Analysis Techniques for Asynchronous Multiprocessor Algorithms," *IEEE Trans. Software Engineering*, **SE-5**, 24–31 (1979).

A seminal paper in the use of extreme value theory to analyze task graphs where the task execution times are independent random variables. Both static and dynamic problem decompositions are studied.

11. A. THOMASIAN and P.F. BAY, "Analytic Queueing Network Models for Parallel Processing of Task Systems," *IEEE Trans. Computers*, **C-35**, 1045–1054 (1986).

Analysis of task graphs with resource contention, using a combination of Markov chain and queueing network analysis. The transition rates for the Markov model are the throughputs of a queueing network model representing the computer system.

12. V.W. MAK and S.F. LUNDSTROM, "Predicting Performance of Parallel Computations," *IEEE Trans. Parallel and Distributed Systems*, **1**, 257–270 (1990).

The authors model a parallel program as a series-parallel, acyclic task graph. Resources in a parallel processor are represented by service centers in a queueing network. A two-step iterative process uses queueing network analysis techniques to find approximate solutions for a system that includes task precedence constraints.

13. R.A. SAHNER and K.S. TRIVEDI, "Performance and Reliability Analysis Using Directed Acyclic Graphs," *IEEE Trans. Software Engineering*, **SE-13**, 1105–1114 (1987).

Describes a graph-based modeling technique for analyzing concurrent systems with stochastic events. The graphs are required to be series-parallel, but the distribution functions associated with activities are equivalent to Coxian distributions.

14. J.B. SINCLAIR, "Distribution Approximation for Parallel System Analysis" (TR9206, Dept. of Electrical and Computer Engineering, Rice University, 1992).

A detailed discussion of the method used to approximate distributions in the ES performance prediction tool by moment matching with a simple m-step distribution function.

CHAPTER 3

PERFORMANCE MODELING THROUGH FUNCTIONAL ALGORITHM SIMULATION

Marios Dikaiakos   Anne Rogers   Kenneth Steiglitz

1. INTRODUCTION

A fundamental problem in parallel processing is to identify sources of
performance degradation in parallel applications, both quantitatively
and qualitatively. This is critical for conducting optimizations to improve the performance, efficiency and scalability of parallel applications,
as well as to guide the development of architectures and programming
environments. In this chapter we address some of the issues involved
in the modeling and evaluation of parallel scientific computations running on message-passing systems. In particular, we present **Functional
Algorithm Simulation**, an approximate simulation scheme that enables us to model and study parallel executions of much larger problem
sizes and more processors than those reported so far in a workstation
environment. Also, it allows us to collect detailed information characterizing parallel executions on various message-passing architectures,
analyze the effects of communication overhead on parallel performance,
and study the scalability of parallel algorithms.

Current methodologies for parallel performance analysis range from
trace collection and analysis to modeling. The former approach is incremental; it uses instrumentation and monitoring tools to collect trace-
data from parallel runs. Traces are processed by analysis tools seeking to expose actual overheads. Users interpret the output of analysis

engines and adapt their codes so as to eliminate apparent bottlenecks. Then, they repeat the instrumentation - tracing - analysis process. This approach is sufficiently accurate in terms of capturing the performance behavior of parallel programs. Instrumentation and tracing, however, inherently consume many resources, making it expensive and tedious to explore parallel performance for different program and machine configurations. Moreover, it is often difficult to associate the performance degradation observed with bottlenecks inherent to the programs or the algorithms studied.

Performance evaluation of parallel systems through **modeling** relies on **models**, that is, abstractions expressing system components and interactions among them. Models abstract hardware and system-software performance characteristics, parallel algorithms and programs, the scheduling of parallel tasks to processors, input data and their partitioning. Typical examples of abstractions are sets of parameters such as the number of processors expressing the size of a multiprocessor system, the CPU clock-rate marking the speed of its processors, the number of grid-points in a grid-structured application representing the size of input data, etc. Interconnection topologies and parallel programs are typically modeled with graphs.

In comparison with instrumentation and measurement, modeling represents a more structured approach to parallel performance analysis. It can be used effectively to explore a wide space of system and program configurations as it is not subject to the various tracing overheads and costs. It simplifies performance prediction, allowing users to simply change model-parameters in order to estimate performance effects with a varying parallel execution setup. Moreover, modeling can elide artifacts that implementation-specific issues have on observed performance. Developing proper models for parallel performance analysis, however, is difficult: simple models usually make simplifying assumptions that restrict their applicability to a coarse level of detail; more complex models, on the other hand, are much more difficult to design, gauge and implement. Finally, models are not as accurate as instrumentation and monitoring systems in estimating actual values of specific performance metrics.

Practical experience shows, however, that program optimization consists of two distinct activities: First, the rough program behavior must be observed to identify performance bottlenecks. Once these bottlenecks have been isolated, the second task of performing more detailed instrumentation and analysis is considerably simplified. Clearly, the former task is akin to performance modeling whereas the latter requires the use of instrumentation and tracing tools.

1.1. Theoretical Modeling

Several approaches have been developed to model parallel performance and guide parallel program development. Most of them can be classified into two broad categories: **theoretical** and **structural** modeling. Theoretical models abstract selected features of a parallel system using sets of parameters, parameterized functions, theorems or statistical distributions. Typical examples of theoretical models for parallel computation are the various flavors of **PRAM**[1], **BSP**[2] and **LogP**[3]. These models associate performance estimates with a small number of key parameters such as the number of processors, the problem size, the average message latency, etc. They provide algorithm designers with a convenient platform for expressing new algorithms formally and proving theorems about their complexity. Nevertheless, they abstract parallel architectures using unrealistic assumptions, like zero communication costs and infinite bandwidth (in the case of PRAM's). Moreover, they have restricted capabilities for expressing communication behavior (e.g. congestion) and evaluating the performance of parallel algorithms with irregular structure and dynamic behavior.

A popular approach to theoretical modeling for performance prediction employs, along with scalar parameters, parameterized mathematical formulas that model interesting aspects of parallel performance behavior. For instance, Sun and Shu[4] use mathematical definitions of scalability to study and predict application scalability on shared-memory parallel architectures. Their formulas include parameters describing system characteristics, which are obtained experimentally. This approach, however, models applications at a high level of abstraction. Therefore, it is applicable mainly when studying coarse characteristics of application kernels, like the effects of machine and problem size on speedup.

Another approach to theoretical modeling relies on probability distributions and queueing models to abstract workload characteristics. The combination of statistical models with theoretical analysis or simulation proves to be useful in the study of certain aspects of parallel systems, like interconnection network performance, scheduling policies, and workload scalability. For example, measurement of interconnection network performance can be carried out with simulations of queueing models or with the use of synthetic computation and communication benchmarks[5]. These methods are applicable when comparing different interconnection strategies and establishing general principles about network design.

1.2. Structural Modeling

In contrast to theoretical modeling, structural modeling is based on software-based abstractions of parallel architectures and/or parallel programs. An example of structural modeling is execution-driven simulation, that is, a combination of simulation and direct execution. Execution-driven simulation uses software simulators as a way of modeling parallel architectures accurately and at a low level of detail. Notably, execution-driven simulators can capture the behavior of interconnection networks, on-processor caches and cache-coherence protocols. The simulators run on workstations[6,7] or parallel machines[8,9], executing application programs directly. At the occurrence of a modeled event, like the dispatch of a message or access to a shared variable, execution is interrupted and the simulator takes over simulating the behavior of the communication or the cache subsystem, respectively.

Execution-driven simulation has thus far been successful in studying modest-size applications[10], but it appears to have limitations in studying large parallel systems and issues of scalability. In such cases, the memory required to hold program and computer system state and the time to simulate execution on many processors become prohibitively high.

In order to overcome simulation overheads, researchers are developing methods for modeling parallel applications and conducting performance prediction based on such models[11,12,13]. Parallel program modeling can be manual, semi-automated or fully automated. Parallel program models are combined with models for parallel architectures of interest, in order to produce performance results like running time and scalability estimates, measurements of communication overhead, etc.

In this chapter we describe **Functional Algorithm Simulation**, a structural approach for modeling a large class of parallel scientific computations on message-passing multiprocessors. Furthermore, we describe **FAST** (Functional Algorithm Simulation Testbed), a prototype system that we built to assess our methodology. Functional Algorithm Simulation incorporates models for:

- Parallel scientific programs;

- Data partitioning;

- Mapping tasks to processors;

- Processor speed;

- Interconnection network topology and performance.

In the Functional Algorithm Simulation approach, the model of a parallel program describes the **skeleton** of its corresponding computation on a given set of input data. The skeleton represents the set of computations and communications executed during a parallel run of the program considered, on the input data at hand. FAST parses the skeleton into a task-flow graph and provides software libraries for mapping this graph to a set of processors. Subsequently, it interprets the mapped task-flow graph and generates a sequence of communication events (message sends and receives) that drive an interconnection network simulator for the topology of choice. A number of parameters are used to describe processor speed in terms of clock cycle time and cycles-per-instruction figures. Also, parameters describe interconnection network performance in terms of message setup and receive overheads and communication channel bandwidth. FAST provides a number of simulators for different interconnection topologies: hypercubes, rings and multi-rings.

Using FAST, we can model various aspects of parallel performance like parallel time, speedup, scalability, profiles of parallelism, and the effects that communication overhead has on application performance. Furthermore, we can compare the effectiveness of various algorithms for mapping tasks to parallel processors and the relative efficiency of different interconnection topologies.

In the following sections we give a detailed description of Functional Algorithm Simulation and FAST. We present a case study showing that FAST can provide accurate and detailed information about the algorithms examined, with minimal resources. This is a study on **SIMPLE**, a popular **Computational Fluid Dynamics** benchmark simulating the hydrodynamics of a pressurized fluid inside a spherical cell. Other case studies with FAST can be found in the first author's dissertation[15]. Finally, we conclude with a discussion and suggestions for future work.

2. FUNCTIONAL ALGORITHM SIMU-LATION

We seek methodologies for modeling and evaluating parallel computations that satisfy the following requirements: (1) They should be flexible to allow the assessment of a large variety of parallel machines with processor numbers ranging from tens to thousands, with different topologies and message-passing interface primitives, and various hardware characteristics. (2) They should be general enough to apply in the study of a comprehensive group of algorithms running on realistic sets of data. (3) They should allow algorithmic and architectural assessments with a moderate cost in terms of development and evaluation time, and invested money. (4) They should be accurate enough to guide the further development of algorithms and architectures.

To satisfy these requirements, we developed a method which exploits two properties common to many parallel scientific applications:

- Most of the parallel execution time is spent in expensive numerical operations/procedures;

- The number and the nature of these operations as well as the data-dependencies and communication occurring among them can be determined during the initialization phase of the algorithms, after the input of data and the setup of data structures. Another underlying assumption is that the initialization phase takes an insignificant portion of the overall parallel time.

Both assumptions are valid for many important scientific algorithms having applications in Computational Fluid Dynamics, Finite Difference Methods, Astrophysics and Computational Molecular Biology (tree-algorithms for the N-Body problem), Multigrid techniques, Lattice-Gas computations, as well as for numerous signal processing algorithms.

By generating the computational domain of an algorithm and identifying the set of "core" operations and communications performed on it, we are able to derive profiles characterizing an algorithm without having to simulate most instructions involved in its parallel execution.

With this remark in mind we introduced **Functional Algorithm Simulation**, a method for **approximately** simulating real parallel executions.

By not doing the numerical calculations, Functional Algorithm Simulation achieves orders of magnitude savings in terms of processor cycles and memory space. These savings enable us to increase the flexibility of simulations, study the performance and scalability of algorithms on parallel machines with thousands of processors, and compare the performance of different interconnection networks under realistic traffic loads.

3. DESCRIPTION OF FAST

To test the Functional Algorithm Simulation method we developed a prototype system called **Functional Algorithm Simulation Testbed (FAST)**. We used FAST to perform functional simulations on a number of interesting scientific algorithms and extract information related to their implementation on message-passing multiprocessors with various configurations and machine sizes[15]. In order to perform a functional simulation of an algorithm, one has to provide FAST with:

1. A sequential implementation of the algorithm, modified so as to generate at run-time the sets of calculations and data-dependences composing the computation, instead of executing actual instructions.

2. The input data that would be provided to a sequential implementation of the algorithm.

3. The target parallel architecture, which is described by specifying a number of processors, selecting one out of a set of available interconnection topologies and message-passing interface paradigms (e.g. asynchronous, blocking), and specifying hardware characteristics such as processor speeds and communication bandwidth.

4. The strategies for partitioning the problem and mapping it onto the target architecture.

FAST generates a **task-flow graph** describing the parallel execution of the algorithm at hand on the chosen architecture for the specific input data. From the task-flow graph, it extracts useful information such as the parallel-time of the execution, speedups achieved for a large range of processor numbers, utilization of processors and communication links, computation-to-communication ratios, distribution of message sources and destinations, and effects of congestion and communication overhead on parallel-time.

FAST is split in two parts: a front-end and a back-end. The front-end generates the task-flow graph that encapsulates operations and data exchanges performed according to the algorithmic description for a given setup of algorithmic parameters and input data. The back-end performs the mapping of the task-flow graph onto a parallel architecture and generates a modified task-flow graph representing the parallel execution on the chosen architecture.

3.1. Front-End

The task-flow graph generation is accomplished by the front-end in two phases. The first one depends on the algorithm studied: given a sequential implementation, the user modifies it by inserting code that produces dynamically the set of calculations and communications that define the corresponding parallel execution. The modified program is the first phase of FAST's front-end for the specific algorithm. Running this program on some appropriate input configuration produces an architecture-independent **Intermediate Representation (IR)** of the parallel execution.

The Intermediate Representation is given in terms of a simple **intermediate language** comprised of **IR-operations** and **Send/Receive** communication primitives. Each IR-operation is an abstraction of a "medium-grain" group of successive numerical instructions. These groups correspond to the **basic computational blocks** of the algorithm. **Send/Receive** primitives correspond to data-dependences between IR-operations and represent the data-flow.

As an example we give a small piece of pseudo-code and present the steps taken to derive the code that produces its Intermediate Representation. This pseudo-code computes upon a two-dimensional grid of size $siz\_x \times siz\_y$ and calculates values of variables at each point of the grid as a function of variables from this point and neighboring ones. It is a simplified version of the routine that calculates temperature and heat variables in the SIMPLE application[16]

```
for j=0 to siz_Y do
 for i=0 to siz_X do
  D[i,j]=s[i,j]+R[i,j]+R[i,j-1]*(1-A[i,j])
  A[i,j]=R[i,j]/D[i,j]
  V[i,j]=(R[i,j-1]*V[i,j-1]+
       s[i,j]*H[i,j])/D[i,j]
 endfor
endfor
```

We notice that in every grid-point (i,j), the computation above requires the values R[i,j-1] and V[i,j-1] from the neighboring point (i,j-1), as well as values of "local" variables, that is, s[i,j], R[i,j], etc. This computation can be represented in an intermediate language format as follows (for every i, j such that $0 < i$, $j < siz\_x$, siz_y) :

```
Grid-point[i, j] :
 RECEIVE from [i,j-1]: R[i,j-1], 8 bytes
 RECEIVE from [i,j-1]: V[i,j-1], 8 bytes
 DAV_comp: DAV_COMP
 SEND to [i,j+1]: R[i,j+1], 8 bytes
 SEND to [i,j+1]: V[i,j+1], 8 bytes
```

DAV_comp denotes an IR-operation corresponding to the basic computational block of instructions that compute D[i,j], A[i,j], and V[i,j]. DAV_COMP is a constant representing the time spent for the calculation of values D[i,j], A[i,j], and V[i,j]. Such constants are expressed in terms of seconds, machine cycles, or instruction counts. In the current implementation of FAST we compute them manually by counting the corresponding machine instructions (e.g. three floating-point multiplications, one floating-point division, etc.). If necessary, the machine instruction counts are transformed into machine cycles or seconds by taking into consideration **cycles-per-instruction** figures from some specific hardware platform.

The first part of FAST's front-end generates an intermediate description of the algorithm examined for a certain input data-set. For instance, the following piece of C-code generates the Intermediate Representation for our example and can be used as the first part of a FAST simulator for this example application.

```
for (i=0; i<siz_X; i++)
  for (j=0; j<siz_Y; j++) {
   if (j-1 > 0) {
    printf("RECEIVE [%d,%d]:%d",i,j-1,siz(*R));
    printf("RECEIVE [%d,%d]:%d",i,j-1,siz(*V));
```

```
  }
  printf("DAV_comp: %lf", DAV_COMP);
  if (j+1 < siz_Y) {
    printf("SEND [%d,%d]:%d",i,j+1,siz(*R));
    printf("SEND [%d,%d]:%d",i,j+1,siz(*V));
  }
}
```

The actual values that would be received, computed, and sent in a real implementation of this example are not of interest. Functional algorithm simulation focuses on extracting information about the **sets** of computations performed and about the sources, destinations, and sizes of messages exchanged; not the numerical values of the results.

In the second phase of the front-end a parser transforms the Intermediate Representation into a weighted **task-flow graph** that follows the **Macro-Dataflow** model of computation[17]. Task-nodes in the graph contain a number of Intermediate Representation primitives. Their "boundaries" are defined by **Send** and **Receive** primitives occurring in the IR. The tasks start executing upon receipt of all incoming data and continue to completion without interruption. Upon completion their results are forwarded to adjacent nodes. Edges correspond to **Send-Receive** pairs and represent the data dependencies between the nodes. Tasks are generated by FAST with no implicit assumptions regarding partitioning and placement of data.

FAST takes into account the case where the data-structures of the parallel execution studied are partitioned into blocks: this option corresponds to the static data-partitioning approach used frequently in practice when parallelizing scientific applications. To this end, the user of FAST has the flexibility to have the system partition the data-structures into blocks structured either according to a given geometry or in compliance to some specified heuristic. Tasks belonging to the same partition will eventually be merged into a sequential thread of execution.

3.2. Back-End

The back-end of FAST (see Figure 1) receives the output from the front-end and maps the task-flow graph onto a message-passing multiprocessor architecture. The mapping process is accomplished in a number of successive steps: first, FAST maps the task-flow graph onto an idealized architecture with a number of processors equal to the number of

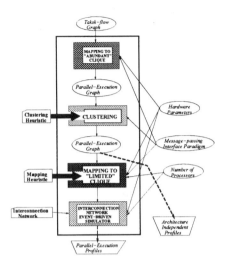

Figure 1: Back-end of the FAST.

tasks, forming a fully-connected network (**"abundant" clique**). The resulting graph is called the **parallel-execution graph**. Furthermore, the user can select a communication paradigm for the message-passing interface, from a couple of available choices such as synchronous or asynchronous blocking **Send**'s and **Receive**'s.

The parallel execution graph is subsequently passed through **clustering**, a stage seeking to minimize the communication overhead of the parallel execution, without sacrificing parallelism[17]. Clustering has been proven to be NP-Complete. A library of different heuristics has been implemented in FAST to allow experimentation with different clustering methods. After clustering, FAST performs a **mapping** of the clustered parallel-execution graph onto a message-passing architecture. The number of processors is provided by the user of the system. This mapping problem is also NP-complete[17]. To map the task-clusters onto processors we have implemented and incorporated in our system another library of heuristics similar to those included in the clustering stage[18]. A detailed description of the clustering and mapping stages are presented in Dikaiakos et al.[18].

A number of different interconnection schemes are available in the current version of FAST: a "limited" clique (a clique with a limited number of processors), a ring, various multirings, and a binary hypercube. The **limited clique** represents the fastest possible parallel implementation of the applications studied, for the number of available processors and the clustering and mapping heuristics adopted. Although it is not a realistic interconnection topology, it is useful for benchmarking the efficiency of architectures with the same number of processors and sparser topologies.

4. MODELING SIMPLE

The SIMPLE computation simulates the hydrodynamics of a pressurized fluid inside a spherical cell. The computer simulation of each time-step solves a number of equations on a two-dimensional grid with size proportional to the size of the spherical cell examined, and updates the values of various physical variables. Every time-step in SIMPLE can be split in five successive phases, according to different types of data dependencies and communication patterns occurring in the algorithm[16]: **Delta** phase (computation of the length of the next time-step), **Hydro** phase (computation of new acceleration, velocity, coordinates, Jacobian, volume of revolution, new density, artificial viscosity, new energy, and pressure), **Heat** phase (computation of the new temperature and heat), **Energy1** phase (computation of energy and work), and **Energy2** phase (computation of total heat, and error). Computation and communication patterns are identical across different time-steps. Therefore, it suffices to simulate and study one time-step only.

4.1. Experiments with SIMPLE

We chose to study SIMPLE because there exist a number of published performance measurements by different research groups[16,19]. Therefore, we can use it to assess the validity of the Functional Algorithm Simulation method and the accuracy of FAST. We compare published measurements and estimations of parallel time and speedup with the respective figures reported by our system. The data reported by Rogers[16] and Lin & Snyder[19] were collected from implementations of SIMPLE on the iPSC/2 multiprocessor. Thus, for the functional simulations of SIMPLE, we provided FAST with the hardware parameters of the iPSC/2. Furthermore, FAST partitioned SIMPLE's two-dimensional grids into blocks, according to a block-partitioning scheme.

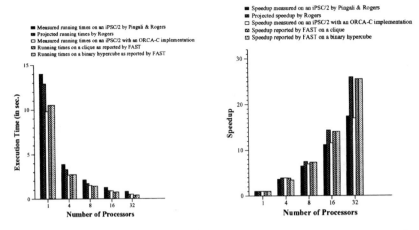

Figure 2: Parallel Time and Speedup for SIMPLE on 4096-point grid.

We should point out, however, that far as parallel time is concerned, different implementations of SIMPLE report different execution times because of differences in machine configurations and software platforms.

Figure 2 (left), shows the parallel execution times of SIMPLE on a 4096-point grid for one time-step. The plots labeled "Measured running times" and "Projected running times" present data from Rogers' thesis[19]. The "Measured running times" correspond to a SIMPLE-implementation with Pingali and Rogers' parallelizing compiler. The "Projected running times" were extracted from a model of a hand-written implementation of SIMPLE which takes into consideration the extra overhead representative of the functional language used [19] (e.g. time spent for array allocations), as well as times spent for floating-point computations and message transmissions. This model is optimistic because it assumes that the workload can be divided evenly among all processors and that the processors are fully utilized during parallel execution. Times reported by FAST correspond to two different interconnection networks: a (limited) clique and a binary hypercube. The clique and the hypercube show almost identical performance characteristics since communication overhead is dominated more by the high setup times and less by propagation and congestion delays. Figure 2 (right), gives the respective speedups, plus the speedup achieved with an ORCA-C implementation of SIMPLE by Lin and Snyder[16].

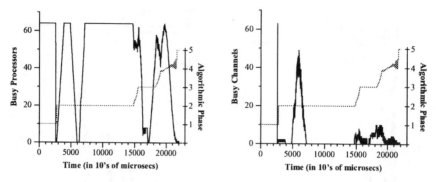

Figure 3: FAST results for 4096 grid-point SIMPLE on a 64-processor **clique** (Parallel Time = 220,022 μs).

From these diagrams, we can see that our system reports numbers that are quite close to measurements and projections by other researchers. In fact, the parallel times given by FAST are slightly smaller than those of the optimistic model for the hand-written implementation. This does not come as a surprise since the code that generated the Intermediate Representation of the parallel execution was hand-written, and also we did not take into consideration other parameters besides computation and communication times (for instance, system overhead). FAST gave us the flexibility, however, to experiment with much larger problem sizes and more processors than those reported so far. We have conducted experiments with up to 2^{20} grid points and predicted performance for machines with up to 1,024 processors[15].

4.2. Using FAST to collect profiles for SIMPLE

To illustrate the use of FAST further, we used it to gather profiles of SIMPLE executions over a wide range of problem and machine sizes. In Figure 3, we present the time-histogram of busy processors and channels during a parallel execution on a 64-processor **clique** of a 4096-point grid problem (solid line). Moreover, we present an approximate estimate of FAST for the duration of the five algorithmic phases of SIMPLE during this execution; the nodes of the task-flow graph can be ascribed to one of these phases.

From the left diagram in Figure 3 we can see that available parallelism is very high in the first phase when all processors simultaneously compute a tentative value for the next time-step. Then, they send their outcome to a single processor, which calculates and broadcasts back the global time-step. This results in the first spike of busy links in the right diagram of Figure 3 and the corresponding sharp drop in the number of busy processors. At the beginning of the second phase (**Hydro**), processors compute acceleration, velocity, and new coordinates for their assigned parts of the grid, and forward the new values to their neighbors. This explains the high number of active tasks, the subsequent sharp drop in processor activity, and the corresponding second spike of busy communication-links. Parallelism starts increasing as processors resume their local execution of the second phase, after having sent and received messages to and from neighboring processors. The third phase (**Heat**), consists of a short, highly parallel computation and two "sweeps" of the grid along its horizontal and vertical directions. Thus, it is mostly sequential and requires limited data-exchange between grid-points[16]. Parallelism drops sharply and active links are few. In the fourth phase (**Energy1**), computations are local in nature and parallelism is high. Finally, the fifth phase is very short and its effect on overall parallel time is negligible. It performs a fast aggregate operation over all grid-points to accumulate the total energy and work. An almost identical computation profile is derived from the functional simulation of a 4096 grid-point SIMPLE simulation running on a 64-processor **binary hypercube**.

4.3. Scalability Analysis of SIMPLE with FAST

FAST gives us the opportunity to study the scalability of an algorithm. Figure 4 (left) presents FAST-predictions of maximum speedups extracted from a large set of FAST-runs simulating different problem and machine sizes.

The right diagram in Figure 4 presents speedup curves for cliques (dotted lines) and hypercubes (solid lines) with 16 to 1024 processors. We notice that there is a point in the number of processors after which the speedups saturate. This is due to communication overhead and to inherently sequential sections of the program. FAST helped us identify these sequential sections: besides the third phase (Heat), which is largely sequential, there is a long sequential part in the first phase of SIMPLE (**Delta**). This corresponds to the time when one processor computes the global time-step by taking the minimum over all tenta-

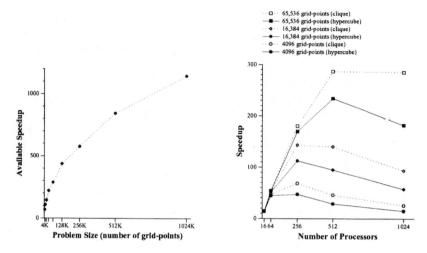

Figure 4: Speedups reported by FAST for SIMPLE executions.

tive time-steps computed locally by other processors. An estimate of
the effects that inherently sequential parts of SIMPLE have on performance scaling is given in Figure 5. It displays the ratio of the portion
of SIMPLE's **parallel execution** that runs sequentially in the absence
of communication overhead, over the total sequential execution time.
We can see that for a given problem size, the non-parallelizable portion
of the algorithm increases with the number of processors. According to
Amdhal's law, this results in a decrease in the efficiency of parallel executions as processor numbers increase. It represents one of the reasons
for the saturation of speedups observed in Figure 4 (right).

To explore this further, in Figure 6 (left) we give a diagram of the
upper bound on speedup derived from a generalized version of Amdhal's
law. Also, we give a diagram of speedups reported by FAST for the
16,384-point grid case on the clique and the hypercube. The generalized
version of Amdhal's law that we use to estimate a tighter upper bound
on speedup is as follows : $speedup = 1/\sum_1^P f_i/i$, where f_i is the fraction
of the sequential computation time which attains a speedup of i on a
P-processor parallel implementation with zero communication costs. f_i
can be easily computed by FAST as the product of i times the portion of
the parallel execution during which there are exactly i busy processors,
over the total sequential execution time. From the plot in Figure 6

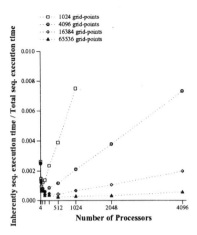

Figure 5: Fraction of sequential execution time that cannot be parallelized.

(left) we see that the speedup reported by the generalized version of Amdhal's law saturates when the number of processors exceeds 2048. On the other hand, speedups corresponding to functional simulations of cliques and hypercubes saturate for numbers of processors beyond 256.

This discrepancy is due to communication costs which have not been accounted for in the Amdhal's law speedups. This is shown in the right diagram of Figure 6, which displays the change of average task processing time and average message delay with respect to the number of available processors for the 16384-point grid. With the increase in machine-size, task-granularities decrease and average message delays increase, in both clique and hypercube interconnection. From Figure 6 (right), we notice that speedup-saturation occurs at the point where the average communication delay exceeds average task execution time.

5. CONCLUSIONS

In this chapter we presented the Functional Algorithm Simulation method, a methodology for modeling the performance of parallel scientific computations that run on message-passing multiprocessors. We described

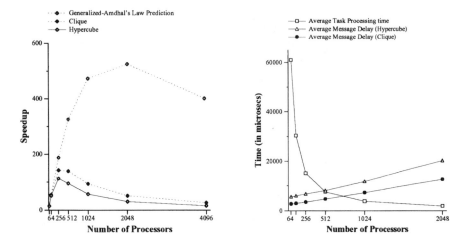

Figure 6: Speedups, average task-execution times and average message delays (16,384-point grid).

the Functional Algorithm Simulation Testbed (FAST), a prototype system that we built to evaluate our approach. We presented results from a functional algorithm simulation of a CFD kernel called SIMPLE which provided us with strong evidence about the soundness of our technique and the validity of our system. Using FAST, we were able to gain further insight into the SIMPLE application by: (a) collecting detailed data on the time-histograms of computation and communication "intensities" during parallel execution, and associating these with the phases of the algorithm; (b) identifying inherently sequential parts of the algorithm and analyzing their effects on speedup and scalability, and (c) studying the way communication overhead affects performance and scalability. Running times of the functional simulations of SIMPLE were very short; for example, it took *0.63 secs* of wall clock time to simulate a 4,096-point grid instance of SIMPLE on a Sparc-2.

Experience with FAST underlines the need for software tools that scientists can use to design, develop, and evaluate new computational algorithms. To this end, we are pursuing cost-effective ways of studying parallel applications and developing Modeling and Evaluation Tools for Parallel Computations. In particular, we are studying the combination of Functional Algorithm Simulation with high-level parallel languages. Our goal is to use the same parallel program for Functional Algorithm

Simulation and actual parallel execution. Having such a tool will provide scientists with the opportunity to describe parallel algorithms and study their inherent properties in reasonable time and with modest computing resources.

REFERENCES

1. A. GIBBONS and W. RYTTER, "Efficient Parallel Algorithms", Cambridge University Press, 1988.

2. L. G. VALIANT, "A Bridging Model for Parallel Computation", Communications of the ACM, **33**, 8, pp. 103-111 (August 1990).

3. D. CULLER, R. KARP, D. PATTERSON et al, "LogP: Towards a Realistic Model of Parallel Computation", Fourth ACM SIGPLAN Symposium on Principles and Practices of Parallel Programming, San Diego, CA (May 1993).

4. X.-H. SUN and J. ZHU, "Performance Prediction: A Case Study using a multi-ring KSR-1 machine", ICASE, NASA Langley Research, Center Technical Report, **95-24** (April 1995).

5. W.J. DALLY, "Performance Analysis of K-ary N-cube Interconnection Networks", IEEE Transactions on Computers, **39**, 6, pp. 775-785 (June 1990).

6. R.G. COVINGTON, S. MADALA, V. MEHTA, J.R. JUMP and J.B. SINCLAIR, "The Rice Parallel Processing Testbed", 1988 ACM SIGMETRICS Conference on Measurement and Modeling of Computer Systems (May 1988).

7. H. DAVIS, S. GOLDSCHMIDT and J. HENNESSY, "Multiprocessor simulation and tracing using Tango", 1991 International Conference on Parallel Processing (August 1991).

8. P. DICKENS and D. NICOL, "LAPSE: Large Application Parallel Simulation Environment", ICASE NASA Langley Research Center, Technical Report, **94-50** (May 1994).

9. S. REINHARDT, M. HILL, J. LARUS, A. LEBECK, J. LEWIS and D. WOOD, "The Wisconsin Wind Tunnel: Virtual Prototyping of Parallel Computers", Sigmetrics 1993 (1993).

10. E. BREWER and W. WEIHL, "Developing Parallel Applications

Using High-Performance Simulations", ACM/ONR Workshop on Parallel and Distributed Debugging (May 1993).

11. M.D. DIKAIAKOS, A. ROGERS and K. STEIGLITZ, "FAST: A Functional Algorithm Simulation Testbed", MASCOTS 94 - International Workshop on Modeling Analysis and Simulation of Computer and Telecommunications Systems, IEEE Computer Society, (February 1994) pp. 142-146.

12. P. MEHRA, M. GOWER and M.A. BASS, "Automated Modeling of Message-Passing Programs", MASCOTS 94 - International Workshop on Modeling, Analysis and Simulation of Computer and Telecommunications Systems, IEEE Computer Society, (February 1994) pp. 208-213.

13. G. HERMANNSSON, A. LI and L. WITTIE, "Analysis of Memory and Time Using EC/DSIM", Systems - MASCOTS'94, International Workshop on Modeling, Analysis and Simulation of Computer and Telecommunications Systems, IEEE Computer Society (February 1994) pp. 187-192.

14. S. SARUKKAI, "Scalability Analysis Tools for SPMD Message-Passing Parallel Programs", MASCOTS'94, International Workshop on Modeling, Analysis and Simulation of Computer and Telecommunications Systems, IEEE Computer Society, (February 1994), pp. 180-186.

15. M.D. DIKAIAKOS, A. ROGERS and K. STEIGLITZ, "Functional Algorithm Simulation: Implementation and Experiments", Department of Computer Science, Princeton University, Technical Report, **TR-429-93** (June 1993).

16. C. LIN and L. SNYDER, "A Portable Implementation of SIMPLE", International Journal of Parallel Programming, **20**, 5, pp. 363-401 (1991).

17. V. SARKAR, "Partitioning and Scheduling Parallel Programs for Multiprocessors" (MIT Press, 1989).

18. M.D. DIKAIAKOS, A. ROGERS and K. STEIGLITZ, "A Comparison Study of Heuristics for Mapping Parallel Algorithms to Message-Passing Multiprocessors", Parallel Algorithms and Applications, **7**, pp. 283-302 (1995).

19. A. ROGERS, "Compiling for Locality of Reference", Ph.D. Thesis, Department of Computer Science, Cornell University (1991).

CHAPTER 4

AN INTEGRATED APPROACH OF PERFORMANCE PREDICTION ON NETWORKS OF WORKSTATIONS

Xiaodong Zhang and Yongsheng Song

4.1. INTRODUCTION

Networks of Workstations (NOW) have become important distributed platforms for large-scale scientific computations. In practice, a NOW system is heterogeneous and time-sharing. Two classes of methods have been used for parallel computing performance studies: experimental methods that employ simulation tools to construct and run a detailed system model or direct measurements on target architectures, and analytical methods that use modeling techniques. Experimental methods are time-consuming, and it may be more suitable to focus on studying a certain part of architecture and system performance. In addition, measurements provide precise data but give little prediction information. Analytical models may provide relatively quick estimates of performance, but often lack sufficient accuracy due to unrealistic assumptions and difficulties of characterizing dynamic behaviors of programs by models. Intensive studies reported in [1] indicate that a highly effective performance evaluation approach is to combine both analytical and experimental methods, where analytical methods are used to capture as many deterministic performance factors as possible, implicit and dynamic factors are obtained through experiments. Applying the same principle, we present a performance prediction method and its software implementation using both experimental and analytical techniques, such as program instrumentation and monitoring, performance measurements, performance simulation at different levels and performance modeling.

To predict the execution performance, major questions include determining what the deterministic and nondeterministic factors are in distributed computing on a heterogeneous NOW, and what performance methods should be used. A single evaluation method is insufficient to handle multiple performance factors of a heterogeneous NOW. We provide static analysis to program source code for two purposes: to characterize the program's structures and execution flows, and to instrument the programs at necessary points for measurements. Important architecture dependent factors, such as network latencies, message latences and iteration overheads are measured using small sample data sets on small-size systems. The instrumented program could also be used for direct simulation which measures the run time of major computation blocks on a target host workstation. The center of the performance prediction system is a heterogeneous NOW simulator which takes the input from both the dynamic and static sources described above. The network traffic and contention are presented by either a software simulation or a stochastic model. Time-sharing effects of dynamic job distributions are also modeled stochastically. Combining the simulation results and performance metrics for heterogeneous NOW, we are able to obtain various performance results, such as execution predictions and other system comparisons. Our execution prediction results indicate that this approach is effective for performance analysis on heterogeneous NOW.

The organization of the paper is as follows. Section 2 overviews the system organization of the integrated environment. Section 3 presents performance prediction case studies. We summarize the paper in Section 4.

4.2. SYSTEM ORGANIZATION

Our integrated approach provides multiple evaluation techniques and options to study performance at different detailed levels. Information items needed for performance evaluation of a NOW system are classified as follows:

- *Program structures.* A parallel program structure can be characterized by some graphs, such as task/thread graphs [1]. The process of characterizing program structures should be done automatically by systems. An example of such a system is Fortran D compiler [2] which translates a Fortran D source code to a SPMD code on multiple processors. The execution flow and related parameters of the SPMD program can be used to characterize the parallel program. Motivated by the Fortran D compiler approach, we have built a software pre-processor to capture necessary information to characterize a parallel program to be executed on a heterogeneous NOW.

- *Architecture dependent timing factors.* These timing factors include communication latencies, synchronization overheads, and computing powers at different workstations, which must be measured on the target NOW system. In addition, direct simulation also needs to measure some part of the computation on target workstations. The pre-processor in the integrated environment instruments a source parallel program at the necessary points for the measurements.

- *Network models.* Network activities are dynamic. If the network structure is not complex, and certain architecture dependent factors can be obtained through precise measurements, the entire network system and its activities can be well presented though a stochastic model. A complex network system can also be simulated at a more detailed level.

- *Workload models.* The execution time of a parallel job on a nondedicated heterogeneous NOW is affected by other possible time-shared jobs in the system. The workload patterns are application dependent. The workload patterns can be modeled by a discrete time model using workload distribution as a variable. Thus, many workload patterns can be characterized by the model. For example, The workload may be assumed to be a geometric distribution with mean $1/P_i$ for the time-shared jobs' think time, where P_i is the average probability of the time-shared jobs on workstation i, for $i = 1, ..., m$, [3].

- *Performance metrics.* The unique features of a nondedicated heterogeneous system make traditional performance metrics for ho-

mogeneous multiprocessor system evaluation not suitable. Zhang
and Yan [4] present a set of metrics which quantifies the heterogeneity and time-sharing effects of NOW and characterizes
the performance effects. These metrics are general enough to
cover performance evaluation of both homogeneous and heterogeneous computations in dedicated and non-dedicated NOW systems. The metrics are used for the prediction.

4.2.1. The System Structure

Figure 1 describes the structure of the integrated environment. A parallel program is first filtered by *pre-processor* which outputs an *instrumented program* and keeps a detailed *program structure record*. The
instrumented program will be executed with a small problem size on
a target workstation which is one of the target NOW to collect *measurements and direct simulation results*. The *simulator* combines both
program structure record representing static information and measurements and direct simulation results representing dynamic program behavior to predict execution performance of the program with larger
problem size on a larger scale NOW system. The performance evaluation results are finally processed by *performance metrics* of heterogeneous NOW.

4.2.1.1. Pre-processor

A major task of the pre-processor is to instrument programs. We choose
to use software monitoring because this approach does not depend upon
any special hardware support, and is enough to detect those events required for performance prediction. In software monitoring, event detection is done by inserting trace code directly into the user's program
before it runs. These inserted trace codes are actually function calls
which will record event data. All the trace routines are packed into one
module to form a trace routine library. Later when the instrumented
program is executed, performance data will be collected. The effects of
software instrumentation costs are compensated when the performance
prediction results are collected. Thus we predict the performance of
non-instrumented codes using performance data from the instrumented
version.

Two major event interests for the instrumentation are

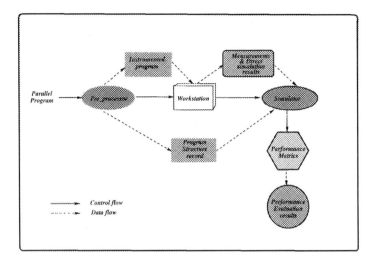

Figure 1: Structure of the integrated performance analysis environment.

- timing cost per parallel iteration loop, and

- measurements of major computation blocks.

Another task of the preprocessor is to characterize program structures by creating a record file. This file record captures the entry to and exit from procedures, loops and message passing library calls. This record file is a machine readable form of the task graph or the thread graph but is automatically generated by the system. Current version of the pre-processor uses PVM programs [5] of C language as source code. Options to process programs expressed by other distributed languages could easily be implemented.

4.2.1.2. Performance Metrics

In heterogeneous network systems, workstations may have different memory systems, different I/O systems, different CPU structures and different networking interfaces. The relative computing power among a set of heterogeneous workstations varies with applications. Hence, one workstation is likely to run faster than another workstation for an application program, but slower for another application program. In order to quantify the relative computing power among the workstations in a heterogeneous network system, for each workstation M_i, a computing power weight $W_i(A)$ with respect to application A is defined as follows:

$$W_i(A) = \frac{S_i(A)}{\max_{j=1}^m\{S_j(A)\}} \quad i = 1, ..., m \tag{1}$$

where $S_i(A)$ is the speed of Machine M_i to solve application A on a dedicated system.

Formula (1) indicates that the power weight of a workstation refers to its computing speed relative to the fastest machine in a system. The value of the power weight is less or equal to 1. Since the power weight is a relative ratio, it can also be represented by measured execution time. If we define the speed of the fastest workstation in the system as one basic operation per time unit, the power weight of each workstation denotes a relative speed. If $T(A, M_i)$ gives the execution time for computing program A on workstation M_i, the power weight can be calculated by the measured execution times as follows:

$$W_i(A) = \frac{\min_{j=1}^m\{T(A, M_j)\}}{T(A, M_i)} \tag{2}$$

By formula (2), we know that if a basic operation executes t_u cycles on the fastest workstation in the network, it executes t_u/W_i cycles on workstation M_i.

Due to limitations of memory size, cache size and other hardware components, the power weights usually change with the problem size of an application. The work reported in [4] shows that the computing power weights of workstations in a network system are constant if the data size of an application is scaled within the memory bound of each workstation. In practice, it is also recommended that an application be partitioned and distributed over a network system under the condition that the data size of each parallel task should be restricted within the memory bound of the workstation. In this paper, we only discuss heterogeneous network computing with constant computing power weight.

To evaluate a parallel computation in a heterogeneous NOW system, *speedup* and *efficiency* are two useful metrics, which have been well-defined in paper [4]. The speedup is

$$SP_A = \frac{min_{i=1}^m\{T(A, M_i)\}}{T_p}, \tag{3}$$

where $T(A, M_i)$ is the sequential execution time for application A on workstation $M_i(i = 1, 2, \cdots, m)$, and T_p is the execution time across the NOW. The efficiency is

$$E = \frac{\sum_{j=1}^{m}(W_j \times |A_j|/S_j)}{\sum_{j=1}^{m}(T_p - T_j^o)W_j}, \tag{4}$$

where $|A_j|/S_j$ represents the CPU busy time needed to execute A_j, the task allocated onto workstation M_j, and T_j^o is the time of workstation M_j executing the owner workload.

4.2.1.3. Simulator

The simulator is the last software component in the intergrated environment, where both static and dynamic data are combined and processed for performance prediction. The simulator consists of a network model, a set of processing element (PE) models, and a user interface. The PE models simulate local computations, while the network model simulates the communications among the tasks executing in the PE models. The user interface provides a set of commands for the users to specify system parameters, to control the execution of the simulated jobs and to output statistics regarding the execution of the simulated jobs and the simulator itself. The system parameters include the power weight of each workstation, the measured network latencies, the network topology and others. The direct simulation time in each workstation can be determined by its power weight and the measured execution time on the single workstation. Users of different applications may have different requirement to the simulator. The nondedicated time-sharing effects and variations of networks can also be simulated. For detailed information about the PE model, the network model and methods of modeling owner workload effects, the interested readers may refer to [3] and [6].

4.2.2. Instrumentation for Predictions

Figure 2 shows an example of m current tasks on m workstations, where the execution time in each node is divided into run time and communication times including waiting time, message-passing latency, message unpackaging time and message packaging time. The communication times are architecture dependent and can be obtained through measurements. The run time can be modeled as a function of the number of workstations (m) and the size of the problem (n). To simplify the discussion, we assume that the size of the problem is a scalar. Let T_i be the total run time in workstation i, then $T_i = \sum_{j=1}^{d} t_j$, where t_j is a run time segment, and d is the number of run time segments in workstation i. A run time segment can be classified into

- A parallel loop: $t_j - \sigma_j = \frac{K_i n}{m}$, where, σ_i is the loop instrumentation overhead, K_i is a system dependent factor on workstation i, and n is the size of the problem (or the loop), and m is the number of workstations. Factor K_i is also dependent on the power weight of workstation i. Thus, $K_i = \frac{(t_j - \sigma_i)m}{n}$, where t_j and σ_i are obtained from measurements on workstation i.

- Parallel tasks: a parallel computation is divided into multiple tasks which can be executed concurrently with the support of communications and synchronization. Loops inside each task are also functions of problems size n and and system size m. Modeling and measurements for the loops inside each task are similar to the ones of parallel loops.

- A block of assignment statements: t_j can be directly measured.

- A conditional statement: both times of *if* block and *else* block statements can be obtained by measurement.

- A function/procedure: t_j can be further divided into assignment blocks, loops and conditional statements.

In general, most computations of a parallel program are formed by parallel tasks and loops. Thus, major time segments can be modeled as functions of n and m. The loop timing models in each workstation are used to predict the execution time of a program of larger n running on an NOW of larger m. Since the predictions need not be quantitatively exact, prediction errors of 10-20% are acceptable. The more measurements we use, the more precise prediction results we will obtain, but more time-consuming. For example, instead of measuring, blocks of assignment statements and conditional blocks can be estimated based on cycles of instructions.

The following is a subroutine named *smooth* from the Kernel MG program of NAS benchmark suite [7] with two instrumentation points.

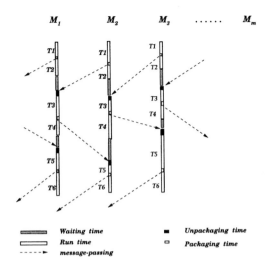

Figure 2: Current tasks on multiple workstations.

```
smooth(u, r, chunk, dim)
        double          ***u, ***r;
        int             chunk, dim;
{
        int             i, j, k;
        double          start_t, t_1, norm, absmax;

        start_t = dsecond();

        for (i = 1; i <= chunk; i++)
          for (j = 1; j <= dim; j++)
            for (k = 1; k <= dim; k++)
              u[i][j][k] += do_op(i, j, k, S, r);

        t_1 = (dsecond() - start_t)/(dim * dim * chunk);
        write_const(t_1);

        communicate(u, chunk, dim, SMOOTH);
}
```

The major operations in the subroutine is the 3 level nested loop. Variable t_1 records the estimated time per each loop iteration on a workstation. The sum of measured run time segments, T_i, $(i = 1, ..., m)$ on each workstation is used for measuring the power weight of each workstation.

In [8], a method is proposed to form a total execution time function in terms of the number of processors (p) and the size of the problem (n). This method was used for predicting data-parallel program execution time on homogeneous multicomputer systems. In a nondedicated heterogeneous NOW environment, this methods may not be effective due to effects of time-sharing and heterogeneity. For example, our experiments in Table 1 show that the prediction errors are significant by using this method to predict the MG benchmark program on a network of up to 8 heterogeneous workstations.

m	n	Predicted (sec)	Actual (sec)	Relative error
4	32	12.55	7.76	+76%
4	64	99.01	52.10	+90%
4	128	790.52	1286.72	-39%
8	32	6.37	4.84	+32%
8	64	49.6	30.05	+64%
8	128	395.37	541.84	-27%

Table 1: The predicted execution times and the comparisons with the actual execution times of the MG program by using the total execution time function on a heterogeneous NOW.

4.2.3. A Target NOW System

Our heterogeneous network system consists of three SPARC 10-30 workstations, five SPARC 5-70 workstations and five SPARCclassic workstations, connected by an Ethernet of 10Mbps bandwidth. The network has maximal throughput of 1000KB/s and minimal latency on the order of 2 milliseconds. Table 2 lists the performance parameters for the three types of workstations.

Model	HZ	Memory(MB)	Cache (KB)	SPECint	SPECfp
S5-70	70	16	16/8	57.0	47.3
S10-30	50	32	20/16	45.2	54.0
Classic	36	16	4/2	26.4	21.0

Table 2: Performance parameters of the three types of workstations, where the cache size is given by the sizes of instruction cache/data cache.

4.3. PREDICTION CASE STUDIES

We selected two programs from NAS (Numerical Aerodynamic Simulation) parallel benchmarks [7]: Programs Kernel EP (EP) and Kernel MG (MG).

The EP benchmark program represents the computation and data movement characteristics of large scale computational fluid dynamics applications. It executes 2^n iterations of a loop, where a pair of random numbers are generated and tested for whether Gaussian random deviates can be made from them by a specific scheme, with n as the input parameter. The number of pairs of the Gaussians in 10 successive square annuli are tabulated. The PVM implementation of this program consists of two main portions— the random number generator, and the main processing loop which tests successive pairs of random numbers for the property that Gaussian deviates can be built from them. Parallelization of the problem is straightforward: each member in a group of workstations works independently on a subset of the random numbers, and the annuli counts are communicated at the end of the processing. A simple front-end PVM process was designed to start the "worker" processes, to communicate to them their starting and ending indices in the loop, and to receive their results in the end of computation. The workload is statically scheduled onto each workstation based on the computing power. The problem size of EP in terms of the number of operations is 2^n. It has a constant memory allocation requirement. Each parallel process only participates in the communication of a 44 byte packet once in the end of processing.

The Kernel MG is a 3D multigrid benchmark program for solving a discrete Poisson problem $\Delta^2 u = v$ with periodic boundary conditions

on a 3 D grid of $256 \times 256 \times 256$. The message passing activities are
mainly conducted between neighboring processor nodes. The amount
of border communications increases as the number of processor nodes
increases.

The experiments and predictions were conducted in a dedicated
heterogeneous environment. Direct simulation was used on host workstations.

Both EP and MG programs are statically divided into concurrent
tasks where loops are major computations. We modeled all the loop
functions inside each task with the aid of measurements. In addition,
network/memory latencies and synchronization overheads are measured
directly from the NOW network. Some direct simulation were also conducted on host workstations for measuring block computations. The
simulator predicted the execution times of the two programs by combining the modeling and direct measurements results, and the program
structure records. We verified the predicted results by running the two
programs on up to 8 workstations. Tables 3 and 4 report the predicted
execution times and the comparisons with the actual execution times
on the NOW of the EP program and the MG program respectively.
The relative errors for most predicted results are under 10%.

m	n	Predicted (sec)	Actual (sec)	Relative error
4	2^{20}	24.508	26.219	-6.5%
4	2^{24}	389.137	405.018	-3.9%
8	2^{16}	0.956	1.034	-7.2%
8	2^{20}	14.32	15.04	-5%
8	2^{24}	194.469	207.520	-6.3%

Table 3: The predicted execution times and the comparisons with the
actual execution times on the NOW of the EP program.

Besides precision, another important factor to evaluate the quality
of predictions is its magnitude of time reduction. The time reduction
is very high by using the integrated environment. For example, the
total computing time used for the prediction of the MG program ($n =$
128 and $m = 4$) from pre-processor, measurements on the NOW and
simulation was about 18 seconds. This was about 72 times reduction
in comparison with the actual execution time of the same problem

m	n	Predicted (sec)	Actual (sec)	Relative error
4	32	8.176	7.76	+5%
4	64	52.603	52.10	+1%
4	128	1219.45	1286.72	-5%
8	32	4.025	4.840	-17%
8	64	29.485	30.05	-2%
8	128	516.47	541.84	-5%

Table 4: The predicted execution times and the comparisons with the actual execution times on the NOW of the MG program.

(1286.72 seconds). When the problem size n and system size m become significantly larger, we expect a much larger time reduction from the prediction.

4.4. SUMMARY

We present a prediction method and its implementation for parallel computing on heterogeneous NOW, where analytical models, experimental techniques and software are integrated. Important static and dynamic execution data are prepared for simulation and performance analyses. Simulation of a NOW system can be conducted at different detailed levels upon evaluation requirement. This method allows application users and system designers to predict the performance of a large program running on a large NOW system based on a set of relatively small sample data. The prediction methods has the other features:

- Only a single workstation is required for the prediction.

- The prediction process can be automatically done promptly.

- The simulator quantitatively characterizes the network structure, the time-sharing workload and the heterogeneity of a NOW.

REFERENCES

1. X. Zhang and Z. Xu, "Multiprocessor scalability predictions through detailed program execution analysis", Proceedings of the 9th ACM

International Conference on Supercomputing, (ACM Press, July, 1995), pp. 97-106.

This paper presents a semi-empirical approach for multiprocessor scalability performance prediction. This approach significantly reduces the time and cost of measurements and simulation by partially applying analytical techniques, while it provides an acceptable prediction accuracy by collecting architecture dependent data and measuring some critical and dynamic program portions. The prediction results were validated on the KSR-1 and the CM-5. This paper received Best Paper Award in the ICS'95 Conference.

2. S. Hiranandani, K. Kennedy and C.-W. Tseng, "Compiling Fortran D for MIMD distributed workstation machines", Communications of the ACM, **34**, 8, pp. 66-80, (August, 1992).

This paper describes the Fortran D compiler for MIMD distributed memory machines. A machine-independent programming model to express data parallelism in scientific programs is proposed. Since it is written in a data-parallel programming style with reasonable data decompositions, it can be implemented on a variety of parallel architectures.

3. X. Zhang and Y. Yan, "A framework of performance prediction of parallel computing on nondedicated heterogeneous NOW", Proceedings of 1995 International Conference of Parallel Processing, (CRC Press, Vol. I, August, 1995), pp. 163-167.

This paper presents an effective framework for performance prediction of parallel computing on nondedicated heterogeneous networks of workstations. The prediction system is based on a two-level model where a task graph is used to capture execution behavior of coarse-grained parallel programs, and a discrete time model is used to quantify effects from nondedicated heterogeneous networks systems. An iterative process is used to determine the interactive effects between network contention and task execution. The prediction model was validated by application programs on a nondedicated networks of workstations.

4. X. Zhang and Y. Yan, "Modeling and characterizing parallel computing performance on heterogeneous NOW", Proceedings of the Seventh IEEE Symposium on Parallel and Distributed Processing, (IEEE Computer Society Press, October, 1995), pp. 25-34.

This paper presents a set of evaluation metrics which quantify the heterogeneity of networks of workstations and characterize time-sharing effects. The metrics were validated by evaluating performance of application programs on networks of workstations.

5. V. S. Sunderam, "PVM: A framework for parallel distributed computing," Concurrency: Practice and Experience, **2**, 4, (December, 1992), pp. 315-339.
This is the original paper describing the software structure of Parallel Virtual Machine (PVM), a message-passing library for parallel computing on networks of workstations and on other parallel architecture platforms.

6. Z. Xu, "Simulation of heterogeneous networks of workstations", MASCOTS'96, Proceedings of the Fourth International Workshop on Modeling, Analysis and Simulation of Computer and Telecommunication Systems, (IEEE Computer Society Press, February, 1996), pp. 59-63.
This paper presents the design and implementation of a simulation system for a nondedicated heterogeneous network of workstations. This simulator provides several options to users to specify and quantify system architectures, network heterogeneity and time-sharing factors. The simulator also supports execution of message-passing parallel programs written in C and the PVM library.

7. D. Bailey, et. al., "The NAS parallel benchmarks", International Journal of Supercomputer Applications, **5**, 3, pp. 63-73, (Fall, 1991).
This paper describes the numerical kernel programs selected from in aerospace applications. These programs have been widely used as benchmarks to evaluate parallel and distributed systems.

8. C. L. Mendes, J-C. Wang and D. A. Reed, "Automatic performance prediction and scalability analysis for data-parallel programs", Proceedings of Workshop on Automatic Data Layout and Performance Prediction, (Rice University, April, 1995).
This paper presents an approach of developing a compiler-aided performance analysis tool. The integration of Fortran 77D and the Pablo software environment provides an automatic process for performance prediction.

CHAPTER 5

Trace-transformation As a Tool For Incremental Simulation of Parallel Program Execution on NOWs

Sekhar R. Sarukkai

5.1 INTRODUCTION

Performance of program executions on *Network Of Workstations* (*NOW*s) are dictated by various, and complex interactions of the hardware, communication library, system software and the applications. In contrast to parallel processors, performance on NOWs are significantly influenced by the heterogeneity in the compute nodes and communication networks, and unpredictable loads placed on them by competing jobs. Another difference lies in the manner in which NOWs evolve or are upgraded: unlike parallel machines, NOWs evolve incrementally over time by the addition of new machines or machine upgrades, replacement of network interconnects and with release of new system software. Studying the effect of such incremental changes on application performance is not only important for meeting quality of service requirements but is essential for making well-informed purchasing decisions as well. For example, investment on reducing communication bandwidth, where most applications executed in the environment are dominated by I/O accesses, will not be as productive as investment in better I/O hardware or better I/O buffer management. The need for tools that give quick and reasonably accurate estimates of the effect of changes in the execution environment on application performance is more important now

79

then ever before, due to the growing number of parallel applications and diverse execution environments.

Literature is replete with performance evaluation experiments on architectures and system-software that fail to deliver the promised performance on applications of interest. Many of these describe experiences in writing or porting applications to new execution environments with different communication and computation characteristics. Though obtaining practical experience in porting software to new architectures, message-passing libraries, operating systems and different computer inter-connection networks and system configurations is valuable, very few organizations can afford the resources to purchase and support many platforms to determine the most suitable execution environment for their applications. Unfortunately, this approach may be unavoidable unless tools that predict the impact of changes in execution environment on application performance are available, especially for applications that are significantly influenced by many architectural or system-software parameters.

There are a few techniques that can be used to develop tools to address this issue:

- Use of analytical models to project expected performance[8].

- Application of Simulation tools:

  - Process-oriented and discrete-event simulators: application workload characteristics are used to drive an abstract or detailed model of the system[2],

  - Direct execution simulators: the application is executed on actual hardware and only selected system component behavior is modeled[1,6].

  - Trace based incremental-simulation: this can be characterized as a hybrid simulation technique. Similar to the direct execution approach in that selected application segments are abstracted out, except that applications need not be re-executed for each simulation – time-stamped trace events of a baseline execution are used to preserve unchanged behavior. Selected events trigger simulation modules that model appropriate system components, much like in a discrete-event simulator.

For analytical tools to be effectively applied widely, a number of difficult barriers have to be crossed: building and validating models of systems that effectively capture system dynamics, building and validating abstract models of the application, and the need for expert skill and training in analytical methods. On the other hand, simulation techniques are simpler to construct for handling dynamic system and application behavior, and are more easily comprehended or developed by a larger audience.

Though process-oriented and discrete-event simulation tools have been used innumerable times to successfully study the interrelationship between applications and the systems, they have been notoriously slow. For example, detailed multi-processor simulations can run 3 to 4 orders of magnitude slower than an actual execution of the application. Direct execution addresses this problem by eliminating simulations of certain modules/components that are not under study. A classic example is the study of the effect of changes in the network characteristic on a distributed application; where the application is executed on the existing hardware and only communication regions are modeled. In such a situation, the need to model the compute nodes and the entire application execution on each node, is completely eliminated. Needless to say, this approach is ill-suited for studying performance issues that arise from heterogenous compute nodes and in situations where multiple parallel jobs compete for the same resources simultaneously. For a comprehensive simulation environment to be effective, multiple levels of simulation detail are essential; SimOS[7] is a good example of a tool that allows both detailed and direct-execution of applications, thus providing the user the choice between accuracy and performance of simulation.

Most of the work presented in the above simulation techniques are targeted towards system design and understanding what system changes effect application performance. While this level of detail is natural from a system design perspective, it is perhaps a bit too detailed from a software design perspective. In the increasingly common situation of commodity components being used to choose and design enterprise-wide computing solutions, rapid evaluation of various trade-offs in selecting the optimal system configuration is vital, for effecient software deployment. In this situation, there will be an increasing need for systems administrators and performance specialists to be able to pose application-oriented queries to a simulation-based performance expert that would determine the effect of various system choices on the applications and workloads that are typically executed in that environment. Application oriented queries such as the following (with respect to performance) are perhaps even more pertinent now than ever before:

- What would be the effect of a two-fold increase in the compute node performance, of selected machines, on the workload of this environment?

- Would increase in IO bandwidth and resources, enable the execution of a larger database/ application?

- Will the application performance benefit more from increasing network or IO bandwidth, and by how much?

- By how much does multitasking effect performance of applications?

A common feature of all these queries is that a large portion of the system performance remains unchanged or abstracted out; the effect of incremental changes or upgrades to specific components in the system, on the overall workload is really at issue. For such an environment, both direct-execution and trace-transformation techniques, both of which are well suited for incremental simulations, can help analyze application sensitivity to changes in system parameters.

The simulations in these cases focus on studying the effect of changes in specific parameters of an already existing system; more so than studying application behavior on completely new systems. Since the former problem is simpler than the latter, more efficient simulation techniques that make use of information about performance on a baseline architecture augmented with specific models of only the incremental changes in the new architecture can be utilized. This paper describes the use of an incremental-simulation environment, based on a trace-transformation approach in predicting program performance with specific emphasis on NOWs. We demonstrate how a close coupling of the simulation environment and a parallel performance visualization environments[3,4], help rapid detection of performance bottlenecks.

There have been other efforts similar in nature, but have either been targeted to designing specific parallel architectures or have been used for other purposes[5,9]. These efforts do not consider critical system issues such as node heterogeneity, message-buffer management, the effect of interrupts and background load on program execution[9], in addition to the application of such an environment in studying application sensitivity to system changes in a distributed environment. In this paper, we demonstrate the use of an event-based technique to rapidly predict the effect of changes in the environment on program execution time. Our methodology starts with measurements of an actual parallel program execution in the form of a trace file. Projections of program performance on different execution environments is then obtained by analyzing and modifying time-stamps of the collected events.

An incremental trace-transformation technique is appealing (as opposed to execution-driven simulation such as in Proteus[1]) for a number of reasons: firstly, since we use actual time stamped traces from the original execution, the characteristics of the environment that do not change are preserved without the need to re-execute them. Secondly, projected performance in the new environment can be studied with a whole suite of trace analysis tools (such as in AIMS[10]) that help pin- point source-code locations that could be potential bottlenecks, as well as their possible causes. However, this technique also has some limitations: it cannot be used to accurately predict the performance of data-dependent programs and for different problem size or an environment with different number of processes. Such predictions require a more comprehensive understanding of application structure; preliminary studies have been carried out based on simulation as well as analytical techniques dealt with the performance prediction tools[9]. The tool discussed here simply provides a convenient means of gauging the impact of changes in the execution environment for one instance of the problem-size and number of processing nodes.

5.2 Analysis Methodology

The analysis methodology is schematically illustrated in Figure 1. A representative set of applications are run on the existing resource in order to generate performance data that is used as an indicator of baseline performance, by the incremental simulator.

In this system, performance data is collected in the form of time-stamped trace files and a representation of the source program in the form of an application-database[9]. Updated execution parameters are passed as command line arguments to the simulator. The simulator interprets each event in the trace file, based on its type, and invokes a

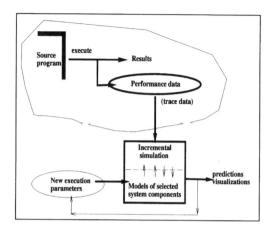

Figure 1: A Schematic representation of the incremental simulation process.

simulator module for appropriate event types. Events that are not to be modified in the new execution environment are left as it is, and no time-stamp modifications are performed for processes in these states. In the simplest form, the resulting trace file contains the same set of events as in the original trace file with updated time-stamps. However, in. more complex situations, new events may be added by the analysis in the resulting trace file. The trace files can be analyzed by using visualization and profile tools that are part of the AIMS toolkit.

Types of execution parameters that can be currently changed and analyzed using the tool, include:

- computation speed of processes

- bandwidth and latency factors of the interconnect

- background load in nodes executing processes

- context switch time and frequency

- modified execution time of selected routines

- communication buffer management

In the rest of this section the trace collection and analysis phases are briefly discussed, followed by a section with some illustrated examples.

5.2.1 Trace Collection

The program is instrumented to generate time-stamped events recorded in a trace file during execution. The types of events captured during program execution captures state information in the various components of the execution environment and any causal dependencies among them. These events can be broadly classified into the following classes:

- Process creation and termination events.

- Processor computation events: These occur in each node and are dependent only on local computa- tions. However, their timing can be affected by execution dependencies that might exist across nodes. These events help determine execution times of computation regions of code in the target environment.

- Message communication events: Messages are used for data exchange, broadcast communication, and synchronization. These events are recorded to help track the effects of communication efficiencies on program performance and to preserve causal relationships. Message communication events recorded include blocking and unblocking of communication calls (such as *pvm_send*, *mpi_recv* and *pvm_msgwait*) and initiation of asynchronous communication calls (such as *pvm_isend* and *pvm_irecv* in PVM).

- I/O events: I/O plays an important role in the performance of parallel applications; state information pertaining to the amount of time and types of IO calls (at application level) are monitored during execution. I/O events include seek, read, write and I/O wait.

Next, this instrumented code is compiled and linked with a monitor library that enables the capture of trace events. Each trace event typically contains a time-stamp, process (or node) id, event type and other relevant data. Events are stored locally in each node until the memory buffer becomes full, at which time the buffers are flushed to disks. This process continues for all nodes during the entire program execution. The set of events generated by all nodes, called th *trace file*, is sorted by time and forms the basis of all further analysis described in this paper.

5.3 Trace Analysis

The time-stamp of the generated events are represented as $t_n^p(i)$; the subscript n indicates the new environment. The granularity of the studies considered in this paper are at the level of gross compute speed, communication speed, communication latency, IO bandwidth and related buffering parameters. Details of node performance – such as cache size and its effect on performance is not considered.

For the performance analysis discussion that follows, we consider as input a trace file consisting of a time ordered set of events. The time stamp of the ith event stored by a node p is represented by $t_o^p(i)$ (where $p < P$, the total number of nodes); the subscript o indicates that the time stamp is the observed value. The trace transformation generates a new trace file with the same number of events, but with recomputed time-stamps.

5.3.1 Computation Events

Computation states are perhaps the easiest to analyze, since changes in execution times are local to a single node, but affected by other processes executing on the same node. Computation event time-stamps are modified based on the speed with which computation can be performed in the new execution environment; event time-stamps are updated based on the ratio of the new and old execution environment speeds. The effect of modifying various parameters such as main-memory bandwidth, cache size, clock rate and so on, translate to changes in node speed in varying levels. Since our interest is in determining the effect of change in the deliverable power of the target environment (without regard to the means by which it is achieved), and in identifying potential bottlenecks in parallel resource utilization caused by changes in the ratio of computation and communication power, this level of abstraction is sufficient for application-oriented performance analysis. Needless to say, access to more specific node or source-code level information will be useful in making the analysis more accurate, but at the cost of time required for building the model and performing the simulation. We should note however, that the methodology itself can easily incorporate any detail of single node performance that the user would like to model, by extracting the appropriate events and analyzing them suitably.

Let us say that the change in computation speed (either increase or decrease) is represented by f. Then, assuming program execution begins at time t0, the new time-stamp value of the first event in the trace is given by: $t_n(1) = (t_o(1) - t0) \times f + t0$. The effect of interrupt handling (due to asynchronous inter-processor communications and IO operations), and process context switching are also incorporated in the analysis. These are incorporated in the analysis, by additional terms in the above equation that considers the number of interrupts (N_i) between events i and $i - 1$, and uses a simple round-robin time-slicing scheme as a means of multi-tasking all active processes on a node. If I_o and I_n are the old and new fixed interrupt handling overheads, and q and q' processes are running in the old and new environments respectively, then

$$t_n(i) = \frac{(t_o(i) - t_o(i - 1))}{q} \times q' \times f \times \tau + t_n(i - 1) - (N_o \times I_o - N_n \times I_n)$$

Here, τ is the difference in context switch overhead in the old and new environments. Care also should be taken to preserve event ordering within the node. Various parameters in the above equation are assigned by parameters to the trace transformation tool. Background loads are injected in each procressor by a selected distribution function.

5.3.2 Global Communications

Global operations include broadcasts, barrier synchronizations and reduction operations. Events related to global operations need to be treated differently from computation events because global operations involve all nodes. Changes to time-stamps of previous events in even one node leads to change in the event time-stamp of the completion of global event on all nodes. If the time for a global operation (say a barrier) on node p, is $g(p)$, then the completion time of the global operation, $t_n^p(end)$, is given by: $t_n^p(end) = MAX(t_n^p(begin)) + g(p))$ Similar modifications to that in equation [1] can be made here in the presence of interrupts. Group communications can be handled in a similar manner for a sub-set of nodes and will not be considered here.

5.3.3 Point-to-point Communications

Inter-processor communication is performed by one node sending data to another node which receives the data. The semantics of the communication operations in various communication libraries have significantly different meanings. For the sake of clarity, we define the terms and meanings of different types communication operations discussed in this paper. These encompass all the point-to-point communication characteristics of MPI, PVM and NX message passing libraries. The receive-send operations can be blocking or non-blocking. Invoking a blocking receive operation causes the calling node to block until the data has been received and copied into the program address space (this corresponds to using crecv in NX, PVM_recv in PVM and MPI_recv in MPI). The node that invokes a blocking send (such as MPI_send in MPI and csend in NX and PVM_send in PVM), blocks until all the data has been copied out of the program address space into the system address space. Two mechanisms may be used for blocking sends: asynchronous and synchronous. In the case of asynchronous sends, the node does not wait for the message to be actually received at the other end (i.e., the send may still block on buffer copy; but may return before the actual receipt). Synchronous communications are implemented by ensuring that both the receiving and the sending nodes have executed their respective communication calls before actually initiating the message transfer. Asynchronous receives are supported in most message passing libraries, including MPI_Trecv in MPI, PVM_Nrecv in PVM and $irecv$ in NX. Non-blocking message passing, is effectively supported in multiprocessors with communication co- processors at each node, allowing computation and message copying to be performed in parallel. In such machines, the time to copy data into a system buffer can be overlapped with useful computation, using non- blocking (instead of blocking) sends. Non-blocked send and receive initiation events affect only local time-stamp values of future events, but the busy wait component that are normally associated with these communications may lead to non-deterministic behavior.

Consider a message of size n and communication cost of C_n. Suppose that trace transformation produces an approximation of the beginning receive and send events such that $(t_n^s(B) + C_n) < t_n^r(B)$. That is, the receiving node invokes the receive before the communication has completed. In this case, the completion of the receive operation depends on the send initiation time since the receive completion time is the sum of the new time of initiation of the send, $t_n^s(B)$, and the new time for communicating the data, C_n, and the receive handling time c, in the receiving node. For the situation where the new receive begin time occurs after the communication is completed, the time of completion of the receive is the sum of the new receive begin time and the receive handling time. If the rate of transfer of a byte is g, the start up time is S, and the per-hop delay is H (most current networks have $H = 0$), then the compensated communication time, C_n, can be estimated by: $Cn = S + n \times g + h \times H$, where h is the number of hops. The transformed time of the completion of the receive operation can then be expressed as:

$$t_n^r(E) = MAX(t_n^s(B) + C_n + s + r, t_n^r(B) + c)$$

In some cases, if the receive is posted after the completion of the communication, an added penalty of copying from system space to programmer space is incurred in the receiving end, leading to

$$t_n^r(E) = MAX(t_n^s(B) + C_n + s + r + t_{copy} \times n, t_n^r(B) + c)$$

For the analysis to be complete, send (and I/O)events should also be considered. Sends (and I/O events alike) have to be treated slightly differently in order to reflect changes in overlap of communi-cations and computations, with changes in the computation and communication overhead character-istics of the new execution environment. Hence, $t_n^s(E)$, the new unblocking time of a message wait event associated with a send event (with finite message buffers) is:

$$t_n^s(E) = MAX(t_n^s(B) + t_n(com_ovhd) + C(\lfloor n/B \rfloor) \times B), t_n^s(B))$$

Here, B is the finite buffer size.

Bloating of send and receive block times due to other load (and buffer usage) is handled as for computation events. One ommision in the communicaiton analysis is contention. This is handled by specifying the expected degradation in link utilization due to mutliple simultaneous requests, that are incorporated in the communication cost. A more elegant and With these simple trace transformation rules, rapid analysis of system behavior is incorporated. For a slightly more detailed study of contention for resources, the events identified above, drive a simplified simulation that handles queuing for resources.

5.4 Examples

In this section we briefly consider some common decisions that have to be made in order to effectively utilize resources in a changing execution environment, and illustrate how this methodology can be useful in such scenarios. The first sub-section considers the effect of change in communication characteristics on the workloads. The next sub-section shows that this approach can also be used to study the impact of processor heterogenity on the workload performance. The succeeding sub-section illustrates a studt of varying system loads placed by competing jobs and its effect on application performance. The last sub-section illustrates the use of this approach in deciding what implementations of applications will be best suited in a new execution environment.

5.4.1 Effect of Communication Characteristics

Consider a parallel implementation of the scalar penta-diagonal solver. The scalar penta-diagonal application (or SP) from the NAS benchmark suite is derived from the diagonalized Beam-Warming approximate factorization scheme for the computation of three-dimensional viscous fluid flow using a structured discretization mesh. SP is a variation on the class of alternating direct implicit (ADI) schemes. A number of approaches can be used to solve this problem in parallel. The two approaches illustrated in the context of tri-diagonal solvers is also relevant in this case; the most significant difference being the number of operations that need to be performed for each communication. In this section, we consider a multi-partition method (class A size) of SP written by Rob Van Der Wijngaart. In this method each node receives grid block cells that line up along the body diagonal of the 3-D grid. All nodes are always busy since cells are positioned such that every coordinate plane that cuts the grid intersects exactly one cell of each node. The resulting collection of pipeline is coarse-grained. The trace events collected for analysis of this benchmark were obtained by a 16 processor run on the Paragon (with co-processor turned off).

First we independently vary the computation and communication-overhead of the nodes in an effort to study the impact of these changes on execution time. Figure 2 (top) shows this comparison. Clearly, there is a nearly linear decrease in execution time as compute nodes are made faster, while reduction in communication overheads has little impact on execution time (a change of about .02 seconds). Such decrease in execution time with increase in compute speed indicates the programs good scalability characteristics since it can tolerate lesser work (or faster processors) and still be compute dominated. Figure 2

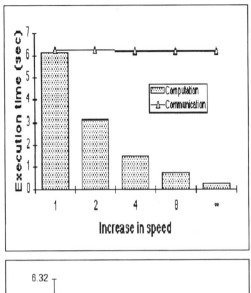

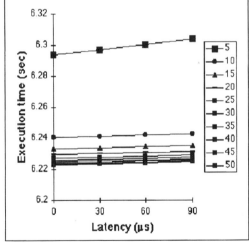

Figure 2: **Top:** Near-linear reduction in execution time with increase in computation speed and no significant impact of change in communication overhead on execution time. **Bottom:** Change in latency and bandwidth have little impact on execution time, indicating good scalability characteristics.

(bottom) shows the effect of change in latency and bandwidth on execution time of program. Increase in bandwidth has little, if any, impact on program execution time. Latency effects has a slightly bigger, though still small, impact on program execution time. This suggests that the program has very good overlap of computation and communication. If this were a representative application of the type of workloads executed in the environment, it suggests little, if any, benefit in upgrading the communication sub-system. In addition, this indicates that competing communication intensive jobs will not significantly degrade the processor utilization exhibited by this application, as this workload can tolerate substantial variations to communication bandwidth.

All the data points in the graph are generated by running simulations with varying latency and bandwidth values, keeping all other parameters the same. Since we do not simulate any other aspect of the program execution, each simulation completes orders of magnitude faster than a full simulation of the program execution. For example, each 16-processor simulation on a standard SGI workstation completes in less than a minute.

5.4.2 Effect of Processor Heterogeneity

In addition to processor, algorithm and communication characteristics, competing jobs and heterogeneity can significantly skew processor utilization. Consider the time-line view of a 16-processor execution trace of the pipeline implementation of a tri-diagonal solver shown in Figure 3, as a representative application with pipelined communications. Here X-axis corresponds to time and Y-axis corresponds to processes. Lines connecting various time-lines indicate inter-process communication. Program execution completes in less than 20 milliseconds. Now if one of the 16 processors is made twice as slow as all the other processors (or conversely, if all but one processors are made twice as fast) reflecting a slower processor or increased background load, does it matter which of the 16 processors is chosen to be the slow one?

Figure 3 compares two options: If the first processor is slow, then the execution time is more than 16 milliseconds (see Figure 3(top)). However if the last processor is the slow one, the execution completes in less than 14 milliseconds (see Figure 3(bottom)). Thus assigning the slow processor to be the logical processor 15, rather than processor 0, leads to more than 12% improvement in performance. Since the

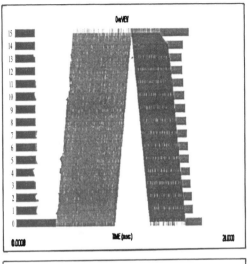

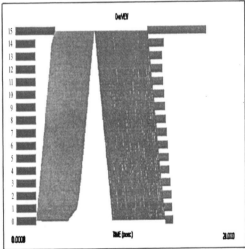

Figure 3: **Top:** A slow first processor results in a delayed start-up of other processors. **Bottom:** A slow last processor does not result in delayed start-up of other processors and reduces completion time of the forward and backward phases.

incremental-simulation technique rapidly provides estimates of application sensitivity to changes in individual processor speeds, informed choices on static processor allocation can be made before production run of applications. A natural use of this capability is the selection of an "optimal" mappping of logical processors to physical processors determined by iteratively invoking the transformations.

5.4.3 Effect of Increase in System Load

Changes in system load are common in a shared environment, where multiple jobs randomly contend for limited resources. These changes in load can have a debilitating effect on some critical application's performance, unless analysis of its sensitivity to varying loads is characterized. Consider the example above, under a heavy, uniformly distributed, workload on 8 of the 16 processors. Many application related questions on the impact of this load on the application performance can be raised. One such question is whether assigning the heavily loaded processors to be the first eight leads to better performance than the assigning them to be the last eight. Trace collected from an execution with no background loads on any of the processors is used to drive the simulation of these two scenarios. Figure 4 compares the two choices. Comparison of the final completion time of the application seems to indicate negligible impact on performance. However, comparison of the completion times in each individual processor indicates that the last 8 processors in the 4(bottom) release the processors for other jobs much earlier than in the case shown in 4(top) – suggesting that it may indeed make a significant difference in the execution of competing heterogenous workloads, to follow the latter approach.

5.4.4 Which Application Implementation to Choose?

The solution of scalar and block tri- and penta-diagonal linear systems is a recurring step in the numerical solution of PDEs using implicit methods. The particular application considered here, called Xtrid, is a Fortran program written for the iPSC/860. It implements different methods for simultaneous solution of N independent scalar tridiagonal systems, each containing N equations in N unknowns. We consider two implementations of the program: one that has clear communication and computation phases using a transpose-based scheme, and another with

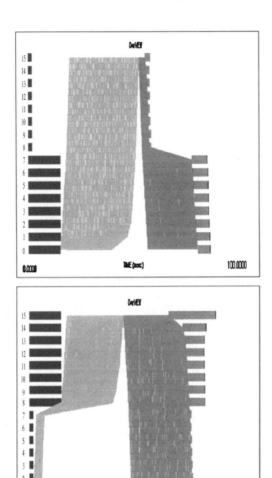

Figure 4: **Top**: First half of processors have 8 times the load as the other half, leading to significant degradation in performance. **Bottom**: When the second half of the processors are subjected to the same load, they are released earlier, thus freeing up the processors to work on other jobs.

overlapped computation and communication using a pipelined scheme. The main difference between the scalar tri-diagonal and block tridiagonal mini-application in the NAS benchmark suite is the solution of block (5 5) tridiagonal systems in the latter case.

Unlike the transpose-based approach, the pipeline approach does not exhibit synchronous communication characteristics. Instead, the Gaussian elimination routine is parallelized using a simple pipelined communication scheme. The nodes are logically arranged in the form of a one-dimensional mesh, with each node sending the intermediate computed results to the next node in the pipeline on each iteration. The completion time is effectively divided into two segments:

- the time to fill the pipeline (i.e. the time the last nodes spends waiting for its first message)

- the remaining completion time for the last node (that includes compute time).

While the execution of the first phase is sensitive to latency and bandwidth changes, the second phase appears to be independent of the communication characteristics.

The question of what approach is best suited to a particular execution environment, largely depends on the characteristics of the environment. This is effectively illustrated by considering the execution of these two versions of the program on two parallel machines with different node and communication characteristics (the Intel iPSC/860 and the Intel Paragon). Performance measurements in the two machines indicate that while the transpose method performs better on the Paragon, the pipeline version performs better on the hypercube. As it turns out, the transpose method performs better in the Paragon since it has a higher bandwidth interconnect. The pipeline method is latency bound and hence does not perform as well on the Paragon. On the other hand, since the hypercube has a slower network, transpose methods perform much more poorly than pipeline methods. Predicting such behavior is important since the choice of implementation changes from the current execution environment to the next.

We successfully used the tool to predict the behavior of the two versions of the program on a paragon, given traces from executions on the hypercube. The difference in compute powers of the two processors were simply accounted for, in the simulation, by a two fold increase in compute speed and the appropriate latency and bandwidth values of the Paragon were input to the tool in order to predict expected performance.

The predicted execution times are quite accurate. Indeed, the simulation correctly points to better performance of the transpose version of the tri-diagonal solver on the Paragon while it picks the pipeline version to perform better on the iPSC/860. This suggests that in spite of many simplifying assumptions made in our simulations, our approach could be used as one means of predicting the general trend in program execution behavior, across successive generations of the execution environment, as long as the environments are not radically different.

	XT(iP)	XT(Pa)	XP(iP)	XP(Pa)
Actual	265	82.68	201.1	138.1
Predicted	264.4	83	217.8	124.6

Table 1: Comparison of predicted and actual execution

In the table above, XT is the tridiagonal solver using the transpose method, while XP is the tridiagonal solver with the pipeline method. iP stands for executions on the iPSC/860 while Pa stands for executions on the Paragon. While these results are on dedicated parallel systems, it illustrates the point that changes in certain characteristics of sub-system performance (such as changes in communication latency and bandwidth) can dramatically impact the choice of implementation. Without this knowledge, it may be impossible for the right mapping of problem solution to the target execution environment. We envison that each of the parameters considered in this section would need to be analyzed before deploying the software in a heterogenous environment.

5.5 Conclusions and Future Work

With the increase in choices of execution environments in which a program can be executed, there arises a need for tools that allow users, architects and system designers alike, to get a rough idea of the impact of design choices on application performance. Determining the relationship between the application and the execution environment (which encompasses all issues that govern program performance, not in user control) implies the determination of communication and computation times as well as any overlap in both. Doing this analysis purely from the application or architecture perspective will not be sufficient. We have instead, adopted the approach of using time-stamped event streams as a means of encapsulating actual workload characteristics, that drives a very simple model of the environment being simulated. We have presented general techniques that project event time-stamps from one execution environment to the other based on simple cost models. Specifically, we have demonstrated the use of an event-based approach to expose performance characteristics of programs in various execution environments. These performance characteristics can lead to a better understanding of the nature of the programs and to the appropriate selection of an execution environment for the problem. Throughout the examples, we have relied on, and found, the use of visual qualitative feedback to be critical in providing better insight into performance tradeoffs.

Clearly, this approach is not suited for detailed system design. This approach is intended to help the user to understand the effect of coarse-grained system changes (such as increased compute power or network bandwidth) on program performance. When more details become needed, traditional simulation techniques may be needed, leading to a costly multi-dimensional system search. It is therefore imperative to carefully tred the fine-line that distinguishes a useful/reliable result from one that is overly simplistic, and use the tool that is most appropriate for the problem at hand. A performance prediction tool with a wide array of choices for abstractions and capabilities for exposing dynamic performance bottlenecks is imperative in making quick and well informed choices for the execution environment.

Since the primary concern in this paper was incremental changes to execution environments, most of the system components that remain unchanged are not modeled – leading to rapid response times. There are still a lot of in-complete ends. Modeling local memory access patterns is being encapsulated as part of the execution speed of the compute node, extension of this work to use load/store counts associated with each event is being considered. In addition, improvements in the program to allow execution environment changes for specific code fragments, subroutines and processors are being incorporated. The primary bottleneck in using this methodology for large traces may be the I/O requirements for reading and writing huge traces. We are further investigating this limitatoin to determine the impact of reading and writing traces and its impact on response time.

REFERENCES

1. E. A. Brewer, C. N. Dellarocas, A. Colbrook, and W. E. Weihl, "PRO-TEUS: A High-performance parallel-Architecture Simulator," Proceedings of the 1992 ACM SIGMETRICS and PERFORMANCE '92 Conference, June 1992.

2. R. Fujimoto and W. B. Campbell, "Efficient Instruction-level Simulation of Computers," Transactions of the Society for Computer Simulation, 5(2), 1988.

3. Michael T. Heath, Jennifer A. Etheridge, "Visualizing the Performance of Parallel Programs," IEEE Software, September 1991.

4. Eileen Kraemer and John T. Stasko, " The Visualization of Parallel Systems: An Overview," Journal of Parallel and Distributed Computing, June 1993.

5. Celso L. Mendes and Daniel Reed, "Performance Stability and Prediction," Proceedings of the International Workshop on High Performance Computing (WHPC '94), Sao Paulo, March 1994.

6. S. K. Reinhardt, M. D. Hill, J. R. Larus, A. R. Lebeck, J. C. Lewis and D. A. Wood, " The Wisconsin Wind Tunnel: Virtual Prototyping of Parallel Computers," Proceedings of the 1993 ACM SIGMETRICS conference, May 1993.

7. Mendel Rosenblum, Stephen Herrod, Emmett Witchel and Anoop Gupta, "Complete Computer System Simulation: The Sim OS Approach," IEEE Parallel and Distributed Technology, Winter 1995.

8. M. J. Clement, and M. J. Quinn, "Analytical Performance Prediction on Multicomputers," Proceedings of Supercomputing'93, Portland, November 1993.

9. Sekhar R. Sarukkai and Jerry Yan, "Event-based Study of the Effect of Execution Environments on Parallel Program Performance," Proceedings of MASCOTS '96,, San Jose, February 1996.

10. J. Yan, S. R. Sarukkai and P. Mehra, "Performance Measurement, Visualization and Modeling of Parallel and Distributed Programs using the AIMS Toolkit," Software -Practice and Experience, 25(4), April 1995.

CHAPTER 6

PERFORMANCE OF DATA DIFFUSION MACHINE ARCHITECTURES

Ting-Li Hu   Fadi N. Sibai

6.1. INTRODUCTION

The main problem with the *uniform memory access* (UMA) architecture is its low potential for scalability and contention elimination. One of the well known solutions to this problem is the *cache-coherent network architecture* [1]. The *Data Diffusion Machine* (DDM) introduced by Hagersten, Haridi, and Warren[2] is an example of a multiprocessor based on this architecture. It incorporates a hierarchical snooping bus architecture and uses a hierarchical search algorithm for finding an item. Since all the memories in DDM are converted into enormous caches, the DDM defines a new architectural type called the *cache-only memory architecture* (COMA).

In general, the performance of multiprocessors can be evaluated either by trace-driven simulation methods or by analytical simulation models. Although a trace-driven methodology is a popular and widely used simulation technique, it generally requires a large amount of disk space to store the program traces. Also, simulations that produce results which would cover a sufficient portion of the design space are very time-consuming. Therefore, methods which can quickly and cheaply produce system performance results are highly desirable. The *Mean Value Analysis* (MVA) model developed by Vernon and Lazowska[3] is one of the analytical models that can evaluate the average performance of multiprocessors efficiently and accurately. Furthermore, it can be easily modified to analyze different multiprocessor architectures; hence, the evaluation methodology of this work is principally based on the MVA model.

The DDM prototype analyzed in this chapter will be referred to as COMA thereafter. The chapter primarily focuses on estimating the *optimal system configuration* of COMA with 3 levels of hierarchy. The optimal system configuration is defined as the configuration (i.e. processor clustering) that leads to peak system efficiency. Under the assumptions of uniform request distribution and uniform system configuration, which means that the number of processors under the directories at the same level of the hierarchy is identical, the performance of 3-level COMA systems can be evaluated and analyzed by modifying the MVA model accordingly. Furthermore, the optimal cluster sizes at each level that optimize the system efficiency are also identified by evaluating the 3-level MVA model.

The organization of this chapter follows. Section 6.2 briefly reviews the cache-only memory architecture (COMA). Section 6.3 describes the mean value analysis (MVA) model and the modifications adopted to analyze hierarchical 3-level COMA systems with different configurations. The optimal configurations of COMA systems are presented and analyzed in section 6.4 for a variety of parameter settings. Finally, section 6.5 concludes this chapter and provides suggestions for future research.

6.2. THE COMA ARCHITECTURE

The smallest instance of a COMA is a fundamental block called *minimal COMA*. The 3-level COMA consists of minimal COMAs connected by a hierarchical interconnection network. The minimal COMA contains a certain number of processing units, a directory, and a single shared bus. The minimal COMA can be a COMA of its own or a subsystem of a larger COMA. A *cluster* is defined as a directory and the subsystem below it. Each processing unit has a high-performance processor, a cache, and a portion of the global shared memory. The memory associated with each unit is augmented to act as a large cache, called the *attraction memory* (AM)[1,4,5]. An *item* is defined as the basic unit of a cache block in AMs. The number of words in an item is called the *block size* or *cache line*. The protocol developed for items in the AMs of a minimal COMA is a snooping protocol which is similar to the write-once protocol proposed by Goodman[6]. The protocol is based on the write-invalidate mechanism for a write operation. Figure 1 illustrates the system architecture for 3-level COMAs. It also

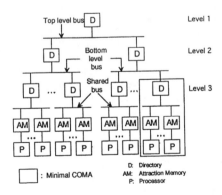

FIGURE 1. Hierarchical 3-level COMA architecture.

defines the terminology which is used by the modified MVA model and the rest of the chapter.

6.3. THE MODIFIED MVA MODEL

Holliday and Vernon developed an accurate analytical technique called the *Generalized Time Petri Nets* (GTPN) model[7,8] to analyze the performance of shared-bus multiprocessors. Based on the GTPN model, Vernon and Lazowska developed a more abstract and significantly more efficient analytical model called the *Mean Value Analysis* (MVA) model[3].

Since the MVA model was designed especially for the snoopy-based UMA machines and the protocol implemented in the minimal COMA is very similar to the write-once cache protocol, the MVA model can be used in the analysis of COMA multiprocessors. Some modifications are however required to apply the MVA model to the COMA systems. First, the hierarchical bus architecture must be included into the MVA model which originally contains only a shared bus. Secondly, since the shared memory does not exist any more, the portion of shared memory in MVA must be modified. Thirdly, data migration is one of the features of COMA, it can increase the hit ratio and thus reduce the need for remote memory references. Since the UMA architecture does not have this capability, the parameters used in the original MVA model will be slightly different from those for COMA. The following paragraphs describe the modifications made to the MVA model.

Figure 2 shows the equivalent MVA Model for 3-level COMAs. The hierarchical architecture in COMA now becomes part of the *virtual shared memory* (VSM), which is equivalent to the shared memory in the UMA architecture plus processors.

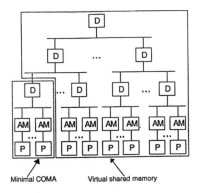

FIGURE 2.   Equivalent MVA model for 3-level COMAs.

The VSM has two properties that are different from the shared memory in UMAs. First, the access latency to the shared memory in the UMA architecture is fixed, which is determined by the access latency of the memory modules used. For the VSM, however, the access latency is no longer a constant. It is a function of how busy the rest of the subsystems are and the location of the serving AM. Secondly, the shared memory in UMA plays a passive role because, other than replying to the request from the shared bus, it does not send any request messages. The shared memory in UMA never interrupts the execution of local processors. On the contrary, the VSM plays an active role in the COMA multiprocessors. It does send requests to the bus (of minimal COMA), interrupts the execution of processors, and therefore competes for the shared bus.

6.3.1. The Workload Model for COMA

We assume that the reader is familiar with the GTPN and MVA models. The workload model and the equations for UMA in references 3, 7, and 8 are still valid for COMA. The GTPN model has been slightly modified to include the distinct characteristics of COMA. The difference between the original GTPN model and the modified one (see Figure 3 and Table 1) is that the operation of writing back the requested block to the shared memory by the serving cache is no longer required in COMA. However, the operation of writing back the replaced item to the shared memory (VSM in COMA correspondingly) by the requesting cache is still necessary.

In the GTPN Model of Figure 3, the big circles marked with P are called *places* while the horizontal bars marked with T are called *transitions*. The places that point to a transition are called *input places* of the transition while those pointed to by a transition are *output places* of the transition. The transitions define actions or requests in the multiprocessor. The tiny circles within places are called *tokens*. The arrows in the GTPN model are the directions that the tokens are going to move across.

The places that initially contain tokens represent the initial conditions for the GTPN model. A transition can *fire* if each of its input places contains at least one token. Each transition is associated with a *firing frequency* which determines the probability that the transition will fire and with a deterministic *firing duration* which defines how long the transition will take. After firing, each input place removes one of its tokens while the output places increase their tokens by one.

In Figure 3, each token in place P1 represents a processor that has just completed an instruction cycle. It is assumed that the memory access behaviors of processors are satistically identical and each processor's token acts independently[8]. The two tokens in place P1 depict the contention of the shared bus between one processor and the other processors because there is only one shared bus available. The tokens in places P2 and P9 indicate that the bus and memory are available, respectively.

Table 1 defines the attributes of the GTPN model for COMA. The third column in Table 1 contains the frequency expressions for the GTPN model. The frequency expressions define relative probabilities of branches

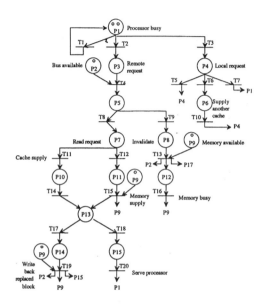

FIGURE 3.   The modified GTPN model for COMA.

TABLE 1.   The attributes of the modified GTPN model for COMA.

Transition	Duration	Frequency	Resources
T1	1	$1 - P_{cpu\_req}$	
T2	0	$(PSRWM + PSWH_{umod}) \times P_{cpu\_req}$	
T3	0	$(PSRH + PSWH_{umod}) \times P_{cpu\_req}$	
T4	0	1.0	
T5	1	1.0 - Freq(T6) - Freq(T7)	spd
T6	0	1 / (# CPUs) * Freq(T14)	
T7	1	$0.5 \times (SRMiss + SWMiss) \times T8 + 0.5 \times (P_{sro} + P_{swo}) \times T13$	
T8	1	$PSRWM/(PSRWM+PSWH_{umod})$	bus
T9	0	1 - Freq(T8)	
T10	0	1 - Freq(T14)	
T11	block size	$P_{csuplro} \times SRMiss + P_{csuplsw} \times SWMiss$	bus
T12	0	1.0 - Freq(T11)	
T13	1	1.0	bus
T14	0	1.0	
T15	block size + d_{data}	1.0	bus
T16	0	1.0	
T17	0	$P_{replprlv} \times P_{prlv} + P_{replsw} \times P_{sro}$	
T18	0	1.0 - Freq(T19)	
T19	block size	1.0	bus
T20	1	1.0	spd

in the net. The resources associated with the net transitions in the fourth column of Table 1 identify performance measures to be calculated. The measures defined in the GTPN model are bus utilization (Bus) and speedup (Spd).

Additionally, to model the new properties of COMA in the MVA model, we need to define two new parameters: n_{equ} and d_{equ}. n_{equ} is defined as the equivalent number of processors seen by the shared bus in a minimal COMA while d_{equ} is defined as the equivalent access latency of the VSM. Once these parameters are determined, they replace the parameters n_{cpu} and T_{mem} in the original MVA model.

From Table 2 and Figure 4, the probability variables used by the modified MVA model to calculate n_{equ} and d_{equ} can be found and calculated by assuming a uniform request distribution. A minimal COMA cluster is called the *client* if it issues a request and the *server* if it serves the request. To determine the equivalent number of processors in the virtual shared memory, let's pick up a minimal COMA cluster in Figure 1 randomly. For a request from any one processor, the local directory, which is actually part of the shared bus, tries to serve it locally, i.e., from any other attraction memories within the requesting cluster. If the request cannot be served

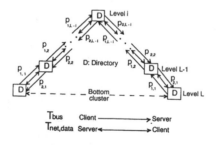

FIGURE 4.   Latency model for global requests in COMA.

TABLE 2.   Summary of parameters in COMA and their ranges.

Parameter	Range
Memory and attraction memory access time	1 clock cycle
Directory update (T_{du})	4 clock cycles
Bus latency (T_{bus})	2 clock cycles
Item transfer latency ($T_{net,data}$)	Block size × clock cycle
Block size	4 - 64 words
Percentage of data sharing	1%, 5%, and 20%

locally, it must go up to the directory of one upper level. Note that in Figure 4, upper level directories (on top) are assigned lower level numbers than the directories on the bottom. $p_{1,1}$, the probability that the request cannot be satisfied by any other attraction memories within the minimal COMA cluster and must be served by the shared virtual memory, is determined by equation 1. L is the number of levels in the hierarchical COMA. For 2-level COMA, the requested item is found since the request has reached the root directory (level 1). For higher level COMAs, the request may either be served by any other sibling cluster at the same level of the directory or go up to the directory of one upper level. $p_{1,j}$ (where j is between 2 and $L-i$), the probability that the request will go to the next upper directory at one upper level, is given by equation 2.

For any level COMA, after the request has reached the first directory (denoted as level i in Figure 4) which contains information on the requested item, this directory is looked up for the attraction memory containing the requested item. Note that the directory at level i does not necessarily mean the root directory. It can be the top directory of any subsystem in the definition of the $p_{2,j}$'s. By assuming a uniform system configuration and uniform request distribution, $p_{2,L-i}$, the probability that the request is going to be forwarded down (from the directory at level i) to a specific subcluster, is equal to one over the number of clusters attached to the directory at level i, minus one, since the request will not select the subcluster that sent the request. The probability $p_{2,j}$, where j is between 1 and $L-i-1$, is calculated in a similar way for the hierarchical buses below until the request reaches the directory at the bottom level ($=L$) except that the denominator (in equation 3) is now replaced by the total number of clusters attached to the directory at level j since any cluster at level j is a possible candidate for serving the request. The probability variables for multi-level COMA are given by:

$$p_{1,1} = PSRWM \tag{1}$$

$$p_{1,j} = \frac{n_{total} - n_{req,L-j+1}}{n_{total} - n_{req,L-j+2}} \qquad j=2, ..., L-i \tag{2}$$

$$p_{2,L-i} = \frac{n_{ser,i+1}}{n_{ser,i} - n_{ser,i+1}} = \frac{1}{c_i - 1} \tag{3}$$

$$p_{2,j} = \frac{n_{ser,L-j+1}}{n_{ser,L-j}} = \frac{1}{c_{L-j}} \qquad j=1, ..., L-i-1 \tag{4}$$

where $PSRWM$:   Probability that a read or write miss hits a private or shared block;

          n_{total}:   Total number of processors in the COMA system;

$n_{req,i}$:   Number of processors attached to (below) the
                        directory containing the client cluster at level
                        i;

$n_{ser,i}$:   Number of processors attached to the
                        directory containing the server cluster at level
                        i;

c_i: Number of clusters attached to any directory
                        at level i.

From Figures 1 and 3 and Table 1, n_{equ} and d_{equ} can be determined
as follows. Recall that a cluster is defined as a directory and the subsystem
below it. Thus, for a specific cluster of minimal COMA, which contains a
directory, a shared bus, and all the attraction memories and processors
attached to the shared bus, n_{equ} is equal to the sum of the number of
processors in that cluster and the equivalent number of processors in the
virtual shared memory. The equivalent number of processors in the virtual
shared memory is equal to the product of the number of processors in the
virtual shared memory and the probabilities (along the requesting path) that
a request from any processor in the virtual shared memory will reach the
shared bus in the minimal COMA cluster. The equations for n_{equ} and d_{equ} for
3-level COMA are given by

$$n_{equ} = [(n_{total} - n_{req,2}) \times \prod_{i=1}^{L-1} (p_{1,i} \times p_{2,i})] +$$

$$\sum_{j=2}^{L-1} [(n_{req,j} - n_{req,j+1}) \times \prod_{m=1}^{L-j} (p_{1,m} \times p_{2,m})] + n_{MC}$$

$$= (n_{total} - n_{req,2}) \; p_{1,1} \, p_{1,2} \, p_{2,2} \, p_{2,1} + (n_{req,2} - n_{req,3}) \; p_{1,1} \, p_{2,1} + n_{MC} \tag{5}$$

$$d_{equ} = (\frac{T_{dir}}{3} + T_{bus} + t_{O,2}) + p_{1,2} \sum_{j=1}^{3} (\frac{T_{dir}}{3} + T_{bus} + t_{O,j}) +$$

$$(1 - p_{1,2}) (\frac{T_{dir}}{3} + T_{bus} + t_{O,3}) \tag{6}$$

$$t_{O,i} = n_{C,i} \times t_{O,L} \times \prod_{j=1}^{L-i} p_{1,j} \tag{7}$$

where L: Number of hierarchical levels in COMA;

              $n_{C,i}$:   Number of minimal COMAs under
                              a directory at level i;

              $t_{O,i}$:   Bus overhead time at level i;

n_{MC}:   Number of processors in a minimal COMA.

d_{equ}, the mean access latency of the VSM, is determined in a similar way. Figure 4 defines the latency model for global requests in a multi-level COMA. Table 2 shows the system parameters used by the modified MVA model for evaluating the performance of multi-level COMAs. From Figure 4, it can be seen that whenever the request goes one level higher, the access latency increases by T_{dir} plus the access latency of the bus (T_{bus}). Therefore, the modified model determines d_{equ} by calculating the sum of the additional latencies along the path of the request, T_{dir} and T_{bus}, as specified by equation 6. Note that each directory module contains a queue which can buffer three requests[5]. Although the requests are usually handled serially, we assume that the internal mechanism implemented in the directories is able to service three requests simultaneously.

Since the requested item in some AMs must wait until the shared bus in the server minimal COMA is available, the mean access latency of the VSM is also a function of the single bus overhead time in the minimal COMA. To incorporate this property, the model assumes that the overhead time at level i, $t_{O,i}$, is a function of the overhead time at the bottom level, $t_{O,L}$, which is the overhead time of the shared bus in minimal COMA (see equation 7). Note that this equation assumes that the volume of the requests from the upper level is negligible because the probability that a request comes from the upper level is much smaller than that from the lower level.

6.3.2. Evaluation Methodology

The inputs to the COMA simulator (we will refer to the performance evaluation program as "the simulator") are the maximum number of processors in a minimal COMA, the cache line, and the number of clusters attached to the top level bus. The simulator generates the results for three different cases of percentage data sharing, 1%, 5%, and 20%. The percentage of data sharing reflects the probability that an item is shared among the AMs.

The performance of COMA is evaluated by first finding the response time (t_{req}) from the response time equation defined in reference 3. The response time is equal to the sum of the processor execution time between requests ($T_{exec,cpu}$), the overhead time ($t_{overhead}$, which is the probability-weighted average of the mean local response time, the mean response time for broadcasting an invalidate operation, and the mean response time of a remote read operation), and the cache supply time ($T_{lat,cache}$, which is the latency of the cache memory). The unit for time is expressed in terms of system cycle, which is independent of the actual clock time.

After having determined the mean response time, the MVA model can now evaluate the performance of COMA multiprocessors by calculating the efficiency and speedup of multiprocessors. Equations for efficiency and speedup are given below.

$$Efficiency = \frac{T_{exec,cpu} + T_{lat,cache}}{t_{req}} \qquad (8)$$

$$Speedup = n_{total} \times Efficiency \qquad (9)$$

where n_{total}:   Total number of processors;

                 $T_{exec,cpu}$:   Average time that a processor is not in idle
                                      state (=2.5 cycles);

                 $T_{lat,cache}$:   Access latency of cache memories (=1 cycle);

                 t_{req}:   Response time or mean number of cycles
                                      between two consecutive memory references
                                      issued by a processor.

The equations of the modified MVA model for COMA are solved iteratively by first setting all waiting times of buses and memory modules to zero, calculating the values of n_{equ} and d_{equ}, and determining the initial t_{req}. The waiting times are then updated in each iteration by using the previous values of the waiting times, n_{equ}, and d_{equ}. n_{equ}, d_{equ}, and t_{req} are then updated correspondingly. Next, the system efficiency and speedup are calculated according to equations 8 and 9. The computation terminates if the absolute value of the difference between the current efficiency and the previous efficiency converges to a certain predetermined tiny value. Since the access latency of the VSM is a function of the overhead time of the shared bus in the minimal COMA, the analytical model may become unstable if the shared bus saturates. To avoid this situation, the simulator is forced to terminate automatically if the results do not converge after a predetermined number of iterations.

6.4. RESULTS FOR 3-LEVEL COMA

Using the modified MVA model and assuming a uniform request distribution and a uniform system configuration, the performance of 3-level COMAs is analyzed by varying the number of top level (level 2 in Figure 1) clusters, data sharing percentage, and cache line. By varying the latter two variables for a specific number of top level clusters, the efficiency and speedup of COMA under various configurations (number of bottom level -- level 3 or minimal COMA -- clusters under each level 2 bus, and number of processors per bottom level cluster) are found. From these results, the efficiency-optimal system configurations can be identified.

Tables 3, 4, and 5 summarize the optimal system configurations for 3-level COMA for various data sharing percentages and cache line settings. The optimal system configuration is defined as the system configuration (number of top level -- i.e. level 2 -- clusters; number of bottom level -- i.e. level 3-- clusters per top level cluster; and number of processors per bottom level cluster) which generates the maximum or peak efficiency for a certain data sharing percentage, cache line, and number of top-level clusters.

TABLE 3.   Optimal 3-level COMA configurations with 1% data sharing.

	Cache line (word)				
	4	8	16	32	64
Top = 16****	2 (32,768)*	2 (8,192)	2 (8,192)	2 (512)	2 (2,048)
	1,024**	256	256	16	64
clusters	29,547***	7,217	6,869	386	1,236
Top = 64	2 (131,072)	2 (32,768)	2 (8,192)	2 (32,768)	2 (2,048)
	1,024	256	64	256	16
clusters	118,176	28,864	6,869	24,702	1,237
Top = 256	2 (131,072)	2 (131,072)	2 (32,768)	2 (32,768)	2 (8,192)
	256	256	64	64	16
clusters	118,202	115,439	27,479	24,714	4,946
Top = 1024	2 (524,288)	2 (131,072)	2 (32,768)	2 (131,072)	2 (131,072)
	256	64	16	64	64
clusters	472,705	115,455	27,476	98,807	79,102
Top = 2048	2 (262,144)	2 (262,144)	2 (65,536)	2 (65,536)	2 (65,536)
	64	64	16	16	16
clusters	236,402	230,871	54,961	49,435	39,557

* Number of processors per bottom cluster (total number of processors)
** Number of bottom clusters
*** Speedup
**** Number of top clusters

TABLE 4.   Optimal 3-level COMA configurations with 5% data sharing.

	Cache line (word)				
	4	8	16	32	64
Top = 16****	2 (8,192)*	2 (8,192)	2 (2,048)	2 (2,048)	2 (512)
	256**	256	64	64	16
clusters	7,305***	7,099	1,673	1,474	286
Top = 64	2 (32,768)	2 (8,192)	2 (8,192)	2 (2,048)	2 (8,192)
	256	64	64	16	64
clusters	29,218	7,102	6,691	1,475	4,560
Top = 256	2 (32,768)	2 (32,768)	2 (32,768)	2 (8,192)	2 (8,192)
	64	64	64	16	16
clusters	29,224	28,404	26,756	5,897	4,565
Top = 1024	2 (131,072)	2 (32,768)	2 (32,768)	2 (32,768)	2 (32,768)
	64	16	16	16	16
clusters	116,868	28,408	26,764	23,576	1,8240
Top = 2048	2 (65,536)	2 (65,536)	2 (65,536)	2 (65,536)	2 (65,536)
	16	16	16	16	16
clusters	59,109	57,736	54,961	49,435	39,557

* Number of processors per bottom cluster (total number of processors)
** Number of bottom clusters
*** Speedup
**** Number of top clusters

TABLE 5.   Optimal 3-level COMA configurations with 20% data sharing.

	Cache line (word)				
	4	8	16	32	64
Top = 16****	2 (512)*	2 (512)	2 (512)	2 (512)	2 (512)
	16**	16	16	16	16
clusters	452***	435	402	342	252
Top = 64	2 (2,048)	2 (2,048)	2 (2,048)	2 (2,048)	2 (2,048)
	16	16	16	16	16
clusters	1,808	1,741	1,608	1,366	1,008
Top = 256	2 (32,768)	2 (8,192)	2 (8,192)	2 (8,192)	2 (8,192)
	64	16	16	16	16
clusters	28,893	6,961	6,430	5,458	4,024
Top = 1024	2 (32,768)	2 (32,768)	2 (32,768)	2 (32,768)	2 (32,768)
	16	16	16	16	16
clusters	28,904	27,818	25,666	21,740	15,977
Top = 2048	2 (65,536)	2 (65,536)	2 (65,536)	2 (65,536)	2 (65,536)
	16	16	16	16	16
clusters	57,771	55,564	51,194	43,239	31,646

* Number of processors per bottom cluster (total number of processors)
** Number of bottom clusters
*** Speedup
**** Number of top clusters

From Tables 3, 4, and 5, as the cache line increases, the speedup at peak efficiency decreases (related to a decrease in the total number of processors) for all three different data sharing percentages. The bottom cluster size that generates the peak efficiency is dependent on the top cluster size since the system with fewer clusters attached to the bottom level bus increases the probability that a request must go through the top level bus, which consequently degrades the system performance. Once the number of clusters below the level 2 bus becomes small enough, the number of clusters below the level 1 bus can increase because the number of requests from subclusters is reduced. In general, the larger the number of top clusters, the smaller is the number of bottom clusters.

From Table 3, the speedup at peak efficiency generally increases as the number of top clusters increases. The total number of processors also depends on the number of top clusters and cache line. It increases as the cache line decreases or the number of top clusters increases for 1% and 5% data sharing. However, for 20% data sharing (Table 5), the total number of processors (as well as the number of bottom clusters and the number of processors per bottom cluster) is a constant for a particular number of top clusters (i.e. it is independent of the cache line) because the impact of the cumulative overhead times due to the hierarchical bus contentions on the access latency, and consequently on the optimal system efficiency, becomes critical. If the total number of processors for a fixed number of top clusters were to increase further (leading to an increase in the bottom level clusters and/or the number of processors per bottom cluster), $p_{1,2}$ $(= (n_{total} -$ number_of_bottom_clusters x n_{MC})/$(n_{total} -n_{MC}))$ would increase so much that the second term in equation 6 would dominate the expression for d_{equ} (and consequently the access latency), leading to the system efficiency no longer being optimal. Generally, with only two processors per minimal COMA cluster, the efficiency-optimal 3-level COMA system structure approaches the structure of the 2-level COMA system.

6.5. CONCLUSION

As the number of processors in multiprocessors becomes larger and larger, the efficiency of the UMA-based multiprocessors decays exponentially and eventually approaches zero. Consequently, the speedup of the UMA-based system saturates. The overhead of the system is dominated by the bus contention instead of the access latency. To minimize bus contention, the structure of the shared bus must be changed. Hierarchical COMA is a solution to the high scalability requirements of today's multiprocessors.

In order to minimize the access latency and the global contention, the COMA architecture uses a hierarchical bus structure when the system becomes large. It was shown herein that this hierarchy can support a large number of processors far beyond the range of the UMA architecture since the directories on every level of COMA behave like filters to the requests arriving either from their bottom clusters or from their top directories. Therefore, contention is drastically reduced.

However, the hierarchical bus structure and the directories add overhead time to the access latency. The deeper the hierarchy, the longer is the access latency. Hence, the number of levels in the hierarchy depends on the size of the system. Our results show that the hierarchical 3-level COMA architecture can support multiprocessor systems with hundreds of processors without much degradation of system performance.

This chapter also presented the optimum system configurations that optimize the system efficiency. When the volume of the requests from above is negligible, the system efficiency is optimized when the number of processors in the minimum COMA (and consequently, the amount of request coming from below) is minimum, i.e. 2. Future work includes repeating the study with different parameters and request distributions (other than the uniform request distribution) accounting for hot spots and spatial locality of items.

REFERENCES

1. P. STENSTROM, IEEE Computer, **23(6)**, 12-24 (June 1990).

2. E. HAGERSTEN, S. HARIDI, D. H. D. WARREN, "The Cache Coherence Protocol of the Data Diffusion Machine," in Cache and Interconnect Architectures in Multiprocessors, edited by M. Dubois and S. Thakkar (Kluwer, Norwell, MA, 1990), 165-188.

3. M. K. VERNON, E. LAZOWSKA, "An Accurate and Efficient Performance Analysis Technique for Multiprocessor Snooping Cache-Consistency Protocols," in Proc. of 15th An. Int. Symp. on Computer Architecture (1988), 308-315.

4. P. STENSTROM, J. TRUMAN, A. GUPTA, "Comparative Performance Evaluation of Cache-Coherence NUMA and COMA Architecture," in Proc. of 19th An. Int. Symp. on Computer Architecture (1992), 80-91.

5. E. HAGERSTEN, A. LANDIN, S. HARIDI, IEEE Computer, **25(9)**, 44-54 (September 1992).

6. J. R. GOODMAN, "Using Cache Memory to Reduce Processor-Memory Traffic," in Proc. of 10th An. Int. Symp. on Computer Architecture (1983), 124-131.

7. J. ARCHIBALD, J. BAER, ACM Trans. on Computer Sys., **4(4)**, 273-298 (November 1986).

8. M. A. HOLLIDAY, M. K. VERNON, "A Generalized Timed Petri Nets Model for Performance Analysis," in Proc. of Int. Workshop on Timed Petri Nets (July 1985), 181-190.

CHAPTER 7

MODELING AND PERFORMANCE EVALUATION OF THE HYBRID-CLUSTER MULTIPROCESSOR: AN ARCHITECTURE TO MINIMIZE CACHE COHERENCE TRAFFIC

Ana Pont, José A. Gil

7.1 INTRODUCTION

The use of private cache memories in multiprocessors with common memory introduces the data coherence problem[1]. The most frequently used mechanisms to avoid this problem are hardware based protocols (based on snoopy bus controller or directory schemes). With this kind of solutions an extra traffic in the bus is generated and this traffic becomes an important factor when the number of processors increases.

Other solution consists in the use of software coherence schemes that need to place certain instructions in the program by the compiler or the programmer.

In others approaches the use of private caches are proposed and, new configurations appear. In these configurations different types of caches according to their content can be found: private and shared data caches and instruction caches[2].

But with these solutions it is very difficult to obtain a scalable multiprocessor and usually the number of processors is limited.

On the other hand there is no doubt about the benefits of cache-affinity scheduling in shared memory multiprocessors to reduce the miss ratio[3]. But the cache affinity scheduling can also reduce the coherence traffic in an appropriated multiprocessor architecture.

The Hybrid-Cluster Multiprocessor presented in this chapter is an architecture thought to avoid an important part of the traffic generated because of the need to guarantee the coherence between the different cache memories. The use of private and shared cache memories and the aspects of cache affinity scheduling have been beard in mind to obtain a scalable architecture.

Queuing network models[4] have been choosen to do the performance study because they are one of the most used tools in performance evaluation. Using these tools a complete evaluation of the architecture proposed can be done under several assumptions.

For the workload an analytical model has been developed. This is a probabilistic model based on the idea presented by Dubois and Briggs[5] and used by many other authors[6, 7, 8]. It is a useful and flexible model to implement analytically solvable queuing networks for evaluating the system under different workloads using a lower computational time than the required with simulation techniques.

7.2 THE HYBRID-CLUSTER MULTIPROCESSOR

In the proposed architecture there is a set of C clusters that share an interleaved multimodule main memory. To access this main memory a packet switched bus is used. With this kind of bus when a processor needs a memory operation it transmits its own address and the required operation on the bus (if the bus is available, if not it must wait) and gets off during the rest of the memory cycle. When the data are ready they are sent to the requesting processor using the bus. This solution requires additional buffers and presents additional delays due to the need of packing and unpacking the information. For the studied architecture an asynchronous packet-switched bus with centralized control is considered.

Each cluster has a set of processors (4 for instance) that are placed in the same circuit. Each processor has its own instruction cache and its own private data cache that does not store shared data. In the same circuit there also is a common cache that can be accessed by all the processors in the cluster. This common cache only stores shared data. There are also two buses that connect the common cache with the processors. The common cache is proposed as a double port memory. Therefore, all the processors that belong to the same cluster share the only copy of a shared block and no cache coherence is needed inside the cluster. However all the references of a shared cache must be "snoopied" through the packet switched bus because these data can also be loaded in the shared caches of the others clusters. Obviously with this organization there is an important reduction of the traffic due to consistence actions. For instance, in a traditional multiprocessor with 32 processor it is necessary to guarantee the data coherence between 32 cache memories. But, in the Hybrid-Cluster multiprocessor if there are 4 processor in the same cluster only 8 cache memories will need coherence actions.

Figure 1 shows the Hybrid-Cluster multiprocessor architecture.

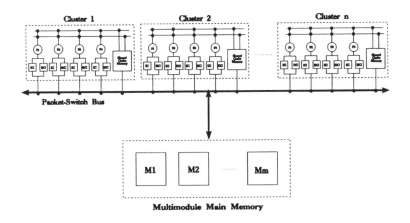

FIGURE 1.   Hybrid-Cluster Multiprocessor architecture.

7.3 MODELING AND PERFORMANCE EVALUATION

For the modeling and the performance evaluation of the Hybrid-Cluster multiprocessor a queuing network has been proposed. This queuing network can be analytically solvable. For this purpose a probabilistic workload is presented.

7.3.1 The Queuing Network

Figure 2 shows the queuing network proposed to model the architecture.

In each cluster the processors ($P_{i,j}$ / i=1,..,C, j=1,...,N) have been modeled as feedback delay centers where memory request are generated. The cache memories associated to each processor (instruction and data caches) are FCFS (First Come First Served) single servers. Its service time is equal to a processor cycle. The double port common cache has been modeled using a FCFS multiple service center. As many servers as ports in the memory are considered (2 in this case). This is a good approach when medium and big cache sizes are considered[9].

The packet-switched bus system is modeled using a Flow Equivalent Service Center (FESC) because it is a load dependent server[10]. The transfer time of a packet (request or response packet) is considered equal to a system cycle. The service time of the system buses depends on the number of packets in the center (load dependent center) and the effective service rate is given by

$$\mu(q) = \frac{Min(q,B)}{\tau}$$

where q is the number of packets in the center, B the number of buses considered (one in this case) and τ the transmission time of one packet.

Each module of main memory (M) is modeled using a FCFS single service center. Its service rate is assumed fixed and constant. An interleaved main memory is considered so, the access for a single data or a block can be the same.

It is a mixed queuing network where there are two kinds of customers: open and closed customers. The closed customers model the memory requirements. The open customers model parallel actions related with the consistency actions. SA (source) and SAK (sink) model the updating of private and shared blocks in main memory. SB (source) and SBK (sink) model the effects of loading a new block in the caches. And, when protocols with write-update policy are studied, it is necessary to consider another class of open customers to model the broadcasting of data, they are SD and SDK source and sink respectively.

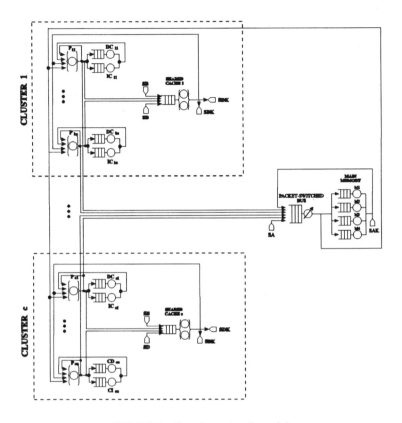

FIGURE 2.   Queuing network model.

7.3.2 The Probabilistic Workload

A probabilistic workload is proposed to solve analytically the queuing network model presented before.

For this purpose an homogeneous system in which all the processors have an identical behavior is considered. After a certain period of internal computation, called Cycle Time, a processor j that belongs to a cluster i generates a memory request. As a on-chip cache is considered, the request will be served in the cache on chip with a probability R, or it will be an external request with probability $1-R$.

The probability of generating an external memory request for instructions is *PI* and, 1-*PI* is the probability of addressing data. It is assumed that there is a degree of data shared called q_S that indicates the probability of accessing to a shared or a private data. Also it is assumed that a request is a write operation with probability *w* and a read operation with 1-*w*.

The hit ratio for private data and instructions is *H*.

Let *Sc* be the size of a cache in blocks. A total of *Ns* shared blocks that can be accessed by all the processors is assumed. *Np* is the number of private blocks.

The behavior of a private block in a cache assuming a Random policy for replacement can be seen in the Markov diagram of the figure 3.

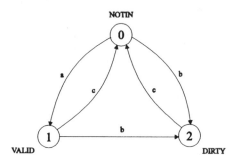

FIGURE 3.   Markov diagram for a private block

Where the states are: NOTIN = 0, VALID = 1 and DIRTY = 2 and the probabilities *a*, *b* and *c* can be calculated as

$$a=\left(1-q_s\right)\frac{(1-w)}{N_p} \qquad b=\left(1-q_s\right)\frac{w}{N_p} \qquad c=\frac{(1-H)}{S_c}$$

Solving this Markov chain it is possible to know the steady state probability distribution π_0, π_1 and π_2. With this values it is possible to obtain the probability of updating a private block in main memory between two successive references (copy-back). This probability is:

$$P_{cb}=\left(1-q_s\right)\left(1-H\right)\pi_2$$

where π_2 is the probability of having a dirty block in steady state.

The behavior of shared blocks depends on the coherence protocol used because the protocol defines all the possible states for a shared block in cache. For each protocol under study it is necessary to develop and solve the associated Markov chain in order to know the steady state probability of each state.

Applying this knowledge to a queuing network the visit ratios of a memory request to each of the servers can be calculated. The visit ratios for the instruction and data cache of a processor are independent of the coherence protocol and they are respectively:

$$v_{IC} = (1-R) \cdot PI \cdot H$$

$$v_{DC} = (1-R)(1-PI)(1-q_s) \cdot H$$

Different snoopy protocols have been studied but in this paper only two of them are considered. The Write-Once[11, 12] protocol to represent the write and invalidate policies and the Dragon[13] that follows a write and update policy.

Write-Once protocol The states for a shared block in a private cache when the protocol Write-Once is used are: π_0=NOTIN, π_1=VALID, π_2=RESERVED, π_3=DIRTY and π_4=INVALID. Figure 4 shows the transition probabilities between the states using a Markov chain.

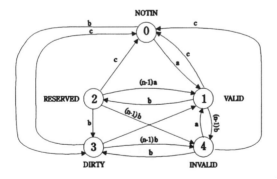

FIGURE 4. Markov chain for the Write-Once protocol

where,

$$a = (1-q_s)\frac{(1-w)}{N_p} \qquad b = (1-q_s)\frac{w}{N_p} \qquad c = \frac{(1-H)}{S_c}$$

Solving this chain the probabilities of each state are known (π_0, π_1, π_2, π_3 and π_4).

Using all of this information the visit ratios for each element in the queuing network can be calculated.

The visit ratio for the common cache in a cluster is:

$$v_{CC(W-O)} = (1-R)(1-PI) \cdot q_s \cdot (1-(\pi_0+\pi_4))$$

According to this protocol the visit ratio for a shared cache placed in other cluster (remote shared cache) is:

$$v_{RSC(W-O)} = (1-R) \cdot q_s \cdot (1-PI)\frac{(\pi_0+\pi_4)\left(1-(1-\pi_3)^{C-1}\right)}{C-1}$$

It is possible to distinguish between two kinds of memory accesses those due to the miss blocks ($v1_{MEM(W-O)}$) and those due to the updating private data and the coherence actions ($v2_{MEM(W-O)}$). The visit ratios in each case are:

$$v1_{MEM(W-O)} = (1-R)\left[PI(1-H)+(1-PI)\left[(1-q_s)(1-H)+q_s(\pi_0+\pi_4)(1-\pi_3)^{C-1}\right]\right]$$

and

$$v2_{MEM(W-O)} = (1-R)(1-PI)\left[(1-q_s)(1-H)\cdot\frac{N_p}{S_c}\cdot\pi_m + \right.$$
$$\left. q_s\left(w\cdot\pi_1+(1-w)(\pi_0+\pi_4)\cdot\left(1-(1-\pi_3)^{C-1}\right)\right)\right]$$

And for the packet switched bus:

$$v_{BUS(W-O)} = 2v1_{MEM(W-O)} + 2v_{CCR(W-O)} +$$
$$(1-R)\left[(1-PI)\left[(1-q_s)(1-H)\frac{N_p}{S_c}\cdot\pi_m+q_s\cdot w\cdot\pi_1\right]\right]$$

Dragon Protocol The Markov chain for this write and update protocol is shown in figure 5. The states for a shared block are: π_0=NOTIN, π_1=VALID-ONLY, π_2=SHARED-CLEAN, π_3=SHARED-DIRTY, π_4=DIRTY.

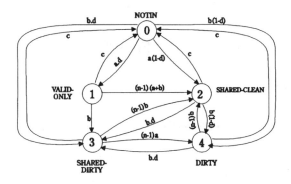

FIGURE 5.   Markov chain for the Dragon protocol

where,

$$a = q_s \frac{(1-w)}{N_S} \quad b = q_s \frac{w}{N_S} \quad c = \frac{(1-H)}{S_C} \quad d = \pi_0^{N-1}$$

Solving the Markov chain the steady state probabilities are known and the visit ratios can be calculated.

The visit ratio for the common cache in a cluster is

$$v_{CC(D)} = (1-R)(1-PI) \cdot q_s (1-\pi_0)$$

And the visit ratio due to the update policy:

$$v_{D(D)} = (1-R) \cdot q_s (1-PI) \cdot w \cdot \left(\pi_2 \cdot \pi_3 + \pi_0 \left(1 - (1 - \pi_3 - \pi_4)^{C-1}\right)\right)$$

For a remote shared cache:

$$v_{RSC(D)} = (1-R) \cdot q_s \cdot (1-PI) \cdot \pi_0 \frac{\left(1 - (1 - \pi_3 - \pi_4)^{C-1}\right)}{C-1}$$

Let $v1_{MEM(D)}$ be the visit ratio for the main memory due to the miss blocks and $v2_{MEM(D)}$ the visit ratio to main memory due to the updating private data and the coherence actions. Their values are:

$$v1_{MEM(D)} = (1-R)\big[PI \cdot (1-H) + (1-PI) \cdot \big[(1-q_s) \cdot (1-H) + q_s \cdot \pi_0 (1-\pi_3 - \pi_4)^{C-1}\big]\big]$$

$$v2_{MEM(D)} = (1-R)(1-PI) \cdot \big[(1-q_s)(1-H)\frac{N_p}{S_c}\pi_m +$$
$$q_s\big(w(\pi_2 + \pi_3) + w \cdot \pi_0(\pi_1 + \pi_2 + \pi_3 + \pi_4)^{C-1} + \pi_0\frac{N_s}{S_c}\pi_3\big)\big]$$

And the visit ratio for the bus is

$$v_{BUS(D)} = 2 \cdot v1_{MEM(D)} + 2 \cdot v_{CR(D)} + (1-R)(1-PI) \cdot$$
$$\big[(1-q_s)(1-H)\frac{N_p}{S_c}\pi_m + q_s \cdot w \cdot ((\pi_2 + \pi_3) + \pi_0(1-\pi_3-\pi_4)^{C-1}) +$$
$$q_s \cdot \pi_0\frac{N_s}{S_c}\pi_3\big]$$

Now, to estimate the mean number of shared blocks (Ns) in cache that can be accessed by all the processors, the birth-and-death process shown in figure 6 is proposed[14].

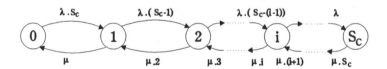

FIGURE 6.   Birth-and-death process

where, $\lambda = q_s(1-H')$ and $\mu = (1-q_s)(1-H)$.

Being $H' = \pi_0 + \pi_4$ the miss ratio for shared blocks. Where, π_0 and π_4 are the probabilities of a miss because the block is not in cache or it has been invalidated. But the misses due to this last cause does not suppose a different number of blocks in cache so, it is possible to consider that $H' = \pi_0$. Therefore,

$$N_s = \frac{S_c \dfrac{\lambda}{\mu}}{1 + \dfrac{\lambda}{\mu}}$$

Although the locality of the references is not so strong for shared blocks than for private ones there is not a big error if the approximation $H \approx \pi_0$ is done. So, $H' \approx H$. Then, $N_s \approx q_s \cdot S_c$.

7.3.3 Analytical Solution

System Power is the most characteristic metric to evaluate performance in computer architecture. In multiprocessors, System Power is defined as the sum of all processor utilization. The analytical solution allows to calculate this metric for different parameters. The program package QNAP-2[14] has been used to solve the proposed queuing network. This package allows to choose analytical or simulation methods to solve the model.

The route for the external close customers in the queuing network is the following: when a processor generates a external memory access it is sent first to the appropriated cache: associated instruction cache (with probability v_{IC}), associated data cache (v_{DC}), or the shared cache placed in the cluster where the requiring processor belongs (v_{SC}). If the access is a hit then the customer goes back to the processor that generated it after it has been served. But, in a miss case, if the missed block is shared it can be served by a shared cache placed in other cluster (if the block is present) or by the main memory according with the protocol considered with probabilities v_{RSC} or vl_{MEM}. Also the consistency actions are different for write or read operations. If the missed block is private it must be supplied by the main memory. But, in both cases a request and a response packet are generated with probability $2(vl_{MEM} + v_{RSC})$. A request for main memory can reach any one of the M modules with equal probability. This is a reasonable assumption if an interleaved main memory is considered. Once the miss block has been served, the customer goes back to the processor that generated it.

The open customers SB (source) and SBK(sink) model the effects of loading a new block in the shared caches as a consequence of a miss. It is possible to consider that this load affects only the shared caches because it degrades the requests of other processors and it doesn't affect the rest of the system when it occurs in a private cache. Their frequency is:

$$\lambda_{load} - \frac{\frac{U \cdot N \cdot C}{Z} \cdot (1-R)(1-PI) \cdot q_s \left(\pi_{notin} + \pi_{dirty} \right)}{C}$$

where U is the processor utilization, Z the cycle time, R the feedback probability, N the number of processor in a cluster and C the number of clusters. The probabilities π_{notin} and $\pi_{invalid}$ depend on the different protocols considered and for instance, the probability $\pi_{invalid}$ does not exist for the write and update protocols.

The customers SA (source) and SAK (sink) model the effect of the copy-back policy. They only affect the packet-switched bus and the main memory. Their visit ratio is:

$$\lambda_{copy-back} = \frac{U \cdot N \cdot C}{Z}(1-R) \cdot v2_{MEM}$$

When write and update protocols are consider (Dragon) it is necessary to consider the effect of the broadcasting. For this case the open customers SD and SDK are introduced. They affect the shared caches and the frequency for the Dragon protocol is:

$$\lambda_{div(D)} = \frac{\frac{U \cdot N \cdot C}{Z}(1-R) \cdot q_s(1-PI) \cdot \pi_0 \left(\pi_1 + \pi_2 + \pi_3 + \pi_4 \right)^{C-1}}{C-1}$$

The involved steps in the analytical solution of the model are the following:
1) The routing probabilities for closed customers can be obtained solving the Markov chains for private and shared blocks.
2) The arrival and departure rates for open customers can also be calculated by setting, initially, the processors throughput (U) to 1. The model is solved using the Convolution method[15] to obtain the performance parameters and a new throughput for the processors.
3) With this new throughput value step 2 is repeated until the required accuracy is reached (e < 0.001 in this case).

7.4 RESULTS

A simulation model was developed to validate these analytical results[15]. The values adopted for the constant parameters are shown in table 1:

Table 1. Constant parameters

PI = 0.7; prob. of addressing instructions
M = 4; memory modules
N = 4; number of processors in a cluster
Z = 2; cycle time
R = 0.6; feedeback probability
H = 0.95; private blocks hit ratio
w = 0.3; write probability
S_p = 16 Kblocks; size of private caches
S_c = 16 Kblocks; size of shared caches
τ_b = 1; bus cycle
τ_{mc} = 4; memory cycle
τ_{ch} = 1; caches cycle

The metric used to compare the architectures is System Power (SP). The graphics presented here show System Power as a function of the number of processors in the system.

Figure 7 shows the comparison between a traditional multiprocessor architectures and the Hybrid-Cluster when the Write-Once protocol is considered in booth cases.

The degree of sharing chosen is 20%. The performance for the Hybrid-Cluster multiprocessor is much better than the traditional one when a high number of processors in the architecture is considered.

A similar study for the Dragon protocol has been done. Figure 8 shows the comparison between the two studied multiprocessor systems when the Dragon write and update protocol is used.

In this case the Hybrid-Cluster also presents an important improvement but it is not so flashy than when the Write-Once protocol is used. This is because the number of misses caused by a write-update protocol as Dragon is much lower than using a write and invalidate policy as Write-Once does. Those misses generate an important amount of traffic in the bus that degrade system performance.

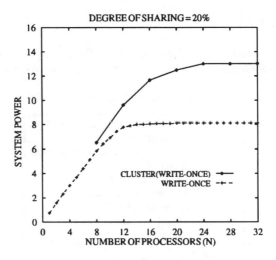

FIGURE 7.   Comparison between traditional multiprocessor architectures and
the Hybrid-Cluster using the Write-Once protocol

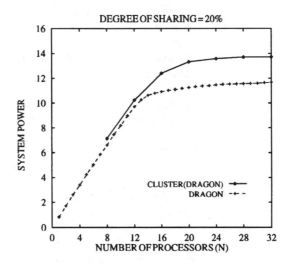

FIGURE 8.   Comparison between traditional multiprocessor architectures and
the Hybrid-Cluster using the Dragon protocol

Figures 9 and 10 show the influence of the degree of sharing in the System Power. The results of the figure 9 have been obtained using the Write-Once protocol to maintain coherence. Figure 10 shows the values using the Dragon protocol.

System performance depends on the workload. This dependence is stronger when write and invalidate protocols are used. The protocols that use an update strategy (as Dragon) are less sensitive to the variation of the degree of sharing, specially when a high number of processors is considered. But in both cases an important improvement can be obtained using a Hybrid-Cluster architecture.

Figure 11 shows the throughput of the bus as a function of the number of processors in the Hybrid-Cluster using the two studied protocols.

When there is a high number of processors in the system the bus becomes the bottleneck. The Dragon protocol generates less traffic in the bus than the Write-Once because the update policy avoids a high number of misses and the updating can be done in a single cycle and sometimes concurrently with other accesses to main memory.

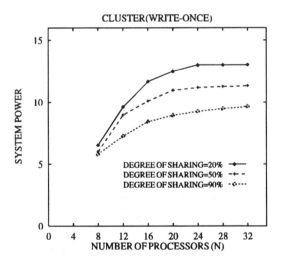

FIGURE 9.   Influence of the degree of sharing using the Write-Once protocol

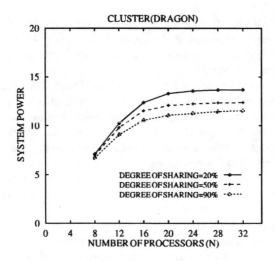

FIGURE 10.   Influence of the degree of sharing using the Dragon protocol

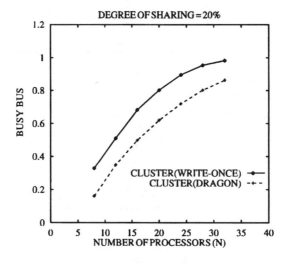

FIGURE 11.   The throughput for the bus in the Hybrid-Cluster multiprocessor

To study the influence of cache affinity scheduling a different degree of sharing in each cluster has been considered. The model has been solved for C=2,...,8 clusters with 4 processors each. The degrees of sharing considered has been:

$C = 2 \Rightarrow q_{s1}=10\%,\ q_{s2}=90\%$
$C = 3 \Rightarrow q_{s1}=10\%,\ q_{s2}=90\%,\ q_{s3}=50\%$
$C = 4 \Rightarrow q_{s1}=10\%,\ q_{s2}=90\%,\ q_{s3}=30\%,\ q_{s4}=70\%$
$C = 5 \Rightarrow q_{s1}=10\%,\ q_{s2}=90\%,\ q_{s3}=50\%,\ q_{s4}=70\%,\ q_{s5}=30\%$
$C = 6 \Rightarrow q_{s1}=10\%,\ q_{s2}=90\%,\ q_{s3}=50\%,\ q_{s4}=70\%,\ q_{s5}=30\%,\ q_{s6}=50\%$
$C = 7 \Rightarrow q_{s1}=10\%,\ q_{s2}=90\%,\ q_{s3}=50\%,\ q_{s4}=70\%,\ q_{s5}=30\%,\ q_{s6}=40\%,\ q_{s7}=60\%$
$C = 8 \Rightarrow q_{s1}=10\%,\ q_{s2}=90\%,\ q_{s3}=50\%,\ q_{s4}=70\%,\ q_{s5}=30\%,\ q_{s6}=50\%,\ q_{s7}=20\%,$
$q_{s8}=80\%$

Note that in all cases there is an average of sharing of 50% therefore figure 12 compare these results with that obtained for an homogeneous degree of sharing of 50%. When the workload is distributed according its cache affinity it is possible to obtain better performance. The improvements are specially important when the number of processors increases.

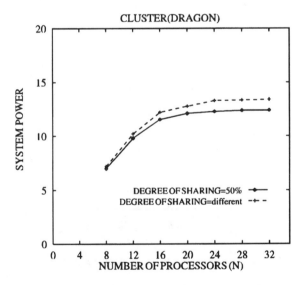

FIGURE 12.   Improvements obtained distributing the workload according cache affinity

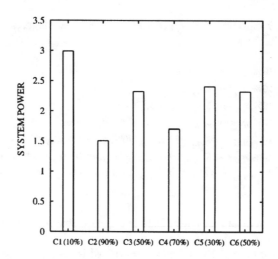

FIGURE 13. The performance obtained in each cluster

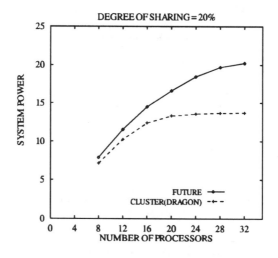

FIGURE 14. The performance forecast for a close future

Figure 13 shows the System Power obtained in each cluster in the multiprocessor system using differents degrees of sharing. Six clusters with

4 processors each has been considered and their degree of sharing are, respectively: 10%, 90%, 50%, 70%, 30% and 50%.

Finally, figure 14 presents the performance forecast for a close future. The following technological advances are considered: CPU's that quadruple its frequency ($Z=0.5$), bigger internal caches that allow a feedback about 90%, memory modules with the half access time and a packet-switched bus with half cycle time.

7.5 CONCLUSIONS

This paper studies the modeling and evaluates the performance of a new multiprocessor architecture called Hybrid-Cluster Multiprocessor. Mixed queuing networks are used to know performance and, a probabilistic workload has been developed.

The Hybrid-Cluster architecture is the result of the performance analysis done for different multiprocessor architectures[15, 16]. Under similar conditions this architecture is less sensitive to the variation of the degree of sharing and therefore presents high scalability than traditional multiprocessors. Also, the arrangement of the processors in the cluster let cache affinity scheduling be used in that cluster. Distributing the workload according its cache affinity important improvements are obtained.

In general, this architecture is a more efficient alternative than the traditional multiprocessors based on common bus for a high number of process units because there is an important decrease of the bus traffic generated because the coherence protocols.

REFERENCES

1.   P. STENSTRÖM, "A Survey of Cache Coherence Schemes for Multiprocessors", Computer, **23**, N° 6, 12-24, (1990).

2.   Y. J. OYANG, "A Multiprocessor Configuration in Accordance with the Aspects of Physical and System Design", Computer Architecture News, ACM Press, **17**. N° 4, 69-73, (1989).

3.   J. TORRELLAS, A. TUCKER, A. GUPTA, "Benefits of Cache Affinity Scheduling in Shared-Memory Multiprocessors", Proceeding of the ACM Sigmetrics Conference on Measurement and Modeling of Computer Systems, **21**, N° 1, 272-274, (1993).

4.   M. AJMONE MARSAN, G. BALBO, G. CONTE, Performance Models of Multiprocessors Systems (The MIT Press Series in Computer Systems, 1986)

5.   M. DUBOIS, F. BRIGGS, "Effect of Cache Coherency in Multiprocessors", IEEE Transactions on Computers, C-31, N° 11, 1083-1099, (1982).

6.   J. ARCHIBALD, J. L. BAER, "Cache Coherence Protocols: Evaluation using a Multiprocessor Simulation Model", ACM Transactions on Computer Systems, 4, N° 4, 273-298, (1986).

7.   Q. YANG et al., "Analysis and Comparison of Cache Coherence Protocols for a Packet-Switched Multiprocessor", IEEE Transactions on Computers, C-38, N° 8, 1143-1153, (1989).

8.   M. K. VERNON, M. A. HOLLIDAY, "Performance Analysis of Multiprocessor Cache Coherence Protocols using Generalized Petri Nets", Proceeding of ACM SIGMETRICS Conference, 9-17, (1986).

9.   J. Y. LE BOUDEC, "A BCM Extension to Multiserver Station with Concurrent Classes of Customers", Proceedings of Performance'86 and ACM SIGMATRICS, 78-91, (1986).

10.   Q. YANG, L. N. BHUYAN, "Analysis of Packet-Switched Multiple-Bus Multiprocessor System", IEEE Transactions on Computers, C-40, N° 3, 352-357, (1991)

11.   J. R. GOODMAN, "Cache Memory Optimization to reduce Processor-Memory Traffic", Proceedings of the 10th. Internantional Symposium on Computer Architecture IEEE, 124-131, (1983).

12.   J. ARCHIBALD, J. L. BAER, "An Economical Solution to the Cache Coherence Problem", Proceedings of the 11th. International Symposium on Computer Architecture IEEE, 355-362, (1984).

13.   E. McCREIGHT, "The Dragon Computer System: An Early Overview", Technical Report Xerox Corporation, (1984).

14.   ___ "The Queueing Network Analysis Package (QNAP-2)". User's Guide, (Simulog, 1994).

15.   A. PONT, J. A. GIL, J.J. SERRANO, "Using Queuing Networks to Evaluate Performance in Multiprocessor Systems with Cache Memories", Proceedings of the 7th Mediterranean Electrotechnical Conference, 1, 321-324, (1994).

16.   A. PONT, J.A. GIL, J.J. SERRANO, "Modeling and Performance Evaluation of a New Multiprocessor Configuration", Proceedings of the IMACS/IFAC International Symposium on Parallel and Distributed Computing in Engineering Systems, 71-75, (1991).

CHAPTER 8

SIMULATION OF DATA PARALLEL PROCESSING IN PARALLAXIS-III

Thomas Bräunl

8.1 INTRODUCTION

Data parallel processing promises a tremendous speedup for certain applications on appropriate SIMD systems. Unfortunately, parallel hardware is quite expensive and there is no generally agreed-on SIMD programming language. In education, the focus is quite frequently on studying efficient parallel algorithms. In this case, the computing power of these systems is not even needed. However, a simulation system can be of advantage for compute-intense applications. Here, all testing and debugging can be done without using the parallel system.

This led us to the development of a data parallel simulation system, together with the creation of a new parallel programming language, called *Parallaxis*. This language is machine independent among SIMD systems, so it avoids the development of software, which can only be executed on one particular system. Sequential Modula-2 (Wirth[5]) was chosen as the base language for Parallaxis, in order to enforce *structured programming*. We do believe that this approach has significant advantages in parallel programming of complex tasks and especially in teaching parallel concepts.

135

8.2 PARALLEL LANGUAGE CONSTRUCTS

Parallaxis (Bräunl[1]) is a data-parallel extension of Modula-2. It is machine-independent among SIMD systems or SIMD-style programming of MIMD systems. Parallaxis also allows the simulation of data-parallel programs on sequential workstations. The Parallaxis language is described in detail in Bräunl[2].

Only a few, well chosen language constructs are used to augment the base language. Parallaxis uses the construct of *configuration* to specify the number and arrangement of processing elements (PEs) in dimensions – just like an array declaration. Parallaxis allows *virtual processors*, which means a programmer may specify any number of PEs, no matter what limitations his computer system may have. Also shown in Figure 1 is the concept of *connection*. Declarations in functional form are used to specify data paths between PEs. With this method, any arbitrary processor and connection structure may be specified.

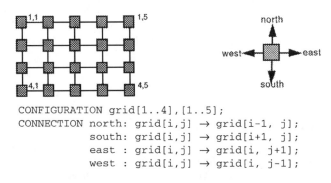

```
CONFIGURATION grid[1..4],[1..5];
CONNECTION north: grid[i,j] → grid[i-1, j];
           south: grid[i,j] → grid[i+1, j];
           east : grid[i,j] → grid[i, j+1];
           west : grid[i,j] → grid[i, j-1];
```

Figure 1: Grid topology with representative PE

Variables may be declared either as *scalars* or as *vectors*. While scalars exist only once (e.g. a loop counter), vector data is spread element-wise over the parallel PEs (e.g. for matrix multiplication, each PE would contain one matrix element). Scalar variables are declared like in standard Modula-2, vectors use the configuration name together with the base data type, e.g.:

```
VAR i  : INTEGER;         (* scalar *)
    x,y: grid OF INTEGER; (* vector *)
```

Parallel program execution is implicit, whenever an expression involves vector data. A scalar value may be used in vector expressions (broadcast), but not vice versa. Vector values in *selections* or *iterations* need an amended semantics. A parallel IF-THEN-ELSE statement executes both branches subsequently, but during the THEN-branch only those PEs are active, for which the selection expression evaluated to TRUE, while only the FALSE-PEs are active during the ELSE-branch. In each iteration of a parallel WHILE-loop, those PEs are eliminated (inactivated), for which the loop expression evaluates to FALSE. The loop terminates when no active PEs are left.

Data exchange between PEs may be performed by using the function MOVE with a previously defined connection name. E.g.:

```
y := MOVE.north(x);
```

moves all vector elements of x one position to the north and assigns it to y. However, arbitrary data exchange (not bound to previously defined connections) is also possible at run time. Data exchange between scalars and vectors is inherently sequential and may be performed by standard procedures LOAD and STORE.

Data *reduction* is facilitated with function REDUCE in combination with an arithmetic function. E.g.

```
i := REDUCE.SUM(x);
```

sums up all elements of vector x and assigns the scalar value to i. Optimal time for data reduction uses data exchanges along the nodes of a binary tree, which requires $\log 2\, n$ steps for reducing n elements, as compared to $n-1$ steps in the sequential version.

8.3 COMPILER

We have developed several compilers for Parallaxis-III. Here, the compiler for generating sequential C-code will be discussed (simulation system). There are further Parallaxis compilers for the MasPar MP-1/MP-2 (SIMD) and the Intel Paragon (MIMD, programmed in SPMD mode) or workstation clusters using PVM (parallel virtual machine). All compilers generate C code (or MPL in case of the MasPar), so a subsequent compilation step is necessary to generate object code. The compiler option list is shown in Figure 2.

```
NAME
      p3 -- Parallaxis-III Compiler User Interface V0.5

DESCRIPTION
      Compile some Parallaxis-III programs and call backend compiler.

SYNOPSIS
      p3 [options] [file] ...

OPTIONS
      -C              Generate C-code for simulation (default)
      -casts          Generate type casts to make C-programs lint free
      -cc name        Name of the backend compiler to use
      -g              Generate debug code (also passed to backend compiler)
      -h, -H, -help   Print this usage
      -headers        Generate header files for imported modules
      -Ipath          Add path to import/include list (Par. and backend)
      -indent i       Set indent of generated code to i blanks
      -koption        Pass option directly to backend compiler
      -Lpath          Add path to library path (backend only)
      -m, -mem        Print statistics about used memory
      -MPL, -mpl      Generate MPL-code for MasPar
      -n, -nocompile  Don't compile, just show comands (implies -v)
      -nop3inc        Don't use standard include paths
      -nop3lib        Don't use standard library paths
      -nodefaults     Same as -nop3inc -nop3lib
      -o name         Name of the generated executable
      -p              Parallaxis compile only, don't call backend compiler
      -c              Paral. and backend compile only, don't call linker
      -Ppath          Add path to import list (Parallaxis only)
      -PVM, -pvm      Generate PVM-code for Paragon
      -r, -rchecks    Don't generate runtime range checks
      -s, -small      Generate small MPL-only model (max. 128KB)
      -t, -time       Print statistics about used time (Parallaxis only)
      -tt, -total     Like -t, but also for backend compiler
      -v              Print version of p3 and the resulting compiler calls
      -vv             Like -v, passes also -v to backend compiler
      -w              Don't generate warnings
      -ww             Like -w, passes also -w to backend compiler

OPTIONS ONLY AVAILABLE DURING DEVELOPMENT
      -Zw             Write code tree
      -Zs             Write symbols tree
      -Zq             Query code tree
      -Zc             Check code tree
      -Z1             Run parser only, no semantic check
      -Z2             Run parser and semantic check only, no code generation

      Every other option is passed unchanged to the backend compiler.

ENVIRONMENT
      P3CC            Name of the backend compiler
      P3INC           ":"-seperated list of paths where to find sources
      P3LIB           ":"-seperated list of paths where to find libraries
      P3OPT           Default options always to set
```

Figure 2: Compiler options

The configurations of Parallaxis, i.e. the PEs, are implemented by linear arrays. Each configuration keeps track about which (virtual) PEs are active and which are not (the "active-set" of the configuration).

8.4 DEBUGGER

A compiler just by itself is not sufficient for parallel program development or even for education purposes. Therefore, we decided to develop also a source level debugger for Parallaxis. Despite starting from scratch, we used the gnu debugger *gdb* and its graphics interface *xxgdb* as a base. First, this C debugger had to be taught to behave as if being a Parallaxis source level debugger. This affects not only the source line window and the positioning of break points, but also (and more difficult) the presentation of Parallaxis data types, especially vector data. Figure 3 shows a typical sample debugging session.

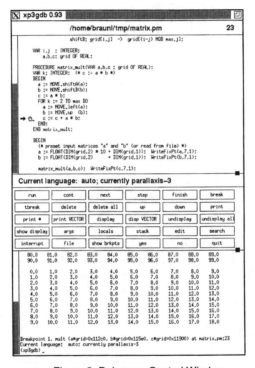

Figure 3: Debugger Control Window

Second, we added a number of graphics facilities. Especially for large vectors (e.g. two-dimensional image or simulation data), it is not very entertaining to examine large lists of data. Instead we provided the possibility to look at vector data *directly* in a graphics window. One- or two-dimensional data is displayed in a window with little boxes representing individual PEs (Figure 4). Each box is colored (rainbow colors or gray scale) according to its data value, and drawn hollow if

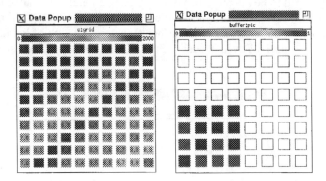

Figure 4: Vector display

inactive. Position numbers may be added and the data range may be fixed. The vector window can display a static state (command *print*) or adapt dynamically to changing data (command *display*).

The PE usage may also be displayed graphically. Here, the program is executed in single step mode and the number of active PEs is determined at each step. Due to the overhead of stepwise evaluation, execution time slows down when using this feature. The PE usage values produce a telltale curve of the application program's parallel characteristics and are a valuable help in localizing critical program regions for optimization of the execution time. Figure 5 shows the PE usage curve for the prime sieve sample program.

```
MODULE prime;
CONFIGURATION list [2..200];
CONNECTION  (* none *);
VAR next_prime: INTEGER;
    removed    : list OF BOOLEAN;
```

```
BEGIN
 REPEAT
  next_prime:= REDUCE.FIRST(DIM(list,1));
  WriteInt(next_prime,10); WriteLn;
  removed := DIM(list,1) MOD next_prime =0
 UNTIL removed
END prime.
```

This tiny program represents the parallel version of the sieve of Eratosthenes. The list of active PEs resembles the candidates for prime numbers not yet removed. In the beginning all PEs are active, which is reflected by the initial peak in Figure 5. But in each step of the REPEAT loop, variable removed becomes true for all multiples of the just found prime, whose PEs will no longer be active in the next iteration of the loop. This explains the exponentially-like decrease in the PE usage diagram.

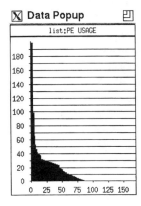

Figure 5: PE usage

8.5 APPLICATION IN SIMULATION

Many simulation models require only SIMD style computation and, furthermore, exhibit a local data exchange pattern. The simulation presented here models a very simplified behavior of cars on a single lane street. If the car concentration exceeds a certain threshold, sudden and unmotivated traffic jams occur.

For this simulation in Parallaxis, two disjoint configurations have been used. One configuration for the cars and one for the street segments. Cars may not take over each other, so they keep their linear order. The street is modeled as a closed ring.

```
CONFIGURATION cars[0..max_cars-1];
CONNECTION
   next: cars[i] <-> cars[(i+1) MOD max_cars] :back;

CONFIGURATION street[0..width-1];

VAR pos, dist,
    speed, accel: cars OF REAL;
    collision   : cars OF BOOLEAN;
    my_car      : street OF BOOLEAN;
    time, z     : INTEGER;
```

At initialization all cars are started at equal distance across the street.

```
pos := FLOAT(DIM(cars,1)) / FLOAT(max_cars);
```

The simulation itself is a large FOR-loop, which generates one graphics line for each iteration. If there is sufficient space in front of a car, it accelerates up to a maximum speed by a constant value plus a small random term. The randomness prevents all cars from maintaining identical distances from each other. Collisions are detected in parallel by measuring the distance of all pairs of subsequent cars. They cause a sudden stop, from which the cars can again accelerate in the subsequent simulation step. The integration required for determining velocity and position from acceleration has been simplified to summation.

```
FOR time := 1 TO steps DO
  ... (* show "collision" at line "time" *)
  my_car := DIM(street,1) =
            TRUNC(pos<:0:> * FLOAT(width));
  ... (* show "my_car" at line "time" *)
  dist := MOVE.back(pos) - pos;
  IF dist < 0.0 THEN dist := dist + 1.0 END;
  (* close street to loop *)

  collision := dist < min_dist;

  IF collision THEN speed := 0.0;
    ELSE (* no collision, accelerate *)
    accel := max_accel + rand_fac *
                            (RandomReal(cars)-0.5);
```

```
(* brake, if necessary *)
IF dist < min_dist THEN accel := - max_accel END;

(* update speed, apply speed limit *)
speed := min(speed + accel, max_speed);

(* do not back up on autobahn ! *)
IF speed < 0.0 THEN speed := 0.0 END;

(* update position *)
IF speed < dist THEN pos := pos + speed
                ELSE speed := 0.0
END;

(* leaving right, coming back in left *)
IF pos >= 1.0 THEN pos := pos - 1.0 END;
END;
END;
```

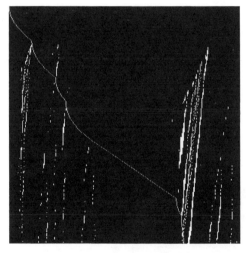

Figure 6: Simulation of traffic congestion

A sample simulation run of the traffic program is shown in Figure 6. The street is modeled as a closed ring, displayed as a horizontal line, while time flows from top to bottom in the figure. Standing cars are marked as bright spots. Also, the route of one individual car is shown, starting in the upper left corner. It is easy to recognize the acceleration phase of the individual car (parabolic curve), leading to a phase of continuous speed (straight line). Sudden breaks occur due to heavy traffic, simply caused by too many cars on the street. Several spontaneous traffic jams occur in this simulation, all slowly propagating in the direction opposite to the driving direction. Some congestions are increasing, while others are decreasing.

8.6 APPLICATION IN IMAGE PROCESSING

Many image processing operations are ideal for SIMD processing. This holds especially for local operators, which use image data only from a limited neighborhood with fast data exchange. We demonstrated the versatility of our approach for a wide range of image operations in a textbook (Bräunl[3]), which is also very well suited for course work in this area. Two of these operators will be discussed in the following.

8.6.1 Edge Detection

The Laplace operator is a very simple local operator for emphasizing edges in gray-scale images (edge detection). The operator carries out a simple local difference pattern. Figure 7 shows the application of the Laplace operator with a subsequent threshold.

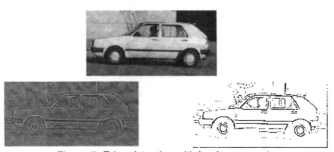

Figure 7: Edge detection with Laplace operator

A procedure for the Laplace operator in Parallaxis, using an open grid structure is defined in the following:

```
CONFIGURATION grid[*],[*], (* open grid *)
CONNECTION north: grid[i,j] <-> grid[i-1,j] :south;
           east : grid[i,j] <-> grid[i,j-1] :west;
```

```
. . .
PROCEDURE Laplace(x: grid OF INTEGER):
                   grid OF BOOLEAN;
VAR temp: grid OF INTEGER;
BEGIN
  temp := 4*x -MOVE.north(x) -MOVE.south(x)
             -MOVE.east (x) -MOVE.west (x);
  RETURN temp > 150;
END Laplace;
```

The new value for each pixel (or each PE) is determined by local data exchange from all four neighbors. The bottom left of the figure shows the intermediate result computed in variable temp (adapted into the gray-scale range [0..255]). The final boolean vector result is obtained by simple thresholding with a scalar constant, selecting only the strongest edges in an image.

8.6.2 Dithering

Dithering transforms a gray. scale image to a binary image by converting the original gray scale intensities to black and white patterns. The apparent increase of intensity levels created by the patterns is being traded against the lower resolution in the binary image. A simple technique with fixed patterns is *ordered dithering* or *halftoning* (Foley[4]). Figure 8 shows dithering with 2×2 patterns, enabling the use of five different intensities.

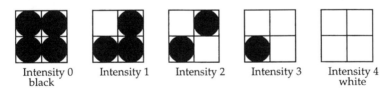

| Intensity 0 | Intensity 1 | Intensity 2 | Intensity 3 | Intensity 4 |
| black | | | | white |

Figure 8: Dithering with 2x2 pattern

The following program is a parallel implementation of ordered dithering. The computation is actually performed only on every fourth PE. Three quarters of the PEs remain inactive, while only the gray scale values of the PEs in the upper left corners of each 2×2 pattern are used. The binary result pattern is set according to this gray scale value. A constant threshold (thres) is used to divide the whole gray scale range in five areas.

The binary result value for the upper left position (res) is set (*black pixel*) if the gray scale input value is less than the threshold. The binary result value for the right neighbor is set (*black pixel*) if the gray scale input value is less than three times the threshold. The remaining two neighbors are determined the same way, according to the patterns in Figure 8. The movement of the neighbor pixels to the right position is performed by standard procedure SEND (moving data to inactive PEs).

```
PROCEDURE dither_ordered(img: grid OF gray):
                        grid OF binary;
CONST thres = g_white DIV 5;
VAR res: grid OF binary;
BEGIN
   IF ODD(DIM(grid,2)) AND ODD(DIM(grid,1)) THEN
      res := img < thres;  (* upper left corner *)
      SEND.right (img < 3*thres,res);
      SEND.down  (img < 4*thres,res);
      SEND.down_r(img < 2*thres,res);
   END;
   RETURN res;
END dither_ordered;
```

The resulting image of *ordered dithering* for 2×2 patterns can be seen in Figure 9. Larger patterns, e.g. 3×3 or 4×4, may also be used.

Figure 9: Ordered dithering

ACKNOWLEDGEMENTS

The author would like to thank all others contributing to the Parallaxis project. Eduard Kappel, Hartmut Keller, Harald Lampke, and Jürgen Wakunda worked on sequential and parallel compiler versions of Parallaxis-III, Jörg Stippa extended the "gnu"-debugger for Parallaxis. We also thank the GMD Karlsruhe for making their compiler construction kit

Cocktail publicly available, and GNU for distributing the sources to *gdb* and *xxgdb*.

Parallaxis-III may be copied over the Internet via "anonymous ftp" from:

`ftp://ftp.informatik.uni-stuttgart.de/pub/p3`

A web page is also available at:

`http://www.informatik.uni-stuttgart.de/ipvr/bv/p3`

REFERENCES

1. T. BRÄUNL, "Parallaxis-III A Structured Data-Parallel Programming Language", Proceedings of the First International Conference on Algorithms and Architectures for Parallel Processing, ICA3PP-95, Brisbane Australia, pp. 43–52 (April 1995)

2. T. BRÄUNL, Parallel Programming – An Introduction, (Prentice Hall, Englewood Cliffs NJ, 1993)

3. T. BRÄUNL. S. FEYRER, W. RAPF, M. REINHARDT, Parallele Bildverarbeitung, (Addison-Wesley, Bonn, 1995)

4. J. FOLEY, A. van DAM, S. FEINER, J. HUGHES, Computer Graphics – Principles and Practice, 2nd Ed., (Addison-Wesley, Reading MA, 1990)

5. N. WIRTH, Programming in Modula-2, (Springer-Verlag, Berlin Heidelberg New York, 1983)

CHAPTER 9

PERFORMANCE ANALYSIS FOR REAL-TIME SYSTEMS DESIGN

Albert Llamosí and Ramon Puigjaner

1. REAL-TIME SYSTEMS

A real-time system is a system in which the time at which it behaves is significant.

This is usually because it interacts with aspects of the physical world that move and the system has to relate to the same movement. Consequently, the correctness of a real-time system depends not only on the logical results of its computation but also on the time at which data are captured or results are produced.

Commonly, a distinction is made between hard and soft real-time systems. In hard real-time systems it is absolutely imperative that responses occur within the specified deadline, otherwise damage can occur to people or beings. In soft real-time systems it is inconvenient —but not a failure— if deadlines are occasionally missed. Actually, most real-time systems are soft with a small hard part.

The timing constraints usually appear in systems devoted to the monitoring or controlling of some equipment. In those cases, the computer is just one component within a larger engineering system. Then the system is said to be embedded.

A common specification for a typical embedded system such as a car computer includes several tasks to be performed. Control theory provides a specification of periodicity (T) and deadlines (D) for each of them. Moreover, each task will have a known worst case computation time (C). Current figures can be:

ABS brake control	T = 25 ms (40 Hz)	D =25 ms	C = 10 ms
Fuel injection control	T = 50 ms (20 Hz)	D =50 ms	C = 20 ms
Temperature control	T =1000 ms (40 Hz)	D = 6 ms	C = 1000 ms

2. ARCHITECTURES FOR REAL-TIME SYSTEMS

Most real-time applications use one of the three software architectures described below, or a combination of them. Namely, cyclic executives, event-driven and message-passing.

2.1. Cyclic executives

Such systems are structured as a main loop which is triggered by a timer. At each step it executes a so called minor cycle, which is a set of procedure calls. The full functionality of the system is made up of a repeating group of minor cycles that is executed indefinitely.

The following pictures describe what a solution could be for the example described above. The timer is assumed to trigger the system each 25 ms. The major cycle is made up of a repeating group of 20 minor cycles of three kinds, as shown by figure 2.1:

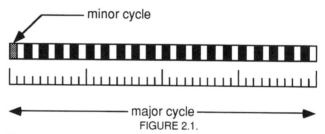

FIGURE 2.1.

The procedure calls issued by each of the three kinds of minor cycles and their worst case execution times are

```
    ABS(10) + Temp(6) + Inj1

    ABS(10) + Inj2(12)

    ABS(10) + Inj1(8)
```

The procedure for fuel injection control has been split in two parts, Inj1 and Inj2, having worst case execution times 8 and 12 respectively.

The worst execution time for each minor cycle is less than 25 ms, so all they can complete its work inside the period. Moreover, each of the three tasks —ABS, injection and temperature control— are activated at the required frequency and complete their work into the specified deadlines, as can be easily checked.

In such an approach, the scheduling is done off line and the resulting structure has as a main advantage, its absolute predictability. So it is well suited for hard real-time systems whose safety is critical. Moreover, it can be very efficient to the extent that the system is sequential in nature and therefore the access to shared data does not require any synchronisation to preserve mutual exclusion.

Nevertheless, it has the very serious drawback of being very hard to maintain. Sparingly, if some of the procedures has to be upgraded and as a result its execution time increases, the full system has to be reorganised.

This is not an easy job, since the problem has been shown to be NP-complete and therefore automatic tools can provide small help. Certainly, some heuristic algorithms have been proposed but they may fail in finding a feasible schedule even if one exists. See [17] for an overview.

2.2. Event-driven systems

An alternative possibility for structuring the system is to assign a task for each of the possible sources of inputs to the system and a task for each output device, so that when an input reaches the system it is processed by the proper task, that sends the resulting outputs to the appropriate device drivers. This structure is shown by the figure 2.2.

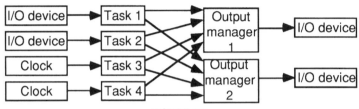

FIGURE 2.2.

Following such an approach, our example would be structured as tasks having the form

```
task      abs_task   task      fuel_task   task      temp_task
is                   is                    is
   loop                 loop                  loop
   abs_control;         fuel_inject;          temp_control;

   next:=               next:=                next:=
   next + 0.025;        next + 0.050;         next + 1.0;
   sleep_until          sleep_until           sleep_until
   next;                next;                 next;
   end loop;            end loop;             end loop;
```

Obviously, such an approach is far much easier to maintain than the previous one. Now, an upgrade of any of the control procedures implies just a local change on that procedure.

However, ensuring that deadlines are met is much harder and requires a careful priority analysis. For many years, priorities have been assigned according to the importance of the elements to be controlled by the procedures but recently this has been shown not to be the good approach. Alternative techniques have raised instead. Namely, rate monotonic analysis (RMA) and deadline monotonic analysis (DMA).

RMA assigns priorities according to the frequency of activation of the tasks (higher priority to higher frequency), whereas DMA assigns priorities according to the deadlines (higher priority to shorter deadlines). In the example, DMA and RMA would assign the same priorities to the tasks because for all them the specified period and deadline are equal.

If the tasks are completely independent, RMA guarantees, as a sufficient but not necessary condition, that deadlines are met if the utilisation of the processor is less than *ln* 2 (i. e. 69%) [6]. DMA has a more complicated condition statement, which is discussed in [1].

Neither DMA nor DMA ensure that deadlines are met if the tasks communicate. However, new sufficient conditions have been stated if either the priority inheritance or the priority ceiling protocols are used for ruling the mutual exclusion on common resources [15].

In the priority inheritance protocol, a lower priority task that has got resource, inherits the priority of any higher priority task that becomes blocked awaiting for the same resource. Moreover, such an inheritance is transitive.

The ceiling inheritance protocol is more elaborated. All tasks have a static priority assigned. All resources have a static ceiling value assigned, which is the maximum static priority of any task using the resource. A task has a dynamic priority, which is the maximum of its own static priority and the priority inherited from blocking a higher priority task. Then a task can only acquire a resource if its dynamic priority is higher than the ceiling of any resources locked by other tasks. Such a protocol, which is easier to implement than it might seem at first sight, makes it possible to obtain less pessimistic estimates of blocking times and moreover it prevents deadlocks.

2.3. Message-passing systems

The third possibility for structuring the system is to organise it in the form of a network of tasks with specific purposes. Each input is then converted in a message or a set of messages that flow through the system, so that each task adds some particular processing on the data, as is illustrated in the figure 2.3. Usually no common data is shared among the tasks. Instead, all persistent data is local to them.

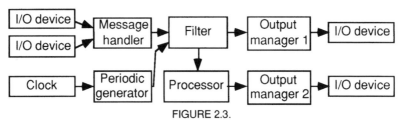

FIGURE 2.3.

Such systems are even easier to maintain than the event-driven ones and have the additional advantage that their implementation can be easily distributed among a set of processors.

In this case priority assignment is done so that it increases along each of the pipelines that make up the system. Otherwise the messages become accumulated at the beginning of the pipes and the system behaves in a strange way.

However, no matter how priorities are assigned, guaranteeing that deadlines are met is even harder but a completely different set of techniques have been developed for analysing the average temporal behaviour of the system, that are discussed below. So, such architectures are only suitable for soft real-time constraints.

Certainly, if a system has a small hard real-time core such a core can be programmed as a cyclic executive task that runs at the highest priority, in parallel with the tasks devoted to the soft part of the system, usually structured in a different way.

3. PERFORMANCE ISSUES IN THE DESIGN OF SOFT REAL TIME (SRT) SYSTEMS

Simplifying, we can consider three phases in the process of designing a SRT system:
- requirement: where the user specifications, functional as well as non-functional (performance, reliability, availability, security, maintainability, performability) are analysed and formalised.
- design: where the solution to build the system is conceived.
- implementation: where the system is implemented and the fulfilment of the functional and non functional specifications is tested.

With conventional design techniques, performance constraints are verified during the testing phase. This is the origin of a lot of effort and time spent in system recoding and, even, redesigning.

With respect to performance, it is convenient:
- at the requirement phase:
  * to discover all the performance characteristics and constraints
  * to define how the performance variables will be measured once the system be implemented.
- at the design phase:
  * to use performance modelling as a help in the design process.
  * to consider the non-functional requirements derived from the measurement needs as the functional ones.
- at the implementation phase:
  * to take measurements of the system behaviour according what has been previously established.
  * to store the resulting measurements in order to be able to re-use them.

4. COMPONENTS OF A PERFORMANCE SPECIFICATION

4.1. General View

The specification of a system's performance defines the temporal behaviour that the system must satisfy under a certain workload scenario. Such specification is compound of a description of the environment where the system is to be run, also called the scenario, plus a set of timing constraints on the behaviour of the system [7, 8].

The scenario should describe both the workload of the system plus the hardware constraints, if any, imposed to the designer, whereas the timing constraints specify both the responsiveness of the system and its resource utilisation rate. The responsiveness being expressed either in terms of ability for throughput absorption or in terms of inter-event duration, or both.

The diagram of figure 4.1. describes such a classification of specification components.

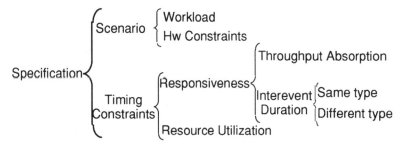

FIGURE 4.1.

In the figure 4.2, the four main components of a performance specification have been classified. The components that are used for building a performance model have been drawn as arrows pointing to the system, whereas the components to be obtained from the model have been drawn as arrows flowing out from the system. They shall be checked against the specified constraints. The same classification applies to a test operation. The components corresponding to arrows flowing in to the system shall be provided in the test, whereas the components corresponding to arrows flowing out from the system shall be measured and checked against the specified constraints.

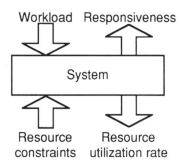

FIGURE 4.2.

The arrows on top represent the characteristics concerning the external behaviour of the system and the arrows below represent those related to the implementation constraints.

In some cases the four aspects are specified in advance. In other cases the designer has some freedom for choosing the proper resource characteristics and resource workload. However, in any real-time system a responsiveness constraint is defined and in general it is related to an expected workload.

4.2. Constraints Definition

The four performance constraint types can be grouped also according another criteria: two of them are probabilistic (throughput absorption and resource utilisation rate) and two of them are times (throughput and duration) [2, 7, 8, 9, 10].

4.2.1. Throughput absorption. This constraint is used to express the capacity of a system to absorb the arriving throughput and is defined by the allowed loss rate (ratio between the lost throughput and the arrived throughput).

4.2.2. Duration. This constraint is used to express the time between two events of different types. Normally it has an upper bound, but it can be asked also to be over a lower bound or between two bounds.

4.2.3. Throughput. This constraint is used to express the characteristics of the output throughput of a system. The constraint can be given as the number of events per unit time or by the time characteristics between two consecutive events of the same type. The conceptual difference between a throughput constraint and a duration constraint comes from the types of the considered consecutive events that are equal for a throughput constraint and different for a duration constraint.

4.2.4. Resource utilisation rate. This constraint specifies the ratio between the total working time of the resource and the observation or connection time. This kind of constraint is used to express that the utilisation rate of a resource must have an upper limit (to allow future workload increasing) or a lower limit (less frequent, but it allows to avoid resource wasting or to allow an appropriate response time) or both.

5. INTERACTION TYPES AND CONSTRAINT TYPES

5.1. Basic types of interactions and constraints

According to [3, 4, 11], the interactions of real-time systems can be classified, as it is shown in figure 5.1., in four categories: stimulus-stimulus (or throughput system), response-stimulus (or interactive system), stimulus-response (or responsive system) and response-response (or timed output system).

5.1.1. Throughput system (stimulus-stimulus). The workload imposed to the system by the environment is modelled as an activity that cyclically sends inputs to the system at the specified rate, no matter the system is able to receive them. Additionally, it shall include some means for estimating (by modelling) or measuring (at testing) the responsiveness of the system. A possible way is the consecutive labelling of inputs, so that possible gaps due to lost inputs can be detected by the system. Another possibility is that the responsibility for checking whether the input has been effectively captured by the system relies on the activity that models the input production. The first approach has the advantage that it can also be applied to test operations and the second approach has the advantage that the system does not need to be extended.

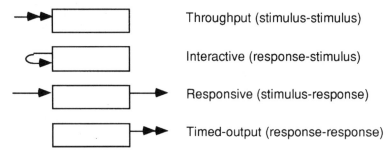

	Throughput (stimulus-stimulus)
	Interactive (response-stimulus)
	Responsive (stimulus-response)
	Timed-output (response-response)

FIGURE 5.1.

The workload is described as the time interval between an input and the previous and the responsiveness as the ability of the system for capturing the inputs at such speed.

5.1.2. Interactive system (response-stimulus). The environment for an interactive system is modelled by an activity that provides an input to the system some delay after the system has sent an output to the activity as answer to the previous input.

The workload is described by the time interval between an input and the previous output of the system and the responsiveness as the time interval between an output and the previous input to the system and can be recorded by the activity simulating the environment.

So described, the time interval corresponding to the full cycle is the sum of the one that describes the workload plus the one that describes the responsiveness. The inverse of the full cycle interval is the throughput of the system. It is often the case that the user's requirements are expressed in terms of such throughput, plus the interval corresponding to the workload. Then, a simple algebraic transformation allows the designer to infer the responsiveness required for the system.

In this case, the need to relate the output with the input that caused it to happen requires the inputs and the outputs to be marked.

5.1.3. Responsive system (stimulus-response). The environment for a responsive system is modelled by an activity that provides inputs to the system plus another activity that receives outputs from the system.

The workload is described as the time interval between an input and the previous one, as in throughput systems and the responsiveness as the time interval between an output and the input that caused it to happen. As stated earlier, the need to relate the output with the input that caused it to happen requires the inputs and the outputs to be marked. The recording of the responsiveness can be done exclusively by the activity that receives the outputs provided that the marks include a time stamp.

5.1.4.   Timed-output   system   (response-response).

The environment for a timed output system is modelled by an activity that receives outputs from the system and that can work as fast as required.

The concept of workload does not apply in this case. The responsiveness is described as the time interval between consecutive outputs, which can be recorded by the activity that receives the outputs.

Summary:

5.2. Compound types of interactions and constraints

However, it is often the case that the different types of workload and responsiveness descriptions must be combined because the systems themselves show the different kinds of interaction in a combined way. A system may, for instance, deal with several sources of inputs or because an input source has both a stimulus-stimulus and a stimulus-response constraints.

Obviously, real systems must have combined. So, in general, the scenario for the system shall be modelled by several of those simple activities. Furthermore, even a single interaction can be addressed under different points of view. A responsive system can have as input a throughput device working at a speed that may lead to the loss of some of the inputs. Then, on one hand a requirement must be specified about the ability of the system for capturing its inputs and on the other hand an additional requirement shall be issued for describing the delay between an output and its causing input. The classification stated above allows the analyser to ensure the completeness of its specifications and to deal with the different concerns separately.

The activities modelling the scenario of a system shall be provided in the terms described above to the system itself (at the testing phase) or to the performance model (at the design phase) in order to obtain an evaluation of the system's responsiveness.

6. PERFORMANCE MODELLING LEVELS FROM A DESIGN

To estimate the system performance during the design phase to verify whether the system responsiveness meet the constraints or to compare from the timing behaviour view point several different design solutions equally acceptable from the functional view point, it is necessary to build a performance model. Building such a model is based on two basic hypotheses [7, 8, 9].

A first assumption is that it is possible to derive performance models from the information of a RT system design.

A second assumption is that the RT system design is an iterative process in which we can distinguish, at least, two phases (fig. 6.1.) that will produce two different modelling levels:
- the logical modelling level, derived from a design without explicitly taking into account its physical implementation.
- the physical modelling level, derived from a design but taking into account its physical implementation.

In the first one a set of logical entities (like access to a DB, send a message, etc.), that we shall call operations, is defined.

On the other hand we shall define a set of classes of active entities, that we shall call transactions, that are executed by a sequential access to different operations and that are activated by some one of the mechanisms described in the previous chapter. These transactions will also carry the information allowing the relate input with their corresponding outputs. During this execution some kind of synchronisation among several transactions can appear (locking the use of an operation, fork and join operations, etc.) and these synchronisation mechanisms will be the main source of execution delays at the present level of the system description.

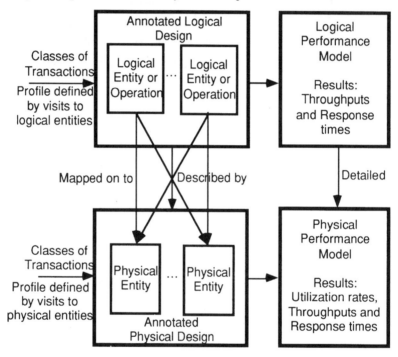

FIGURE 6.1.

To execute these operations, they must be mapped on to physical entities or devices (CPU, disks, specific types of network, etc.) taking into account their capacity and their geographical distribution; this physical implementation constitutes the physical design of the RT system. Once this implementation has been done, each one of the transaction classes can be described by a sequence of accesses to these physical entities. When we look at the system at this level, a second source of execution delays appear due to the waiting queues when several transactions try to use simultaneously the same device.

From the transaction profile (sequence of accesses to logical entities) at the logical level and the mapping of the logical design onto the physical design, it is possible to deduce the transaction profile for the physical level. However, in order to have clearer models it can be useful to deal with several sequential operations as if they were a single one if there are no synchronisation relations among them or with other transactions and/or operations.

A set of different transactions can be included in the same class if they have a similar path through the entities constituting the design. A transaction is bounded by its starting and ending events.

The scenarios defining the RT system workload will be characterised by different mixes of transaction classes.

In both modelling levels it is necessary to represent just those aspects affecting the timing behaviour and avoid those that do not affect the considered working situation. It is necessary to consider just the operations considered in the workload scenario excluding the rest.

From both levels of design, performance models can be derived in order to estimate, whether the performance constraints established in the requirements analysis, are met. From the Logical Design can be derived the Logical Performance Model and from the Physical Design, the Physical Performance Model. However, with the strict information contained in both designs it is just possible to build the model but not to run it because of lack of numerical data. This information must be included in the design by means of annotations including the necessary data.

As the performance constraints are always related to time, the information to be annotated will be either directly time or other magnitudes allowing the computation of times. Another type of information that should be annotated concerns buffer sizes, transaction routing probabilities across the operations, etc.

A third level of performance model can be considered. Once the system is implemented and tested, it is possible to measure the numerical values of the variables describing the transactions and to introduce this values (much more accurate than the previously estimated ones) in the model. From the modelling point of view it is a physical one. However the description of the transactions can be modified by the experimentation with respect to the one established in the design. This phase can be considered as the model calibration. The scheme to build this performance model is shown in figure 6.2.

In the modelling process, manual as well as eventually automatic, it is necessary to create for each design method, a library of modules representing the behaviour of each one of the logical and physical entities normally used in the considered design method. Then model building will consist in the selection and connection of the appropriate modules that must be completed with values incorporated by annotation. Another view of the re-utilisation

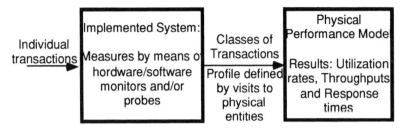

Calibration Process

FIGURE 6.2.

7. ANNOTATIONS

The attempt of putting all the information about a system in a single text or diagram is doomed to failure. The only successful way to deal with complexity is separation of concerns, so that some aspects of a system can be discussed as much independently from the others as possible.

Therefore, the following information to be annotated should not be considered to be included into given descriptions of a system according some design method, but to be, eventually, a separate description that concentrates on its performance aspects. Nevertheless the consistency among the different views of a single system can be checked and even prepared by automatic tools [5, 8, 12, 13, 14].

7.1. At requirements level

A simple way to establish the link between some performance specification and a design is to describe the scenario that makes up the environment of the system in terms close to those used in design methods, i.e. by means of activities that emulate the behaviour of the devices controlled by the system. Such activities shall have a simple cyclic nature that, when it is completed with proper time descriptions for their steps, can model in a unified way the workload imposed to the system and its responsiveness. Different kinds of systems have different kinds of time constraints with such peripherals. For this reason a specific notation has been provided for each kind of interaction.

7.1.1. Interactive systems. When a part of a system is interactive, the workload is described in terms of the expected delay between an output from the system and the next input and the responsiveness of the system is defined in terms of the required delay between the input to the system and its next. For example:

```
device   I;
  is interactive;
  workload: o_i_delay = TIME_SPECIFICATION;
  responsiveness: i_o_delay = TIME_SPECIFICATION;
end.
```

7.1.2. Throughput systems. For throughput systems, the workload is described in terms of the delay between consecutive inputs to the system, and the responsiveness in terms of the percent that it must be able to accept. For example:

```
device   Th;
   is throughput;
   workload:  i_i_delay = TIME_SPECIFICATION;
   responsiveness: lost_ratio = NUMERIC_CONSTANT;
end.
```

7.1.3. Timed output systems. Timed output aspects of a system do not have an associated workload. The responsiveness is described by the time interval between two consecutive outputs. For example:

```
device   O;
   is timed_output;
   responsiveness: o_o_delay = TIME_SPECIFICATION;
end.
```

7.1.4. Responsive systems. Responsive systems are more complex to be specified because each input must be related to the corresponding expected outputs. Moreover, the input must be characterised by a specific workload and the output must be characterised by a responsiveness constraint.

This implies the addition of a linking clause between the input activities and the output activities to the usual constraints. However, an input can have effects on several outputs and for each output the responsiveness constraint may differ. Therefore, the input device will be characterised by its workload plus a list indicating on which output devices this input may have an effect. The output device will be characterised by a listing indicating which input devices may cause an output there and which is its responsiveness constraint. To the extent to which the lists are redundant when taken as a whole, an automated system can check the specification for consistency. For example:

```
device   I;
      is responsive_input:
      output to OUTPUT_PROJECTION_LIST;
      workload:  i_i_delay = TIME_SPECIFICATION;
end.
```

```
device   O;
      is responsive_output:
      input from INPUT_DEPENDENCY_LIST;
end.
```

The characteristics specified for inputs must match the characteristics specified for their related outputs. For details see [7, 8].

7.1.5. Time specification. The time intervals corresponding to the workload conditions for the system must be expressed in terms of some distribution law with its corresponding parameters and, eventually, their upper and lower bounds. Constant and exponential laws (1-parameter laws) shall be the usual ones. The responsiveness constraints will be usually defined as some time limit plus an indication about how rigorously the constraint must be satisfied.

Usually, the constant, exponential, bounded exponential, uniform and user defined laws are used in workload specifications, whereas the uniform, lower bounded, upper bounded and user defined are used in responsiveness specifications. The hyperexponential law is used in the description of physical devices (on to which the system is implemented).

7.1.6. Replication. When multiple agents behave in the same way, they can be summarised by a single description plus the number of instances for the described interaction.

7.1.7. Compound interactions. As stated in section 5.2., time constraints can be compound of several types of the four elementary interactions. Such combinations can be easily expressed by means of the elementary notations.

7.2. At design level

At design level, the annotations will depend on the typical elements used by the design method. However, we can always identify three kind of design elements:
- the activity as the element that makes some manipulation with data.
- the data structure that describes its organisation and encapsulates their data access routines.
- the interface of the system with its environment.

7.2.1. Activities. The making of a performance model for a system requires some knowledge about the structure of the involved activities. Such a description must map the algorithmic structure of the activity where the blocks of sequential operations have been replaced by a description of the associated resource consumption, whereas calls to procedures of access routines, which may lead to delays because of locking operations shall explicitly appear in its proper place.

Therefore, a conventional description for describing algorithms can be applied, with the only differences that some of the code may have been replaced by a special indication about the expected resource consumption associated to the replaced code (in its simplest form, just a time), and that boolean expressions may have been replaced by the expected probability of getting the value *true*. For instance, the activity shown in figure 7.1 would appear in textual form as

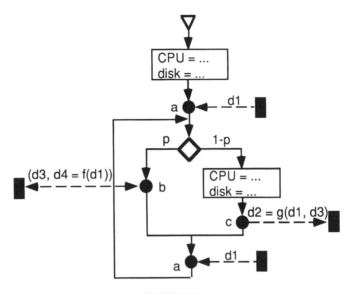

FIGURE 7.1.

```
activity a_name;
    requires a, b, c;
    begin
        RESOURCE_CONSUMPTION;
        a.routine_x;
        while true do begin
            if CHOICE
                then begin
                    RESOURCE_CONSUMPTION;
                    c.routine_y
                end
                else b.routine_z;
            a.routine_u
        end
    end
end.
```

Branching alternatives in the structure of algorithms must be weighted according to the respective probabilities. This can be achieved by the usual boolean expressions.

At the design step, it is not expected that the resources required by activities are assigned to actual ones. Therefore, the resource consumption is dealt with only as a time delay.

7.2.2. Data structures. The interlocking effects of calls to access procedures of a data structure is hard to be described in a high level notation. Therefore, either the designer benefits from using a well known set of data structures for which performance models can be taken from a predefined library or he builds the performance model of the non standard module by his own. In both cases, the only meaningful description, from the performance point of view, is a reference to such modules.

7.2.3. Interfaces. Interfaces are the links of the system with the external environment, which is composed by devices whose behaviour has been formalised as a virtual activity. For performance modelling purposes, the server acts as an data structure that offers an access to the activity emulating what in the actual system will be the physical device.

The problem of characterising the performance aspects of the behaviour of the interface becomes then similar than for any data structure. However, in this case it is even more realistic that a set of modules which represent the performance of the interface is available because interface algorithms are relatively standard for a given device.

7.3. At implementation level

7.3.1. Introduction. So far, sequential code and data access routines have been assumed to consume just time. However, at the implementation level a more refined approach is feasible. Actually, sequential code consumes several types of resources such as CPU, disk, communication links, DBMS etc. Several instances of such resources can exist and it is usual that most of them are shared by different activities and and/or data structures. At the implementation step, a mapping of activities and/or data structures to actual resources is established, as well as the scheduling policy upon them. Therefore, a more precise model can be built, that takes into account the delays introduced by both the effective consumption of the resources and the delays introduced by awaiting for the resources to be available.

Hence, the annotations must describe, on one hand, the available resources, in a notation such as

```
resource r;
     is RESOURCE_DESCRIPTION;
end.
```

As usual, *r* stands then for a template. Actual resources of the type defined can be obtained by instantiation through declarations such as

```
r1, r2, r3: r;
```

On the other hand, the resource consumption declarations, that have been specified so far only as a delay, must now be extended in order to provide a more accurate description of the device behaviour:

```
RESOURCE_CONSUM  →   delay = TIME_SPECIFICATION
                     | consumption
                           RESOURCE_CONSUM_LIST
                     end

RESOURCE_CONSUM_LIST  →
            RESOURCE_CONSUM_ITEM
           | RESOURCE_CONSUM_ITEM, RESOURCE_CONSUM_LIST
```

Resource consumption items ought be different according to the different resource types and will be discussed in detail below. Obviously, annotations for all the existing types of devices will not be given, but just for those appearing more frequently in the RT system design; for the rest of devices an *ad hoc* description similar to those that will be presented, should be built.

7.3.2.   CPU. The CPU is the most important case of a resource, to the extent to that it is always present in RT systems. A CPU is characterised by its computing speed, number of units and scheduling policy.

The description of the amount of such a CPU that will be required for performing a certain operation must be so that the expected computing time can be inferred from it. The most straightforward way of describing such a consumption is to provide the expected execution time directly. Three facts advise for doing so. The first one is to improve compatibility with the delay statements related to resource consumption that appear at design level. The second one is that both experience and intuition lead to express CPU consumption in terms of time. Finally, the way of providing the most accurate consumption estimates for an operation is to measure such consumption on a prototype.

Moreover, a priority description of the process that executes the operation will sometimes be required as part of the description of the resource consumption.

The scheduling policy on a CPU must reflect
- the order in which the attending processes are queued,
- whether or not several queues exist for different levels of priorities,
- whether or not new reaching processes can preempt the executing one.

If the processes are queued in a round robin fashion, so the scheduler uses a time sharing policy, then the quantum of time shall also be specified.

Whenever a single schedule manages a set of identical CPU units, the number of such units must be specified. Note that this is a different situation of that where the different units are managed by independent schedulers, in which case they will be described as independent resources.

7.3.3.   Physical access to disk. The delay introduced by a physical disk access depends on the time spent performing the actual operation, that is compound of four factors:
- the time spent by the arm's placement,
- the time spent awaiting for the proper angular placement,
- the time spent by the proper sector running under the header (during which the data is transmitted)
- the time spent to solve the conflicts at the path to the central unit.

The relative weight of those factors strongly depends on the configuration of the disk units. They may be either alone and associated to a single CPU, or may be several disk units associated in a single CPU or may belong to a cluster organisation with a specific cluster controller having, potentially, a buffer space. In each case, the disk can be single, or a set of them sharing one or several controllers.

Moreover, the information that the designer has about how the data is organised in a disk can be very different in different kinds of applications.

Most often he shall assume that the accesses shall be randomly spread throughout the disk but under some circumstances, he can have some control about the extent to which his data is stored in a contiguous fashion.

The typical scheduling techniques for providing access to a disk are:
- first in first out (FIFO),
- shortest seek time first (SSTF) which is only theoretical because its implementation is too much CPU consuming,
- SCAN, shortest seek in the same direction, although it is still too CPU consuming,
- n-steps SCAN, that can be performed by the control unit itself. In this case, the operating system provides sequentially sets of at most n requests to the control unit of the disk. Requests are grouped in sets and the sets are sent to the control unit following a FIFO policy but the requests belonging to each set are served following a SCAN policy.

Once the header is placed in the proper position, the following phases depend on the policy of the control unit to solve the conflicts of the disk depending on it. The more frequent policies are:
- first in first out (FIFO). In this case the control unit manage the petitions by means of a FIFO queue and the disk seizes the control unit during the rotational latency time plus the record transfer time.
- shortest latency time first (SLTF). In this case, the disk waits the rotational latency time until the arrival of the record to the head; if the control unit is free it seized it during the transfer time otherwise it looses a full tour before trying to transfer again at the next turn.

In consequence it is necessary to furnish for each disk information related to the above concepts. Typical data to be annotated are:
- the CPU or CPUs to which the disk is connected
- the number of occupied cylinders
- the number of tracks per cylinder
- the number of records per track
- the number of controllers that manage the path between CPU and disk
- the policy used by the controllers
- the size of the cache memory of the controller
- the rotational speed
- the function that relates the number of cylinders moved by the arm and the time spent in this operation or, equivalently the maximum, mean and minimum times of the arm movement
- if the n-SCAN policy is used, the value of n
- other characteristics of the disk subsystem, like mirrored disks, RAIDs, cluster configurations, etc.

The modelling levels of a disk subsystem range from a simple FIFO queue with service time equal to the seek time plus the latency time plus the transfer time to a very detailed one in which it is taken into account the precise record being accessed.

7.3.4. Logical access to disk. Application software deals with files at a logical level, where the organisation of data into tracks is often ignored, as well as the policy of the operating systems for assigning blocks at the moment of file creation or appending. Even more, the user often ignores the links imposed by the operating system or the DBMS until the proper data is reached, or the pages that are kept resident in main memory.

In those cases, the performance model for the resource, now a file or a database, must be built from statistically collected data, with figures relating the delays, the CPU consumption and the disk consumption with the volume of the recorded files, the kind of request and the level of concurrence.

In simplest cases, however, distribution of probabilities indicating the number of physical accesses to disk implied by each kind of logical access will suffice.

7.3.5. Communication network. In order to build a performance model of a communication link, it must be specified the kind of protocol and the proper parameters for each case, which usually must be complemented by the transmission speed of the physical layer. Indeed, for a given protocol, the model can be built at different levels of detail. For instance, an ethernet configuration can be modelled specifying only as a transmission delay without taking into account the conflicts and retransmissions, or from its length and the number of stations considering a simplified version of the protocol, or with a further level of detail, specifying also the exact positions of each station in the communication bus.

The resource consumption must specify the length of the message to be sent and information, statistical or of any other type, concerning the routing and the destination of the messages.

7.3.6. Operating system. The operating system introduces some overhead on the resource consumption implied by application programs. Such a consumption is due essentially to scheduling activities and memory management (e.g. the management of virtual memory).

Some alternative approaches can be used for estimating such overheads. A simple possibility is to increase in a certain percent the resource consumption involved by the application programs. A more precise approach is that the modelling of the system takes into account some CPU consumption and some disk accesses at a constant rate or, better, at a rate depending on the number of processes in execution at any instant. In all cases, statistical information on such consumption is necessary.

7.3.7. Resource instances and utilisation rate constraints. So far, means for describing resource types have been provided. Actual resources should be obtained by means of proper instantiation, in the usual fashion. Moreover, some utilisation constraints can apply to such instances, which must, therefore be indicated for them. In general, a rate indicating the maximum rate that the system is allowed to maintain the resource in a busy state suffices. The default value is 1, indicating absence of restrictions.

7.4. Transactions

The algorithms involved in a system will, in general, process the input data as a function of an internal state. In some cases, the degree in which this relationship influences the performance of the system is not meaningful and therefore their details can be ignored in the performance model or simply characterised as a law of probability distribution.

However, as stated earlier, in other circumstances the way in which the algorithms relate the contents of the inputs with their internal state is so critical for the performance of the system that can be the key feature to be modelled. This is the case, for instance, of the adaptive routing algorithms in computer networks.

Some kind of marking of inputs, and the transmission of the marks through the system is also required in responsive systems, in order to relate the outputs with the inputs and to be able to properly measure the corresponding duration.

In such cases, the description of activities and data structures must be extended with a characterisation of the key aspects to be taken into account for input data and internal states, and to provide a version of the algorithms to be analysed expressed in this terms. In order to do it, however, it suffices to include data definitions and procedures in the description of activities and access routines to data structures as well as to include data communication in the inputs and outputs to data structures. All those aspects can be included in the model without a further extension of the design method notation.

Obviously, the same addition of procedural details must be applied to the activities emulating the behaviour of external devices, which must describe the generation of input according to some statistical rules.

The appropriate distribution of marks can be easily described by the user through a procedure.

The need to mark data with source identifier and time stamp for relating inputs and outputs can be inferred from the system specification. The couples that shall be compared in the performance model can be inferred from the linking clauses.

8. RELATION BETWEEN PERFORMANCE EVALUATION AND DESIGN

The goal of this section is to establish the relationships existing between the entities used in the different activities related with the dynamic behaviour of the system[8, 11], namely:
- expression of the performance constraints.
- modelling and design help.
- measuring.

This relationship can be seen in figure 8.1.

9. CONCLUSION AND OPEN PROBLEMS

This work shows that performance model derivation from the system design description is possible and that this task can be automated. The ability to estimate the performance of real-time systems has evident consequences in savings of implementation effort because the designer has estimations of the system performance during the design process and, obviously, before the system implementation. Therefore, the backtracking process of redesign becomes strongly pruned because only feasible designs progress.

However there are two critical aspects for the real application of the proposed technique:

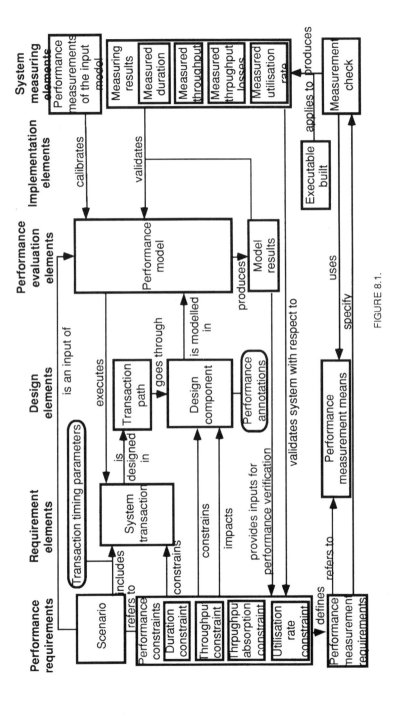

FIGURE 8.1.

- the creation of some kind of automated procedure to allow the designer to derive the performance models; the way is the definition of a set of models of the basic design elements and a set of rules about how to choose the models (depending on the desired accuracy and on the quality of the available data) and how to relate them.
- the estimation of the information which is required to be annotated on the design in order to execute the model; only the empirical data coming from similar modules run on compatible hardware support can provide reusable and reliable values.

REFERENCES

1. N. AUDSLEY, A. BURNS, M. RICHARDSON, A. WELLINGS, Deadline-Monotonic Scheduling, Dept. of Computer Science, YCS 146, University of York, 1990.
2. S. AYACHE, E. CONQUET, R. PUIGJANER, Taxonomy of Performance Requirements. Complement doc. TFP07-2.0. August 1992. 12 pp.
3. A. BENZEKRI, A., R, PUIGJANER, Types of Systems and Types of Timing Constraints. Complement doc. TFP15-2.0. June 1992. 7 pp.
4. A. M. DAVIS, Software Requirements. Analysis and Specifications. Prentice-Hall, 1990.
5. K. JACKSON, A. LLAMOSÍ, R. PUIGJANER, Towards Automatic Building of Performance Models: Formal Specification of Performance Constraints. In Proceedings of the IEEE SEKE'94, edited by Alf Berzstis. IEEE Computer Society Press 1994. pp. 148-155.
6. C. LIU, J. LAYLAND, Scheduling Algorithms for Multiprogramming in a Hard Real Time Environment, Journal of the ACM, XX, 1 (January 1973), pp. 46-61.
7. A. LLAMOSÍ, R. PUIGJANER, Performance Annotations for MASCOT. Complement doc. UIB77-5.0. March 1993. 61 pp.
8. A. LLAMOSÍ, R. PUIGJANER, Performance Issues of Real-Time Systems Design. In Performance and Reliability Evaluation, edited by R. Marie, G. Haring, G. Kotsis. R. Oldenburg & Österraichische Computer Gesellschaft 1994. pp. 9-60..
9. R. PUIGJANER, Information Annotation for Performance Modelling. Complement doc. TFP16-2.0. August 1992. 10 pp.
10. R. PUIGJANER, A. LLAMOSÍ, New Performance Constraint Type: Throughput Absorption. Complement doc. TFP39-1.0. January 1993. 4 pp.
11. R. PUIGJANER, A. BENZEKRI, S. AYACHE ET AL, Estimation Process of Performance Constraints during the Design of Real-Time and Embedded Systems. In Advanced Information Systems Engineering, edited by C. Rolland, F. Bodart, C. Cauvet. Springer-Verlag, 1993. pp.629-648.
12. R. PUIGJANER, J. SZYMANSKI, Towards the Automatic Derivation of Computer Performance Models from the Real Time and Embedded Systems Design. In Proceedings of IEEE MASCOTS'94. IEEE Computer Society Press 1994. pp. 397-398.

13. R. PUIGJANER, A. LLAMOSÍ, Steps towards the Automatic Derivation of Performance Models from the Mascot Design. In Memorias de la XX Conferencia Latinoamericana de Informática. Editorial Limusa. 1994. pp. 705-716.
14. R. PUIGJANER, Performance Aspects of Real-Time Systems. In Proceedings of IEEE MASCOTS'95. IEEE Computer Society Press 1995. pp. 17-21.
15. L. SHA, R. RAJKUMAR, J. LEHOCZKY, Priority Inheritance Protocols, Dept. of Computer Science, ECE and Statistics, Carnegie Mellon University, 1987.
16. C. U. SMITH, Performance Engineering of Software Systems, Addison-Wesley, 1990.
17. J. XU, D. PARNAS, On Satisfying Timing Constraints in Hard-Real-Time Systems, IEEE Transactions on Software Engineering, IX, 1, January 1993, pp. 70-84.

CHAPTER 10

Best-Case Analysis of
Systems with Global Spares and its
Application to Performability Modeling[*]

Meng-Lai Yin, Douglas M. Blough

10.1 INTRODUCTION

In this chapter, we analyze, under best-case conditions, fault-tolerant systems that make use of *global spare* modules. A global spare is a module which can replace any failed module in the system that performs an equivalent function. Global spare modules can be contrasted with *local spare* modules, which serve as dedicated replacements for a particular system module. Local spares can not replace any failed modules other than their dedicated partners, even if those modules perform the identical function. The use of global spares is efficient because one spare module can provide a potential replacement for many system modules, whereas the use of local spares would require at least one spare per system module. Due to their efficiency, global spares are commonly used in large fault-tolerant systems which contain some identical modules.

Despite the widespread use of systems with global spares, the amount of research that has analyzed these systems is relatively small. Most of this research makes the simplifying assumption that module failure distributions are exponential, e.g. Avizienis [2] and Goel[5]. However, in practice, this

---

[*]This work was supported in part by NSF under Grant CCR-9318495, by the Hughes Aircraft Company Doctoral Fellowship Program, and by the University of California MICRO program.

assumption is rarely satisfied. No analytical study of systems with global spares that assumes arbitrary module failure distribution is known to the authors. Some specific non-exponential distributions have been considered, such as the phase-type distribution [7,14], the lognormal distribution [15], and the Coxian distribution [16]. Of these, only the phase-type distribution can approximate arbitrary distributions. However, the papers that use phase-type distributions consider only systems with local spares [7,14]. Systems with global spares are more difficult to handle because they introduce dependence between modules that does not exist in systems having only local spares. An interval of time performability solution for degradable nonrepairable systems has also been proposed [1]. Although this method is applicable to systems with global spares, it requires calculation of all state sequences which takes exponential time.

Finally, a general method for analyzing large systems, known as the hierarchical composition method, has been proposed [12]. However, in the hierarchical composition method, it is assumed that individual modules are independent. Since systems with global spares introduce dependence between modules, the hierarchical composition method does not produce an exact solution when analyzing systems with global spares. Although this method could be used to analyze such systems, it would produce only an approximation that does not necessarily constitute a lower bound or an upper bound.

In this chapter, we present an analysis of systems with global spares and arbitrary module failure distribution under best-case conditions. This analysis leads to an efficient algorithm to numerically evaluate such systems in the best case. When combined with our previous work [12,13] that provided an exact solution for part of the problem and a worst-case analysis, this allows us to efficiently calculate upper and lower bounds that can be used in performability analysis of such systems. To be precise, our approach calculates probabilities for all possible performance levels in a system with global spares and arbitrary failure distribution, under both best-case and worst-case conditions. In a performability evaluation, exact performance level probabilities would be combined with performance values for each of the levels. Substituting our best-case and worst-case probabilities in such an evaluation yields upper and lower bounds on performability. We present the details of our best-case analysis and show an example of how our analyses can be used to upper and lower bound the performability of a system.

10.2   BACKGROUND

10.2.1   Problem Definition

A performance non-degradable system has only two states, *i.e.,* the system is working and providing service or the system is failed. In contrast, in a performance-degradable system, failure of a component of the system will not cause the system to fail. Instead, the system degrades its performance and continues providing service, although at a reduced level. Therefore, more than two performance levels are considered for performance-degradable systems. Traditional measures of dependability such as reliability and availability are insufficient for performance-degradable systems such as many fault-tolerant multiprocessor systems. Dependability, which is usually represented by reliability or availability, indicates a system's ability to perform its functions in the presence of faults. In detail, reliability, a function of time, is defined as the probability that a system does not fail during a given time interval. Availability, also a function of time, is defined as the probability that a system is operational at time t, whether or not it fails prior to that time. Despite the fact that these measures have been widely used in the fault tolerance community, they consider only two levels of system performance, *i.e.,* operational or failed. For performance-degradable systems, dependability is therefore not sufficient.

The performance-degradable non-repairable system considered here has $(n + m)$ identical modules to start with, where n modules provide service and m modules serve as global spares. When one of the n modules fails, and at least one global spare is available, then the failed module will be replaced by a global spare. Otherwise, the system degrades its performance and the remaining $(n - 1)$ modules provide service. A second failure can occur either on the newly-replaced module, or on any of the $(n - 1)$ surviving modules. In both cases, the second-failed module will be replaced by a global spare if there is a spare available; otherwise, the system will degrade its performance. This scenario continues until no global spare and no working module is left. In this situation, the system is considered to be totally failed.

Refer to the number of modules that are providing service as the *performance level*. The problem considered here is to determine the probability that at time t, the system specified above is working at performance level i, where $0 \leq i \leq n$. Note that for performability modeling [6] the probability and the *performance* of each level have to be determined. Here, we assume that the performance value (often called reward) for each level is given.

Moreover, we assume that the performance is *monotone-non-decreasing*. In other words, the loss of a module does not result in a higher reward.

The hierarchical composition method has been used as an efficient modeling method for large systems [10]. However, the independence assumption between individual modules is required. The systems discussed here violate the independence assumption since the *global order* of a failure occurrence determines whether the failed module is replaceable. If a failure's global order is no later than m (the number of global spares), then the failed module can be replaced by a global spare. Otherwise, it can not be replaced.

10.2.2 Assumptions

In this chapter, we make the assumption that spares do not fail while they are off-line. Once a spare is brought on-line, we assume that it has the same failure distribution as the working module that is replaced. Moreover, all modules are assumed to be identical which means they all have the same failure distribution. Two kinds of standby spares can be distinguished. Hot-standby spares operate in synchrony with the on-line modules and are prepared to take over at any time; cold-standby spares are unpowered until needed to replace a faulty module. As a result, hot-standby spares have non-zero failure rate, while cold-standby spares are usually assumed to have zero failure rate while they are off-line. Note that since a global spare can replace *any* module in the system, it can not be a hot-standby spare. Although some work assumes that global spares have a non-zero failure rate which is different than that of the on-line modules [2,5,11], most work follows the assumption that the spares don't fail until they are brought into the system. Systems with global spares that have non-zero failure rate are an interesting topic for future research.

Denote the failure distribution for a module by $F(t)$. We assume that some numerical method has been applied and the values for all i-fold convolutions of $F(t)$, denoted by $F^{(i)}(t)$, $0 \le i \le m + 1$, are determined. When i is small, the value of $F^{(i)}(t)$ can be calculated numerically from the i-dimensional integral. When i is large, the calculation of the i-dimensional integral becomes prohibitive. However, Ross[8] has developed a method of closely approximating $F^{(i)}(t)$ for general distributions, and Robinson and Neuts[7] have given a method of calculating $F^{(i)}(t)$ when $F(t)$ has phase-type distribution.

A final assumption is that reward values are monotone-non-decreasing, *i.e.,* the loss of a module does not result in higher performance.

10.2.3   Overview

For the exact solution of this problem, an algorithm which applies the work of Furchtgott and Meyer [1] was proposed [12]. However, this algorithm requires exponential time and therefore is not a practical solution for large systems. This makes it important to find efficient algorithms that provide upper and lower bounds on the expected performance. When reward values are monotone-non-decreasing, our best-case analysis provides an upper bound on the expected performance. Previously, we presented a worst-case analysis which yielded a lower bound [12,13].

Our method of attacking this problem is to model each module by a renewal process. Thus, n modules are modeled by n independent renewal processes; combining the statuses of these renewal processes gives a state of the system. While spares exist in the system, renewal of a module represents that module's failure and subsequent replacement by a spare. The first renewal of a module after the global spares are exhausted represents that module's failure which results in the module being failed forever and the system's performance being degraded. Although subsequent failures of such a module are not possible in an actual system, such modules continue to experience renewals in our model because renewal processes are infinite. However, these renewals do not correspond to any physical events in the system.

Consider, for example, a 2-module system. As stated, each module is modeled by a renewal process. Combining these two renewal processes yields the state space shown in Figure 10.2.3. Each state in Figure 10.2.3 is specified by the values of two random variables, X_1 and X_2. X_1 and X_2 take non-negative integer values, and represent the number of renewals occurring in the corresponding module by time t.

For a 2-module system, the state space is two-dimensional, as shown in Figure 10.2.3. When an n-module system is considered, the state space is n-dimensional. Each dimension represents the renewal process for one module. The renewal processes are represented by non-negative integer-valued random variables $X_i, 1 \leq i \leq n$. Furthermore, the renewal processes are all independent. Thus, a state of an n-module system, denoted by $(a_1 a_2 ... a_n)$, is specified by the values of n random variables. The probability that the system is in state $(a_1 a_2 ... a_n)$ is $\prod_{i=1}^{n} P\{X_i = a_i\}$. Denote $P\{X_i =$

a_i} by p_{a_i}. From renewal theory, $p_{a_i} = F^{(a_i)}(t) - F^{(a_i+1)}(t), 1 \leq i \leq n$. Recall that all i-fold convolutions of $F(t)$ are assumed to be calculated already.

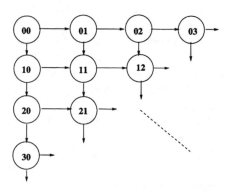

Figure 1: State Space for a Two-Module System

For a system to be in the highest performance level, the sum of the n renewal processes' values must be no greater than m (the number of global spares). The sum of the probabilities of the states with this property is the probability that the system is in the highest performance level. On the other hand, the system will be in a degraded performance level if the sum of the n renewal processes' values is greater than m. Unfortunately, the state space can not be used to obtain the exact probability for degraded performance levels. The problem is that, for a state with total number of renewals greater than the number of global spares, different renewal orders may result in different performance levels, as shown in Figure 2.

Consider a 2-module system with one global spare, *i.e.*, $n = 2$, and $m = 1$. State (21) has a total of 3 renewals, which is larger than the number of global spares. As shown in Figure 2, the performance level for state (21) could be 1 or 0, according to the order of these renewals. In Figure 2a and 2b, the system ends up with both modules not working, *i.e.*, in performance level 0. However, in Figure 2c, module 2 remains working and, hence, the performance level is 1.

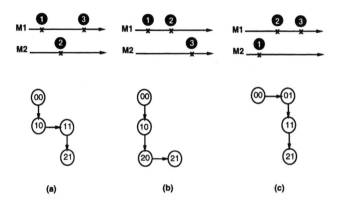

Figure 2: Different Ordering for state (21)

Recall that we assume the performance is monotone-non-decreasing, that is, the loss of a resource does not result in a higher performance. Therefore, when all states in the state space are in their highest possible level, the system has the highest possible (best-case) expected performance. The probability that the system is in a performance level under this situation is referred to as the *best-case* probability. Similarly, when each state is in its lowest possible level, the system has the lowest (worst-case) expected performance. The probability of a performance level under this situation is referred to as the *worst-case* probability. Previous work presented efficient algorithms which calculate the highest-level's probability and the worst-case probabilities of degraded levels [12,13].

The remainder of the chapter is organized as follows. We first briefly introduce the algorithms for the highest performance level's probability and for the worst-case probabilities. We then present the details of the efficient algorithm which provides the best-case probabilities for degraded performance levels. Finally, we analyze an example system to show the application of our method.

10.2.4 Our Previous Work

Algorithm for the highest performance level's probability

The algorithm for the highest performance level's probability applies matrix multiplication. Define matrix B as

$$\begin{bmatrix} p_0 & 0 & 0 & 0 & \cdots & 0 \\ p_1 & p_0 & 0 & 0 & \cdots & 0 \\ p_2 & p_1 & p_0 & 0 & \cdots & 0 \\ \cdot & \cdot & \cdot & p_0 & & \cdot \\ \cdot & \cdot & \cdot & & \cdot & \\ \cdot & \cdot & \cdot & & \cdot & 0 \\ p_m & p_{m-1} & p_{m-2} & p_{m-3} & \cdots & p_0 \end{bmatrix}_{(m+1)\times(m+1)}$$

where $p_i = F^{(i)}(t) - F^{(i+1)}(t)$. An element $b_{i,j}$ in matrix B is defined as 0 if $i < j$; otherwise, $b_{i,j} = p_{i-j}$. This is a lower triangular Toeplitz matrix [3,4], because the elements in the jth column are the same as the elements in the $(j-1)$st column except that they are shifted down by one row with the first row filled by 0. Define vector V_0 as $\begin{bmatrix} 1 \\ 0 \\ \cdot \\ \cdot \\ 0 \end{bmatrix}_{(m+1)\times 1}$. and

define $V_k = B * V_{k-1} = B^k * V_0$, for all $k \geq 1$. It was proven that the sum of all elements in vector V_n is the probability that an n-module system is working in the highest performance level [12]. Moreover, the value in row $(i+1)$ $(0 \leq i \leq m)$ is the probability that the n modules have renewed a total of i times. Therefore, generating B^n obtains the highest performance level's probability. If we generate B^n by $(n-1)$ matrix multiplications, the time complexity is $O(m^2 n)$. If n is represented by a binary number, B^n can be calculated as products of powers of 2, and the time complexity is $O(m^2 \log n)$.

Algorithm for the worst case probabilities

From previous work[12,13], the worst-case probability that the system is in level $n - l$, denoted by $P\{L_{n-l}(t)\}$, can be expressed as:

$$P\{L_{n-l}(t)\} = \binom{n}{l} p_0^{n-l} Q(l, m+l) \sum_{y=l+1}^{k} \binom{n}{y} p_0^{n-y} R(y, m+l) \qquad (1)$$

In this equation, $R(y, m+l)$ is the probability that y modules (which have renewed at least once) have renewed *exactly* $(m+l)$ times in total, and $Q(l, m+l)$ is the probability that l modules (which have renewed at least once) have renewed *at least* $(m+l)$ times in total. Matrix multiplication is also used in the algorithm for obtaining the value of $P\{L_{n-l}(t)\}$.

Define matrix C as

$$\begin{bmatrix} p_1 & 0 & 0 & 0 & \cdots & 0 \\ p_2 & p_1 & 0 & 0 & \cdots & 0 \\ p_3 & p_2 & p_1 & 0 & \cdots & 0 \\ \cdot & \cdot & \cdot & p_1 & & \cdot \\ \cdot & \cdot & \cdot & \cdot & & \cdot \\ \cdot & \cdot & \cdot & \cdot & & 0 \\ p_m & p_{m-1} & p_{m-2} & p_{m-3} & \cdots & p_1 \end{bmatrix}_{m \times m}$$

As before, each $p_i = F^{(i)}(t) - F^{(i+1)}(t)$. Similar to matrix B, this is a lower triangular Toeplitz matrix. However, differing from B, this matrix excludes the cases where a module has no renewal (p_0). Also, define vector

U_0 as $\begin{bmatrix} 1 \\ 0 \\ \cdot \\ \cdot \\ 0 \end{bmatrix}_{m \times 1}$ and define $U_y = C * U_{y-1} = C^y * U_0$, for $y \geq 1$. It was

proven that the ith row of U_y is equal to $R(y, n+i-1)$ [12]. In other words, all $R(y, m+l)$ necessary to evaluate $P\{L_{n-l}(t)\}$ are available once all U_y's are calculated. Furthermore, $Q(l, m+l)$ can be calculated from the $R(y, m+l)$'s. Thus, obtaining all U^y will give us the value of $P\{L_{n-l}(t)\}$. The overall complexity of this procedure is dominated by the time to calculate all U_y which is $O(m^2n)$.

10.3   BEST CASE ANALYSIS

10.3.1   Basis

Consider a class of states where every state in it has best-case level l. Refer to this class as *BCL-l*. All other states in the state space do not have best-case level l. Denote a state by $(a_1a_2...a_n)$. For a state to be in class *BCL-l*, it must satisfy the following two criteria.

Criterion 1: *the sum of the smallest l a_ks is no more than the number of global spares (m)*

Criterion 2: *the sum of the smallest $(l+1)$ a_ks is greater than m*

Criterion 1 makes sure that the best-case level is at least l. The smallest l a_ks correspond to the l modules whose renewals result in replacement in the best case. The best case happens when each of these renewals has global order less than m. Criterion 2 assures that the system can not perform in a level higher than l. With these two criteria, the system's best-case level must be l.

In the following discussion, the state representation $(a_1a_2...a_n)$ is assumed to be ordered suc that the smallest l a_ks are in the left part, and the remaining $(n-l)$ a_ks are in the right part.

$$\overbrace{\underbrace{a_1a_2\cdots a_l}_{l}a_{l+1}\cdots a_n}^{n}$$

We refer to "$a_1a_2...a_l$" as the *left* part, and "$a_{l+1}a_{l+2}...a_n$" as the *right* part. For distinction, any a_k in the left part is denoted by a_i, and any a_k in the right part is denoted by a_j. Note that the minimum value of a_j in the right part can be the same as the maximum value of a_i in the left part.

If a state is in *BCL-l*, then Criteria 1 and 2 state that $\sum_{i=1}^{l} a_i \leq m$, and $(\sum_{i=1}^{l} a_i) + a_j > m$. Therefore, $a_j \geq m + 1 - \sum_{i=1}^{l} a_i$, $l+1 \leq j \leq n$. The best-case probability for performance level l is the sum of all states' probabilities in class *BCL-l*.

10.3.2   Detailed Analysis

Consider the state representation for a state in class *BCL-l*. The sum of the left part, denoted by k, $k = \sum_{i=1}^{l} a_i$, is in the range of $[0, m]$, according to Criterion 1. In addition, the maximum value in the left part, denoted as q, is also a number in the range of $[0, m]$. Otherwise, Criterion 1 can not be satisfied. Figure 10.3.2 shows all the possible combinations of k and q for states in class *BCL-l*. Corresponding this figure to the state space, an element in the figure represents a set of states with the same values of k and q. Note that the total number of states for each element is infinite since there is no upper bound for the value of a_j. However, in our analysis, states with the same values of k and/or q can be combined together.

Note that q (the maximum value in the left part) can not be larger than k, otherwise, the sum of the l a_is would be larger than k. Therefore, all $q > k$ cases need not be considered. In addition, when q is 0, the only possible value for k is 0, since $\sum_{i=1}^{l} 0 = 0$. Hence, only the first element exists in the first column ($k = 0, q = 0$).

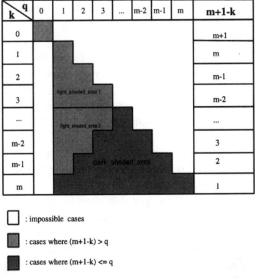

q / k	0	1	2	3	...	m-2	m-1	m	m+1-k
0									m+1
1									m
2									m-1
3									m-2
...									...
m-2									3
m-1									2
m									1

☐ : impossible cases

▨ : cases where (m+1-k) > q

■ : cases where (m+1-k) <= q

Figure 3: Cases for Different k and q in the Best Case

All elements in the same row have the same value of k, hence the same value of $(m + 1 - k)$, as listed in the right-most column. Note that $a_j \geq q$, because any a_j in the right part must be greater or equal to the maximum value of a_i in the left part (this was denoted as q). The light-shaded area represents the cases where $(m + 1 - k) > q$. In these cases, the value of $a_j \geq (m + 1 - k) > q$, and any a_j in the right part is different than any a_i in the left part. On the other hand, the dark-shaded area represents the cases where $(m + 1 - k) \leq q$. In these cases, $a_j \geq q \geq (m + 1 - k)$. Therefore, it is possible that some a_j in the right part have the same value as q. The reason for this distinction is that in the dark-shaded area case, the number of occurrences of q is essential in the probability calculation, as will be explained later.

Note that there are rows where *no* element is in the dark-shaded area. These are the rows that have $q \leq k < (m + 1 - k) \Rightarrow 2k < m + 1 \Rightarrow k < \frac{m+1}{2} \Rightarrow k \leq \lceil \frac{m+1}{2} \rceil - 1$. Thus, for rows with $k \leq \lceil \frac{m+1}{2} \rceil - 1$, any a_j in the right part is different than any a_i in the left part. Let $k' = \lceil \frac{m+1}{2} \rceil - 1$. Then for rows with $0 \leq k \leq k'$, only light-shaded-area exists. Refer to this area as light-shaded-area 1. For rows with $k > k'$, both a light-shaded-area and a dark-shaded-area exist. Refer to the light-shaded-area part in these rows as light-shaded-area 2.

Consider the probability of light-shaded-area 1. For a state belonging to light-shaded-area 1, its processed representation is $(a_1 a_2 \cdots a_l a_{l+1} \cdots a_n)$, where $\sum_{i=1}^{l} a_i = k$ and $a_j \geq (m + 1 - k) > q \geq a_i$. An element in light-shaded-area 1 includes a group of states where each of them has the above property. Note that a state's probability can be calculated as the product of the left-part probability and the right-part probability, *i.e.*, $P_{left} \times P_{right}$. The probability for the group of states with same value of k and $a_j \geq (m+1-k)$ is $P_{right} = (F^{(m+1-k)})^{n-l}$. Since each a_j in the right part is no less than $(m + 1 - k)$, $F^{(m+1-k)}$ is the probability for all possible cases for each module in the right part. In addition, since there are $(n - l)$ modules in the right part, the probability for all possible cases for all a_j is $(F^{(m+1-k)})^{n-l}$.

Refer to $D(l, k)$ as the probability that l modules have renewed exactly k times in total. For example, $D(2, 2)$ is the probability that 2 modules (module a_{i_1} and module a_{i_2}) have renewed twice in total. That is, $a_{i_1} = 1$ and $a_{i_1} = 1$, or $a_{i_1} = 0$ and $a_{i_2} = 2$, or $a_{i_1} = 2$ and $a_{i_2} = 0$. Our approach of calculating the probability of the states in light-shaded-area 1 is to represent the probability in terms of $D(l, k)$ and $F^{(m+1-k)})^{n-l}$, since $D(l, k)$ can be obtained in polynomial time. Recall that in Section 2, for vector V_n, the value in row $(i + 1)$ $(0 \leq i \leq m)$ is the probability that the n modules have renewed a total of i times. Note that $D(l, k)$ is the kth row of vector V_l.

Also, note that $D(l, k)(F^{(m+1-k)})^{n-l}$ is *not* the probability for all states with $\sum_{i=1}^{l} a_i = k$ and $a_j \geq (m+1-k)$. To see this, consider the case where $n = 3$, $m = 4$, $l = 2$, and $k = 2$, hence, $m + 1 - k = 3$. The probability represented by $D(2,2)(F^{(3)})^1 = D(2,2)F^{(3)}$ is for states $(a_{i_1} a_{i_2} a_3)$ that satisfy $a_{i_1} + a_{i_2} = 2$ and $a_3 \geq 3$. This includes states $(11\hat{3})$, $(02\hat{3})$, and $(20\hat{3})$, where $\hat{3}$ means $a_3 \geq 3$. However, there are totally 9 cases for states that satisfy Criteria 1 and 2, e.g., $(11\hat{3})$ $(1\hat{3}1)$ $(\hat{3}11)$ $(02\hat{3})$ $(0\hat{3}2)$ $(\hat{3}02)$ $(20\hat{3})$ $(2\hat{3}0)$ $(\hat{3}20)$.

In fact, the probability for all states in light-shaded-area 1 is $\binom{n}{l}D(l,k)(F^{(m+1-k)})^{n-l}$. In this expression, $\binom{n}{l}$ represents the number of ways that l out of the n modules can be selected without order to be in the left part. Since $\binom{n}{l}D(l,k)(F^{(m+1-k)})^{n-l}$ is the probability for all elements in one row of light-shaded-area 1, where $0 \leq k \leq k'$, the probability for all states in *light-shaded-area 1* is

$$P_{light-shaded-1} = \binom{n}{l} \sum_{k=0}^{k'} D(l,k)(F^{(m+1-k)})^{n-l} \qquad (2)$$

When $k \geq \lceil \frac{m+1}{2} \rceil$, each row contains two parts, the light-shaded-area part and the dark-shaded-area part. Note that when $k = m$, $m + 1 - k = 1 \leq q$, and only the dark-shaded-area part exists. For light-shaded-area 2, we expand each $D(l,k)$ to an array of q elements, each element is denoted by $D(l,k,q)$, where $1 \leq q \leq (m + 1 - k) \Rightarrow 1 \leq q \leq (m - k)$. $D(l,k,q)$ is the probability that l modules, where the maximum number of renewals in these l modules is q, have renewed a total of k times. The reason for distinguishing a maximum number of renewals (q) is that for a state covered in $D(l,k,q), q \geq (m+1-k)$, it belongs to the dark-shaded area. Therefore, the sum of the states' probabilities for states in *light-shaded-area 2* is

$$P_{light-shaded-2} = \binom{n}{l} \sum_{k=k'+1}^{m-1} \sum_{q=1}^{m-k} D(l,k,q)(F^{(m+1-k)})^{n-l} \qquad (3)$$

When $k \geq \lceil \frac{m+1}{2} \rceil$, and $(m + 1 - k) \leq q \leq k$, this is the dark-shaded area. As stated before, in the dark-shaded area, a_j in the right part can have the same value as a_i in the left part. Denote the number of occurrences of q in the left part by r, where $1 \leq r \leq l$. Since $\sum_{i=1}^{l} a_i = k$, it follows that $\sum_{i=1}^{l-r} a_i = k - qr$. $(k - qr)$ must be greater than or equal to 0, because the sum of non-negative numbers (a_i) is non-negative. Thus, $k - qr \geq 0 \Rightarrow k \geq qr \Rightarrow r \leq \lfloor \frac{k}{q} \rfloor$. Therefore, $1 \leq r \leq \min(l, \lfloor \frac{k}{q} \rfloor)$.

For states in the dark-shaded area, the $(l - r)$ smallest a_is in the left part have a sum $(k - qr)$, and each $a_i \leq q$. Denote the probability that $(l - r)$ modules have renewed $(k - qr)$ times, where each module has renewed no more than q times by $D_q(l - r, k - qr)$. Note that $D_q(l - r, k - qr)$ can be calculated like $D(l - r, k - qr)$ except that we replace all $p_{q'}$, $q' > q$, by zeros.

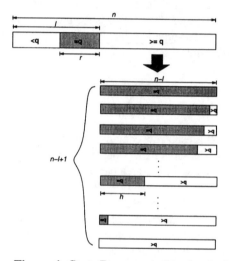

Figure 4: State Representation Analysis

Denote the number of appearances of q in the right part by h, $0 \leq h \leq n - l$. Then each of the remaining $(n - l - h)$ modules in the right part must have renewed more than q times. Figure 10.3.2 shows all the cases considered for an element in the dark-shaded area in Figure 10.3.2. As shown in Figure 10.3.2, the state representation is further divided into three parts: the "$< q$" part which has $(l - r)$ elements, the "$= q$" part which has $(r + h)$ elements, and the "$> q$" part which has $(n - l - h)$ elements. For any one of the $(n - l + 1)$ cases, the probability is calculated as

$$D_q(l - r, k - qr)(p_q)^{r+h}\left(F^{(q+1)}(t)\right)^{n-l-h}.$$

Denote this as $P_{one-case}$. Then, the sum of the probabilities of all states in the dark-shaded area in Figure 10.3.2, referred to as $P_{dark-shaded}$, is

$$\sum_{k=k'+1}^{m} \sum_{q=m+1-k}^{k} \sum_{r=1}^{min(l,\lfloor k/q \rfloor)} \sum_{h=0}^{n-l} \binom{n}{l-r}\binom{n-l+r}{r+h} P_{one-case} \qquad (4)$$

Finally, combining (2), (3) and (4) together, the probability that in the best case, the system is in performance level l, is $P_{dark-shaded} + P_{light-shaded-1} + P_{light-shaded-2}$.

10.3.3   Complexity Discussion

Note that $P_{light-shaded-1} = \binom{n}{l}\sum_{k=0}^{k'} D(l,k)(F^{(m+1-k)}(t))^{n-l}$, and the time complexity for preparing all $D(l,k)$ is $O(m^2 n)$. Given that all $D(l,k)$ are available, $\binom{n}{l}\sum_{k=0}^{k'} D(l,k)(F^{(m+1-k)}(t))^{n-l}$ can be calculated as

$$\binom{n}{l}\left[\; (F^{(m+1)}(t))^{n-l} \quad \cdots \quad (F^{(m+1-k')}(t))^{n-l}\;\right] * \begin{bmatrix} D(l,0) \\ D(l,1) \\ D(l,2) \\ \cdot \\ \cdot \\ D(l,k') \end{bmatrix}$$

To prepare the first row vector, recall that all $F^{(m+1-k)}(t)$ are preprocessed and stored in an array. The time to calculate them is less than $O(n^3 m^2 + n^2 m^3)$. Since each $(F^{(m+1-k)}(t))^{n-l}$ in the row vector takes $O(n)$ time, and there are $O(m)$ elements in the vector, the time complexity is $O(nm)$. The multiplication of the row vector and the column vector takes $O(m)$ time. Therefore, the time complexity for obtaining the probability of the light-shaded-area 1 is $O(nm^2) + O(nm) + O(m) = O(nm^2)$.

For light-shaded-area 2, preparing all $D(l,k,q)$ takes $O(nm^3)$ time. This is because each $D(l,k,q)$ is an extension of $D(l,k)$, and generating $D(l,k,q)$ for one q takes $O(nm^2)$ time. Moreover, there are $O(m)$ choices of q. The matrix multiplication technique used for *light-shaded-area 1* is applied again. Hence, each $\sum_{q=1}^{m-k} D(l,k,q)$ is multiplied by the corresponding $(F^{(m+1-k)}(t))^{n-l}$, and the time complexity is $O(m)$. Again, to prepare all $(F^{(m+1-k)}(t))^{n-l}$ takes $O(nm)$ time. Therefore, the time complexity for getting the probability of *light-shaded-area* 2 is $O(nm^3) + O(nm) + O(m) = O(nm^3)$.

For the dark-shaded-area probability, we prepare all $D_q(l - r, k - qr)$ first. The time complexity for preparing one $D_q(l - r, k - qr)$ is $O(nm^2)$. Since there are $O(m)$ choices of q, the overall time complexity for all $D_q(l - r, k - qr)$ is $O(nm^3)$. Since all p_q and $F^{(q+1)}$ are known, the time complexity to prepare all $(p_q)^{r+h}$ and $(F^{(q+1)}(t))^{n-l-h}$ is $O(n)$. Moreover, the time complexity of summing up all calculated items in (4) is $O(n^2m^2)$. Hence, the overall time complexity for calculating $P_{dark-shaded}$ is $O(\max(nm^3, n, n^2m^2)) = O(n^2m^2 + nm^3)$. Since the best-case probability for level $n - l$ is $P_{dark-shaded} + P_{light-shaded-1} + P_{light-shaded-2}$, the time complexity for the best-case probability for one degraded level is $O(\max(nm^2, nm^3, n^2m^2 + nm^3)) = O(n^2m^2 + nm^3)$.

The above time complexity is only for the calculation of the best-case probability for one degraded level. With $O(n)$ degraded performance levels, the time complexity for obtaining the best-case probabilities for all degraded levels is $O(n^3m^2 + n^2m^3)$.

10.4   MODELING EXAMPLE

The example considered here is a multiprocessor system where each processor unit is a triply redundant module. The failure distribution function $F(t)$ for such a processor unit is $3e^{-2\lambda t} - 2e^{-3\lambda t}$, where λ is the failure rate of one physical processor. For all $F^{(i)}(t), 1 \leq i \leq m + 1$, the values are calculated numerically by using Ross's approximation method [8]. For obtaining the exact expected number of working processors, the tool 'UltraSAN'[9] is used. The performability measure used is a simple one, namely the expected number of working processors at time t. Each physical processor's mean time to failure is assumed to be one year (8760 hours). Thus, the failure rate $\lambda = 0.000114155$. Figure 5 shows the best case, the worst case, and the exact solution as functions of time when there are ten primary processors and five global spares.

In this example, the difference between the best case and worst case solutions is quite small when t is less than 5000 hours. This can be seen more clearly in Figure 6 which shows the same data between 0 and 10,000 hours. Since we provide an exact solution for the highest performance level's probability, our method is highly accurate during the early stage of the system's life. It is only when the performance has degraded considerably that this difference becomes significant. In many applications, particularly mission-oriented ones with relatively short mission times, it is the early

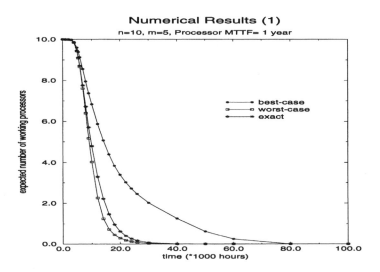

Figure 5: Example (0 to 100,000 hours)

stage of system life which is critical to evaluate. Even if an evaluation of the
middle and latter stages of system life is necessary, our approach provides
best case and worst case values of performability which can be quite useful
in many applications.

Given a large pool of resources, how to use these resources so that the
optimum performability can be achieved is an important design concern.
Figure 7 illustrates how our method can be used to address this issue. Consider how a total of 100 processors should be divided between primaries and
spares for the same example system. Figure 7 shows the expected number
of working processors in such a system for m ranging from 1 to 35 at time
$t = 1/2$ year. Assume this is a mission-oriented system with a mission time
of $1/2$ year and we would like to maximize the expected number of working
processors at the end of the mission. This figure illustrates that the best
design choice is not at either extreme, namely using all 100 processors as
primaries or using the maximum number (35) of spares. Rather, an optimal
design uses 23 spares (best case) and 25 spares (worst case). Hence, our
results can be used to help design an optimal system configuration.

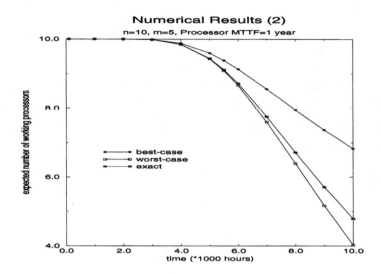

Figure 6: Example (0 to 10,000 hours)

REFERENCES

1. D.G. FURCHTGOTT, J.F. MEYER, "A Performability Solution Method for Degradable Nonrepairable Systems," IEEE Trans. on Computers, **Vol. C-33,** No. 6, June 1984, 550-554.

2. L.R. GOEL, R. GUPTA, R.K. AGNIHOTRI, "Analysis of a three-unit redundant system with two types of repair and inspection," Microelectronic Reliability, **Vol. 29,** No.5, 1989, 769-773.

3. R.A. HORN, C.R. JOHNSON, Matrix Analysis, (Cambridge University Press, 1985).

4. I.S. IOHVIDOV, translated by G. PHILIP, A. THIJSSE, Hankel and Toeplitz Matrices and Forms, (Birkhauser Boston, 1982).

5. F.P. MATHUR, A. AVIZIENIS, "Reliability analysis and architecture of a hybrid-redundant digital system: Generalized triple modular redundancy

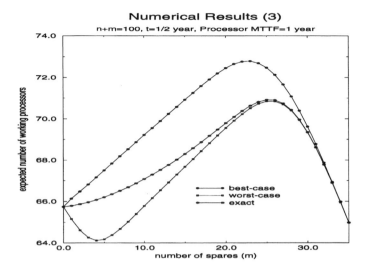

Figure 7: Optimum Performability Example

with self-repair," Spring Joint Computer Conference, 1970, 375-383.

6. J.F. MEYER, "On Evaluating the Performability of Degradable Computing Systems," IEEE Trans. on Computers, **Vol.** **C-29,** No.8, August 1980,720-731.

7. D.G. ROBINSON, M.F. NEUTS, "An Algorithmic Approach to Increased Reliability Through Standby Redundancy," IEEE Trans. on Reliability, **Vol. 38,** No.4, Oct. 1989, 430-435.

8. S.M. ROSS, "Approximations in Renewal Theory," Probability in the Engineering and Informational Sciences, 1987, 163-174.

9. W.H.SANDERS, W.D.OBAL II, M.A.QURESHI, F.K.WIDJANARKO, "The UltraSAN Modeling Environment," Performance Evaluation Journal, Special Issue on Performance Modeling Tools, 1995.

10. R.A. SAHNER and K.S. TRIVEDI, "Reliability Modeling Using

SHARPE," IEEE Trans. on Reliability, **Vol. R-36,** JUNE 1987, 186-193.

11. B.D. SIVAZLIAN, K.H. WANG, "Economic Analysis of the M/M/R Machine Repair Problem with Warm Standbys," Microelectronic Reliability, **Vol. 29,** No.1, 1989, 25-35.

12. M.L. YIN, Hierarchical-Compositional Performability Modeling for Fault-Tolerant Multiprocessor Systems, Ph.D. Dissertation, Information and Computer Science Department, Univ. of Cal. Irvine, 1995.

13. M.L. YIN, D.M. BLOUGH, L. BIC, "Modeling Systems with Global Spares,"   Proceedings of the Pacific Rim International Symposium on Fault-Tolerant Systems, 1995, 52-57.

14. C.E. WELLS, Replacement vs Repair of Failed Components For a System With a Random Lifetime," IEEE Trans. on Reliability, **Vol. 37,** No.3, August 1988, 280-286.

15. W.B. JOYCE, P.J. ANTHONY, "Failure Rate of a Cold or Hot-Spared Component with a Lognormal Lifetime," IEEE Trans. on Reliability, **Vol. 37,** No.3, August 1988, 299-308.

16. K.S. TRIVEDI, Probability and Statistics with Reliability, Queuing, and Computer Science Applications, (Prentice Hall, Inc., Englewood Cliffs, NJ, USA, 1982).

CHAPTER 11

MARKOV RENEWAL THEORY APPLIED TO PERFORMABILITY EVALUATION

Ricardo Fricks   Miklós Telek
Antonio Puliafito   Kishor Trivedi

11.1. INTRODUCTION

Computer and communication systems are designed to meet a certain specified behavior. The procurement of metrics to establish how well the system behaves, that is, how closely it follows the specified behavior, is the objective of quantitative analysis. Traditionally, performance and dependability evaluation are used as separate approaches to provide quantitative figures of system behavior. Performance evaluates the quality of service, assuming that the system is failure-free.[1] Dependability focuses on determining deviation of the actual behavior from the specified behavior in the presence of component or subsystem failures.[2]

Beaudry[3] proposed the aggregated measure *computation before failure*, while Meyer[4] proposed the term *performability*, which has been used since then. Performability analysis aims to capture the interaction between the failure-repair behavior and the performance delivered by the system. Its results are fundamental to the analysis of real-time system performance in the presence of failure.[5]

Performability measures provide better insight into the behavior of fault-tolerant systems. Basic metrics used to evaluate fault-tolerant designs are reliability and availability. The conditional probability that

193

a system survives until some time t, given it is fully operational at $t = 0$, is called the reliability $R(t)$ of the system.[6] Reliability is used to describe systems which are not allowed to fail; in which the system is serving a critical function and cannot be down. Note that components or subsystems can fail so long as the system does not. The instantaneous availability $A(t)$ of a system is the probability that the system is properly functioning at time t. Availability is typically used as a basis for evaluating systems in which functionality can be delayed or denied for short periods without serious consequences.[7] Reliability and availability do not consider different levels of system functionality.

Performability analysis of real systems with non-deterministic components and/or environmental characteristics results in stochastic modeling problems. Several techniques for solving them for transient and steady-state measures have been proposed and later combined under the framework of Markov reward models.[8] The traditional framework allows the solution of stochastic problems enjoying the **Markov property**: *the probability of any particular future behavior of the process, when its current state is known exactly, is not altered by additional knowledge concerning its past behavior.*[6,9] If the past history of the process is completely summarized in the current state and is independent of the current time, then the process is said to be *(time-) homogeneous.* Otherwise, the exact characterization of the present state needs the associated time information, and the process is said to be *non-homogeneous.* A wide range of real problems fall in the class of Markov models (both homogeneous and non-homogeneous), but problems in performability analysis have been identified that cannot be adequately described in this traditional framework. The common characteristic these problems share is that the Markov property is not valid (if valid at all) at all time instants. This category of problems is jointly referred to as *non-Markovian* models and can be analyzed using several approaches:

- *Phase-type expansions* - [10,11] when the past history of the stochastic process can be described by a discrete variable, an expanded continuous-time homogeneous Markov chain can be used to capture the stochastic behavior of the original system.

- *Supplementary variables* - [12] when the past history is described by one or more continuous variables, the approach of the supplementary variables can be applied and a set of ordinary or partial differential equations can be defined together with boundary conditions and analyzed.

- *Embedded point-processes* - [13,14] when the temporal behavior of the system can be studied by means of some appropriately chosen embedded epochs where the Markov property applies. Several well-known classes of stochastic processes such as regenerative, semi-Markov and Markov regenerative processes are based on the concept of embedded points.

The object of this chapter is to present a theory based on the concept of embedded point-processes that encompass semi-Markov and Markov regenerative processes. This theory, named Markov renewal theory, is reviewed in the first three sections of this chapter and later applied to several non-Markovian performability models.

Our purpose is to provide an up-to-date treatment of the basic analytic models to study non-Markovian systems by means of Markov renewal theory and an accurate description of the solution algorithms. In particular, we develop a general framework which allows us to deal with renewal processes and specifically with semi-Markov and Markov regenerative processes. We hope that this chapter will serve as a reference for practicing engineers, researchers and students in performance and reliability modeling. Other surveys on Markov renewal theory applied to reliability analysis have appeared in the literature,[15,16] but none of them as complete or as didactic as the present one.

The rest of this chapter is organized as follows. Section 11.2 introduces the basic terminology associated with the theory, including the concepts and distinction between semi-Markov processes and Markov regenerative processes. Section 11.3 presents basic solution techniques for stochastic processes with embedded Markov renewal sequences.

Markov regenerative Petri nets, useful as a high-level description language of these kind of stochastic models, are reviewed in Section 11.4 and employed in the analyses of three examples presented in Section 11.5. Examples are selected to illustrate the methodology associated with semi-Markov and Markov regenerative processes. Section 11.6 concludes the chapter.

11.2. MARKOV RENEWAL THEORY

Assume we wish to quantitatively study the behavior of a given non-deterministic system. One possible solution would be to associate a random variable Z_t, taking values in a countable set $\mathcal{F}$, to describe the state of the system at any time instant t. The family of random variables Z_t constitutes a stochastic process $\mathbf{Z} = \{Z_t; t \in \mathcal{R}_+ = [0, \infty)\}$.

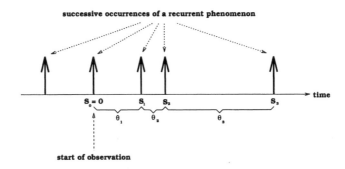

Figure 11.1: A sample realization of a renewal process.

Suppose we are interested in a single event related with the system (e.g., when system components fail). Additionally, assume the times between successive occurrences of this type of event are *independent and identically distributed* (*iid*) random variables. Let $S_0 < S_1 < S_2 < ...$ be the time instants of successive events to occur (as shown in Figure 11.1). The sequence of non-negative *iid* random variables, $\mathbf{S} = \{S_n - S_{n-1}; n \in \mathcal{N} = [1, ..., \infty)\}$ is a *renewal process*. Otherwise, if we do not start observing the system at the exact moment an event has occurred (i.e., $S_0 \neq 0$) the stochastic process $\mathbf{S}$ is a *delayed renewal process*.

Contexts in which renewal processes arise abound in applied probability. For instance, the times between successive electrical impulses or signals impinging on a recording device are often assumed to form a renewal process. Another classical example of renewal process is the item replacement problem explored in [9,17] where $S_1 - S_0, S_2 - S_1, ...$ represent the lifetimes of items (light bulbs, machines, etc.) that are successively placed in service immediately following the failure of the previous one.

However, suppose instead of a single event, we observe that certain transitions between identifiable system states j of a subset $\mathcal{E}$ of $\mathcal{F}$,

$\mathcal{E} \subseteq \mathcal{F}$, also resemble the behavior just described, when considered in isolation. Successive times S_n at which a fixed state j, $j \in \mathcal{E}$, is entered form a (possibly delayed) renewal process. In the sample process realization depicted in Figure 11.2 we see that the sequence of time instants $\{S_0, S_4, ...\}$ forms a renewal process, while $\{S_1, S_5, ...\}$ and $\{S_2, S_3, ...\}$ form delayed renewal processes.

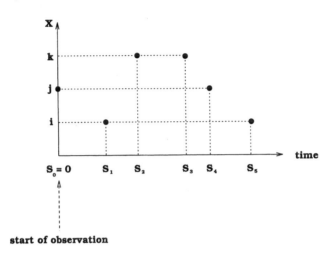

Figure 11.2: A set of renewal processes progressing concurrently.

Additionally, when studying the system evolution we observe that at these particular times the stochastic process $\mathbf{Z}$ exhibits the Markov property, i.e., at any given moment S_n, $n \in \mathcal{N}$, we can forget the past history of the process. In this scenario we are dealing with a countable collection of renewal processes progressing simultaneously such that successive renewals form a discrete-time Markov chain (DTMC). The superposition of all the identified renewal processes gives the points $\{S_n; n \in \mathcal{N}\}$, known as *Markov renewal moments**, and together with the states of the DTMC defines a **Markov renewal sequence** (MRS).

In this section we review the definitions and some of the concepts of **Markov renewal theory**, a collective name that includes MRS's, and two other important classes of stochastic processes with embedded

---

*Note that these instants S_n are not renewal moments as described in renewal theory, since the distributions of the time interval between consecutive moments are not necessarily iid's.

MRS's, named semi-Markov processes (SMP's) and Markov regenerative processes (MRGP's). Our ultimate aim is to study $\{Z_t; t \in \mathcal{R}_+\}$, however, as a first step we need to study Markov renewal theory. Our emphasis in this chapter is "how to" explore the possibilities of this wealthy theory rather than its technical details (or "why" does it work).

The definitions and terminology mentioned here were influenced by [18], but the formalism comes from Çinlar.[19,20] We strongly recommend Çinlar [20] and Kulkarni [21] for a more detailed study of Markov renewal theory. Classical references for the other classes of stochastic processes mentioned in this chapter are: renewal processes,[9,17,22,23] and regenerative processes.[9,24,25] For the general theory of Markov chains good references are [6,9,20].

11.2.1. Historic Overview of Markov Renewal Theory

Semi-Markov processes were independently introduced by P. Lévy [26,27] and W.L. Smith [24] in 1954. Although Smith's work was only published in 1955, its main results were announced in a talk given on the author's behalf by D.V. Lindley at the International Congress of Mathematicians held in Amsterdam in September 1954. At the same congress Lévy announced his results concerning semi-Markovian processes, which were identical with the results given by Smith. Also at the same time, L. Takács [28] introduced and applied the same type of stochastic process to problems in counter theory. Semi-Markov process is a generalization of both continuous and discrete time Markov chains which permit arbitrary sojourn distribution functions, possibly depending both on the current state and on the next state to be entered.

The term Markov renewal sequence is due to R. Pyke, who gave an extensive treatment of many aspects of such processes in 1961.[29,30] Markov regenerative processes were introduced by R. Pyke and R. Schaufele in 1966 where they were called semi-Markov processes with auxiliary paths.[31] Most of the theoretical foundations of Markov regenerative processes were laid out in the work of Çinlar in 1975 [20] under the name of semi-regenerative processes. Later, Kulkarni [21] suggested the name Markov regenerative process that we use in this chapter.

11.2.2. Markov Renewal Sequence

Define, for each $n \in \mathcal{N}$, a random variable X_n taking values in a countable set $\mathcal{E}$ and a random variable S_n taking values in $\mathcal{R}_+$, such that $S_0 \leq S_1 \leq S_2 \leq ...$, assuming $S_0 \doteq 0$. The bivariate stochastic process $(\mathbf{X}, \mathbf{S}) = \{X_n, S_n; n \in \mathcal{N}\}$ is a **Markov renewal sequence** if it satisfies

$$Pr\{X_{n+1} = j, S_{n+1} - S_n \leq t \mid X_0, ..., X_n; S_0, ..., S_n\} =$$

$$Pr\{X_{n+1} = j, S_{n+1} - S_n \leq t \mid X_n\}$$

for all $n \in \mathcal{N}$, $j \in \mathcal{E}$, and $t \in \mathcal{R}_+$. Thus $(\mathbf{X}, \mathbf{S})$ is a special case of bivariate Markov process in which the increments $S_1 - S_0, S_2 - S_1, ...$ are all non-negative and are conditionally independent given $X_0, X_1, ...$

We will always assume *time-homogeneous* MRS's; that is, the conditional transition probabilities $K_{i,j}(t)$, where

$$K_{i,j}(t) \doteq Pr\{X_{n+1} = j, S_{n+1} - S_n \leq t \mid X_n = i\}$$

are independent of n for any $i, j \in \mathcal{E}, t \in \mathcal{R}_+$. Therefore, we can always write

$$K_{i,j}(t) = Pr\{X_1 = j, S_1 \leq t \mid X_0 = i\}, \qquad \forall i, j \in \mathcal{E}, \ t \in \mathcal{R}_+$$

The matrix of transition probabilities $\mathbf{K}(t) = \{K_{i,j}(t) : i, j \in \mathcal{E}, t \in \mathcal{R}_+\}$ is called the **kernel** of the MRS*.

The stochastic sequence $\{X_n; n \in \mathcal{N}\}$ keeps track of the successive states visited at Markov renewal moments and forms a discrete-time Markov chain with state space $\mathcal{E}$. The one-step transition probabilities of this *embedded Markov chain* (EMC) are

$$
\begin{aligned}
p_{i,j} &\doteq Pr\{X_{n+1} = j \mid X_n = i\}, \qquad \forall i, j \in \mathcal{E} \\
&= \lim_{t \to \infty} K_{i,j}(t)
\end{aligned}
$$

---

*Note that $K_{i,j}(t)$ is a possibly defective distribution function, so that $\lim_{t \to \infty} K_{i,j}(t) \leq 1$.

There are no restrictions regarding the structure of the EMC on an
MRS. There is no imposition that $\{X_n; n \in \mathcal{N}\}$ should be irreducible
for instance. Therefore, we can start at time S_0 in a state of $\mathcal{E}$ that
will not be reached again at any other Markov renewal moment in the
future evolution of the process.

Let the *vector of initial probabilities* of X_0 be described by $\mathbf{a} =
(a_0, a_1, ...)$ where (i) $a_i \doteq Pr\{X_0 = i\} \geq 0, \forall i \in \mathcal{E}$, and (ii) $\sum_{i \in \mathcal{E}} a_i = 1$,
then we say that $(\mathbf{X}, \mathbf{S}) = \{X_n, S_n; n \in \mathcal{N}\}$ is an MRS completely
determined by $(\mathbf{a}, \mathbf{K}(t))$. Thus, the vector of initial probabilities $\mathbf{a}$
and the kernel matrix $\mathbf{K}(t)$ completely determine all finite-dimensional
distributions of the Markov renewal sequence.[21]

Embedded MRS's can be identified associated with semi-Markov
and Markov regenerative processes. Hence, we now proceed with a
study of such processes.

11.2.3. Semi-Markov Processes

Given an MRS $(\mathbf{X}, \mathbf{S})$ with state space $\mathcal{E}$ and kernel $\mathbf{K}(t)$, we can
introduce the counting process

$$\mathbf{N}(t) \doteq sup\{n : S_n \leq t\}, \qquad \forall t \in \mathcal{R}_+$$

to count the number of Markov renewal moments up to time t, but not
considering the one at zero. Using the counting process just defined,
we introduce the process $\mathbf{Y} = \{Y_t; t \in \mathcal{R}_+\}$ defined by

$$\begin{aligned}
Y_t &\doteq X_{\mathbf{N}(t)} \\
&= X_n, \qquad if \ S_n \leq t < S_{n+1}
\end{aligned}$$

for all $t \in \mathcal{R}_+$, called **semi-Markov process** (SMP) determined
by $(\mathbf{a}, \mathbf{K}(t))$. An SMP (for a sample realization see Figure 11.3) is
a stochastic process which moves from one state to another within a
countable number of states with the successive states visited forming a
discrete-time Markov chain, and that the time required for each successive move is a random variable whose distribution function may depend
on the two states between which the move is being made. The nomen-
clature "semi-Markov" comes from the somewhat limited Markov prop-
erty which $\mathbf{Y}$ has: the future of $\mathbf{Y}$ is independent of its past provided
the present is a Markov renewal moment.[20] Note that since we consider

$S_0 \doteq 0$, then the initial condition $Y_0 = i$ always means that the SMP has just entered state i at the time origin. Like MRS's, an SMP is specified by its vector of initial probabilities $\mathbf{a}$ and the kernel matrix $\mathbf{K}(t)$.

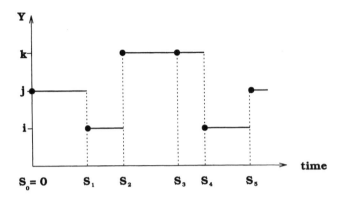

Figure 11.3: A sample realization of a semi-Markov process.

From the SMP definition it should be observed that the process only changes state (possibly back to the same state as shown in Figure 11.3) at the Markov renewal moments S_n. The possibility of transitions not resulting in real state changes can be easily verified by inspecting the kernel matrix $\mathbf{K}(t)$ for non-zero elements on its main diagonal. It follows that, the matrix $\mathbf{K}(t)$ associated with a particular SMP (as well as to an MRS) is not necessarily unique. There are SMP's (as well as MRS's) which can be described by more than one matrix $\mathbf{K}(t)$. A unique kernel matrix can always be defined by its minimal representation, in which all Markov renewal moments represent (real) state transitions. For instance, the minimal representation of the SMP depicted in Figure 11.3 would prevent Markov renewal moment S_3 and, consequently, the time interval between consecutive Markov renewal moments would always represent the sojourn time in each of the EMC states. The derivation of the minimal representation of $\mathbf{K}(t)$ is introduced and explored in [32].

SMP's represent sufficiently general and constructive mathematical models of complex multicomponent systems, whose states are randomly changed by extreme conditions*. The only essential restriction is the

---

*We call these conditions extreme because we assume that after the condition

semi-Markov property, that can be interpreted from two different per-spectives (actually used to simulate the behavior of SMP's):

- The sequence of system states at times of changes must be de-scribed by a homogeneous DTMC, and times to the next Markov renewal moment only depend on the current state and next state of the system.

- The times to the next Markov renewal moment only depend on the current state, and the selection of the destination state only depend on the current one and the time when the state transition happens.

In the subsequent derivations of this paper we consider an extension of SMPs obtained by attaching *reward rates* (r_i) to their states $(i \in \mathcal{E})$. Having introduced these new variables, we can then compute the reward accumulated by **Y** over any interval $(0, t)$. The accumulated reward $B(t)$ is defined by the following integral:

$$B(t) = \int_0^t r_{Y(\tau)} d\tau$$

Several important measures of **Y** can be defined by this extension (such as the cummulative time **Y** spends in a subset of states, etc). These measures are refered to as reward measures of the SMP, and can be characterized by $(\mathbf{a}, \mathbf{K}(t), \mathbf{r})$, where **r** is the vector of the reward rates. Details on this and other analytical results associated with the reward concept can be found in [5,18,32].

11.2.4. Markov Regenerative Processes

A stochastic process $\mathbf{Z} = \{Z_t; t \in \mathcal{R}_+\}$ with state space $\mathcal{F}$ is called *regenerative* if there exist time points at which the process probabilisti-cally restarts itself. Such random times when the future of **Z** becomes a probabilistic replica of itself are named *times of regeneration* for **Z**. This concept may be weakened by letting the future after a time of regeneration depend also on the state of an MRS at that time. We then say that **Z** is a Markov regenerative process.

MRGP's are stochastic processes $\{Z_t; t \in \mathcal{R}_+\}$ that exhibit em-bedded MRS's $(\mathbf{X}, \mathbf{S})$ with the additional property that all conditional

---

appears (or is detected) the system state will change instantaneously.

finite distributions of $\{Z_{t+S_n}; t \in \mathcal{R}_+\}$ given $\{Z_u; 0 \leq u \leq S_n, X_n = i\}$ are the same as those of $\{Z_t, t \in \mathcal{R}_+\}$ given $X_0 = i$.[21] As a special case, the definition implies that

$$Pr\{Z_{t+S_n} = j \mid Z_u, 0 \leq u \leq S_n, X_n = i\} = Pr\{Z_t = j \mid X_0 = i\}$$

It also implies that the future of the process $\{Z_t; t \in \mathcal{R}_+\}$ from $t = S_n$ onwards depends on the past $\{Z_u, 0 \leq u \leq S_n\}$ only through X_n. Observe, that in the regenerative process this future from S_n onwards was completely independent of the past.

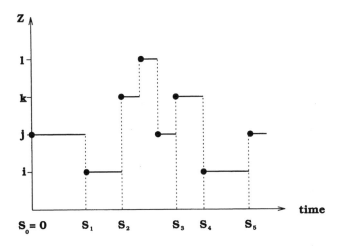

Figure 11.4: A sample realization of a Markov regenerative process.

In contrast to SMP's, state changes (possibly to states outside $\mathcal{E}$) are allowed between two consecutive Markov renewal moments (see Figure 11.4) in MRGP's. It is possible for the system to return to states in $\mathcal{E}$ without these moments constituting Markov renewal moments. For example, suppose we start observing the system when it has just entered a state j, as shown in Figure 11.4. At that particular instant the Markov property is applicable since there is no past history of the process, but because of system characteristics, we know this property will no longer be valid for that state after the first state transition (not necessarily to a state in $\mathcal{E}$). This situation could be understood if we consider that although state j being part of the EMC **X**, it does not communicate with other states of **X** and, hence, the Markov chain **X** is reducible. Although others states of **X** are (possibly) accessible from state i, this state cannot be accessed from any other state of **X**.

The structural complexity of an MRGP depends on two main constituents:

- the stochastic process between two consecutive Markov renewal moments;

- the cause of the occurrence of a Markov renewal moment.

The stochastic process between the consecutive Markov renewal moments, usually refered to as *subordinated process*, can be any continuous-time discrete-state stochastic process over the same probability space. Recently published examples considered subordinated CTMC's [18,33], SMP's [34,35], MRGP's [32], or a more general stochastic reward process.

The occurrence of a Markov renewal moment can be caused by

- the expiration of a random delay:
  - independent of the subordinated process;
  - some preceeding state transition of the subordinated process results in a new Markov renewal moment;

- an acummulated reward measure of the subordinated process reaches a random barrier*:
  - independent of the path of the subordinated process;
  - some preceeding state transitions of the subordinated process results in new Markov renewal monent;

- other more complex reason[†].

The subclass of MRGP's with subordinated SMP's (or CTMC's) and with Markov renewal moments caused by one of the first two reasons is considered in [34,36].

---

*While the preemption policy of the reward process (*preemptive repeat with resampling*) can be considered by means of one of the first reason as well, other preemption policies (*preemptive resume* [34] or *preemptive repeat without resampling* [36]) can result in a more complex situation which falls only into reason 2.

†This last reason results in the wides class of MRGPs, but we believe that the majority of the practically interesting cases are captured by one of the former reasons.

11.3. PROBLEM SOLVING USING MARKOV RENEWAL THEORY

Let $\mathbf{Z} = \{Z_t; t \in \mathcal{R}_+\}$ be an MRGP with state space $\mathcal{F}$, whose embedded MRS is $(\mathbf{X}, \mathbf{S}) = \{X_n, S_n; n \in \mathcal{N}\}$ with kernel matrix $\mathbf{K}(t)$ over a countable state space $\mathcal{E}$, a subset of $\mathcal{F}$ (i.e., $\mathcal{E} \subseteq \mathcal{F}$). For such a process we can define a matrix of conditional transition probabilities as:

$$V_{i,j}(t) \doteq Pr\{Z_t = j \mid Z_0 = i\}, \qquad \forall i \in \mathcal{E}, \forall j \in \mathcal{F}, \forall t \in \mathcal{R}_+$$

In many practical problems involving Markov renewal processes, our primary concern is finding ways to effectively compute $V_{i,j}(t)$ since several measures of interest (e.g., reliability and availability) are related to the conditional transition probabilities of the stochastic process.

In this section we review some of the main techniques to determine transition probabilities. The underlying process discussed is an MRGP.

11.3.1. Markov Renewal Equation

At any instant t, the conditional transition probabilities $V_{i,j}(t)$ of $\mathbf{Z}$ can be computed as:[20,21]

$$
\begin{aligned}
V_{i,j}(t) &= Pr\{Z_t = j, S_1 > t \mid Z_0 = i\} + Pr\{Z_t = j, S_1 \leq t \mid Z_0 = i\} \\
&= Pr\{Z_t = j, S_1 > t \mid Z_0 = i\} + \\
&\quad \sum_{k \in \mathcal{E}} \int_{u=0}^{t} Pr\{Z_{t-u} = j \mid Z_0 = k\} d(Pr\{Z_u = k, S_1 < u\}) \\
&= Pr\{Z_t = j, S_1 > t \mid Z_0 = i\} + \sum_{k \in \mathcal{E}} \int_0^t V_{k,j}(t-u) dK_{i,k}(u) \\
&= Pr\{Z_t = j, S_1 > t \mid Z_0 = i\} + \sum_{k \in \mathcal{E}} \int_0^t dK_{i,k}(u) V_{k,j}(t-u)
\end{aligned}
$$

for all $i \in \mathcal{E}$, $j \in \mathcal{F}$, and $t \in \mathcal{R}_+$. If we define matrix $\mathbf{E}(t)$ by

$$E_{i,j}(t) \doteq Pr\{Z_t = j, S_1 > t \mid Z_0 = i\}, \qquad \forall i \in \mathcal{E}, \forall j \in \mathcal{F}, \forall t \in \mathcal{R}_+$$

then, the set of integral equations $V_{i,j}(t)$ defines a **Markov renewal equation**, and can be expressed in matrix form as

$$\mathbf{V}(t) = \mathbf{E}(t) + \int_0^t d\mathbf{K}(u)\mathbf{V}(t-u)$$

where the Lebesgue-Stieltjes integral* is taken term by term.

To better distinguish the roles of matrices $\mathbf{E}(t)$ and $\mathbf{K}(t)$ in the description of the MRGP[†] we use the following terminology when referring to them:

- We call matrix $\mathbf{E}(t)$ the **local kernel** of the MRGP, since it describes the state probabilities of the process during the interval between successive Markov renewal moments.

- Since matrix $\mathbf{K}(t)$ describes the evolution of the process from the Markov renewal moment perspective, without describing what happens in between these moments we call it the **global kernel** of the MRGP.

The Markov renewal equation represents a set of coupled *Volterra integral equations of the second kind* [37] and in general are hard to solve in time-domain. The research for effetive numerical solution methods of this equation has only started recently. We believe that the best numerical approach should be based on specific features of MRGP's which are not necessarily captured by the kernel matrices $\mathbf{K}(t)$ and $\mathbf{E}(t)$. However, methods based on the kernel matrices are the most general so far, and will be the ones exposed in this chapter.

To summarize, solving problems using Markov renewal theory is a two step process:

- First, we need to construct both kernel matrices $\mathbf{K}(t)$ and $\mathbf{E}(t)$[‡].

- We then solve the set of Volterra integral equations for the conditional transition probabilities $V_{i,j}(t)$ or for some measure of interest.

---

*$\int_0^t dK(u)V(t-u) = \int_0^t k(u)V(t-u)du$ when $K(t)$ possesses a density function $k(t) = \frac{dK(t)}{dt}$.

[†]Actually, this terminology will be adopted even when discussing issues related with SMP's for consistency in our presentation.

[‡]For the case of SMP's, only the global kernel matrix $\mathbf{K}(t)$ is necessary.

11.3.2. Synthesis of the Kernel Matrices

The construction of kernel matrices can proceed by reasoning from particular facts to a general conclusion (*inductive approach*) or reasoning from the general to the specific (*deductive approach*). The inductive approach starts from the analysis of possible state transitions and relies only on basic probability theory to construct both kernel matrices. Conversely, the deductive approach applies general techniques to solve for a particular case. It is hard compare, in general, the two alternative approaches for a particular problem under consideration. Only experience can help in selecting the most suitable technique. Hence, we illustrate both approaches (whenever possible) in the examples in this chapter without discussing their particular merits.

The inductive approach does not have any general formulation. Its application varies from case to case, though the contrustive process of the matrices follows approximately a regular pattern. We illustrate this logical pattern step-by-step along the solution of the examples presented in the end of this chapter. Our main interest in this section is to explore the deductive approach because of its algorithmic nature.

The deductive approach provides a closed form expression in transform domain for the elements of matrices $\mathbf{E}(t)$ and $\mathbf{K}(t)$ based on the kernels of the subordinated processes. Due to the generality of this approach it provides a robust and widely applicable procedure to construct the kernel matrices, and that is why we use it in the analysis of subsequent examples as a deductive method with comparison of the inductive one.

Since the first reason of the occurrence of Markov renewal moments can be considered as the special case of the second reason a unified approach was introduced in [34] to analyze the subclass of MRGPs characterized by the first two reasons. Three matrix functions $\mathbf{F}^i(t, w)$, $\mathbf{D}^i(t, w)$ and $\mathbf{P}^i(t, w)$ (where t denotes the time, w denotes the barrier level, and the superscript i refers to the initial (regeneration) state of the subordinated process) were introduced to quantify the different occasions of the completion of the regeneration period and the internal state probabilities with a fixed barrier height. $\mathbf{F}^i(t, w)$ refers to the case when the next regeneration moment is because of the accumulated reward measure reached the fixed value w of the barrier. For the analysis of this case an additional matrix ($\mathbf{\Delta}^i$ referred to as branching probability matrix) is introduced, as well, to describe the state transition subsequent to the regeneration moment. $\mathbf{D}^i(t, w)$ captures the case when the next regeneration moment is caused by one of the concluding state transitions of the subordinated process. And $\mathbf{P}^i(t, w)$ describes the state transition probabilities inside the regeneration period.

Based on the kernel of the subordinated SMP ($\mathbf{Q^i(t)} = \{Q^i_{k,\ell}(t)\}$) these functions can be evaluated by the following equations [34][*]:

$$F^{i\sim*}_{k,\ell}(s,v) = \delta_{k,\ell}\frac{r_k\left[1 - Q^{i\sim}_k(s+vr_k)\right]}{s+vr_k} + \\ \sum_{u\in R} Q^{i\sim}_{k,u}(s+vr_k)F^{i\sim*}_{u,\ell}(s,v) \tag{1}$$

$$D^{i\sim*}_{k,\ell}(s,v) = \frac{1}{v}Q^{i\sim}_{k,l}(s+vr_k) + \sum_{u\in R} Q^{i\sim}_{k,u}(s+vr_k)D^{i\sim*}_{u,\ell}(s,v)$$

$$P^{i\sim*}_{k,\ell}(s,v) = \delta_{k,\ell}\frac{s\left[1 - Q^{i\sim}_k(s+vr_k)\right]}{v(s+vr_k)} + \\ \sum_{u\in R} Q^{i\sim}_{k,u}(s+vr_k)P^{i\sim*}_{u,\ell}(s,v) \tag{2}$$

where $Q^i_k(t) = \sum_\ell Q^i_{k,\ell}(t)$; s is the time variable and v is the barrier level variable in transform domain; r_k is the reward rate associated to state k; R is the part of the state space from which an exit results in a new regeneration moment; and the superscript $\sim$ ($*$) refers to Laplace-Stieltjes (Laplace) transformation.

Given that $G_g(w)$ is the cumulative distribution function of the random barrier height to reach the next regenerative moment, the elements of the i-th row of matrices $\mathbf{K}(t)$ and $\mathbf{E}(t)$ can be expressed as follows, as a function of the matrices $\mathbf{P}^i(t, w)$, $\mathbf{F}^i(t, w)$ and $\mathbf{D}^i(t, w)$:

$$K_{i,j}(t) = \int_0^\infty \left[\sum_{k\in R^i} F^i_{i,k}(t,w)\Delta^i_{k,j} + D^i_{i,j}(t,w)\right] dG_g(w) \tag{3}$$

$$E_{i,j}(t) = \int_0^\infty P^i_{i,j}(t,w)dG_g(w) \tag{4}$$

---

[*]This subsection summarizes the results only for the cases when the cummulative or reward measure is accumulated according to *prd* and *prs* models; for *pri* models we refer to [36].

11.3.3. Solution Techniques of Markov Renewal Equations

We can classify the existent solution methods in two categories:

- time domain methods;[38]

- Laplace-Stieltjes domain method.[18,34]

One possible time domain solution is based on a discretization approach to numerically evaluate the integrals presented in the Markov renewal equation. The integrals are solved using some approximation rule such as trapezoidal rule, Simpson's rule or other higher order methods:

$$\mathbf{V}(t_n) = \mathbf{E}(t_n) + \sum_{i=0}^{n} a_i \mathbf{K}'(t_i)\mathbf{V}(t_n - t_i)$$

where $\mathbf{K}'(t_i)$ denotes the derivative $\frac{d\mathbf{K}(x)}{dx}$ evaluated at point t_i *. In these equations h is the discretization step and it is assumed constant, and the coefficients a_i depend on the integration technique used. For example, when the trapezoidal rule is used $a_0 = a_n = \frac{h}{2}$ and $a_i = h, i = 1, 2, \cdots, n - 1$. Hence, at any given time $l = t_n = nh$, a linear system of the form:

$$[\mathbf{I} - a_0\mathbf{K}'(0)]\mathbf{V}(t_n) = \mathbf{E}(t_n) + \sum_{i=1}^{n} a_i \mathbf{K}'(t_i)\mathbf{V}(t_n - t_i)$$

needs to be solved. Note that if $a_0\mathbf{K}'(0)$ is a diagonal matrix then the method is explicit, otherwise it is implicit.

A potential problem with this approach is that the right-hand side of the above equation can in general be expensive to compute. Nevertheless, there exist cases where the generalized Markov renewal equation has a simple form and the time-domain solution can be carried out.

Another time domain alternative is to construct a system of partial differential equations (PDEs), using the method of supplementary variables.[12] This method has been considered for steady-state analysis in [33] and subsequently extended to the transient case in [39]. Up to now, this method has been elaborated only for the cases when the occurrence

---

*When the derivative of matrix $\mathbf{K}(t)$ is difficult to obtain Equation can be approximated as: $\mathbf{V}(t_n) = \mathbf{E}(t_n) + \sum_{i=0}^{n}[\mathbf{K}'(t_i) - \mathbf{K}'(t_{i-1})]\mathbf{V}(t_n - t_i)$.

of a new Markov renewal moment is due to one of the first two causes discussed in the previous section.

An alternative to the direct solution of the Markov renewal equation in time-domain is the use of transform methods. In particular, if we define $\mathbf{E}^{\sim}(s) = \int_0^\infty e^{-st} d\mathbf{E}(t)$ and $\mathbf{V}^{\sim}(s) = \int_0^\infty e^{-st} d\mathbf{V}(t)$, the Markov renewal equation becomes

$$\begin{aligned} \mathbf{V}^{\sim}(s) &= \mathbf{E}^{\sim}(s) + \mathbf{K}^{\sim}(s)\mathbf{V}^{\sim}(s) \\ &= [\mathbf{I} - \mathbf{K}^{\sim}(s)]^{-1}\mathbf{E}^{\sim}(s) \end{aligned}$$

After solving the linear system for $\mathbf{V}^{\sim}(s)$, transform inversion is required. In very simple cases, a closed-form inversion might be possible but in most cases of interest, numerical inversion will be necessary. The transform inversion however can encounter numerical difficulties especially if $\mathbf{V}^{\sim}(s)$ has poles in the positive half of the complex plane.

11.4. MARKOV REGENERATIVE STOCHASTIC PETRI NETS

Stochastic Petri nets of various types (SPN [40], GSPN [41], ESPN [42], DSPN [43], etc.) have been proposed as model description languages for analyzing the performance and reliability of systems. The analytical/numerical solution of such models proceeds by utilizing mathematical engines based upon the underlying stochastic processes of each Petri net class - CTMC for SPN's and GSPN's, SMP for a subset of ESPN's and MRGP for DSPN's. In this chapter, we use the class of stochastic Petri net named MRSPN to describe and help solve the sample problems explored in the next section.

Markov Regenerative Stochastic Petri Nets (MRSPN's) were introduced in [18] to overcome limitations on modeling power (notably allowing the solution of non-markovian models) of existing analytical tools. MRSPNs allow transitions with zero firing times, exponentially distributed or generaly distributed firing times. The underlying stochastic process of an MRSPN is an MRGP, and it was proved in [18] that MRSPN's constitutes a true generalization of all the above classes. With a restriction that at most one generally distributed timed transition is enabled in each marking, the transient and steady state analysis of MRSPN's can be carried out analytically-numerically rather than by discrete-event simulation. We now present some of the basic concepts concerning MRSPN's, but to do that we review some of the classical terminology of Petri nets.

A **Petri net** (PN) [44,45] is defined by a set of *places* (drawn as circles), a set of *transitions* (drawn as bars), and a set of *directed arcs*, which connect transitions to places or places to transitions. Places may contain *tokens*. The state of the Petri net, called *marking*, is defined by a vector enumerating the number of tokens in each place.

The states of a PN can be used to represent various entities associated with a system - for example, the number of functioning resources of each type, the number of tasks of each type waiting at a resource, the allocations of resources to tasks, and states of recovery for each failed resource. Transitions represent the changes of states due to the ocurrences of simple or compound events such as the failure of one or more resources, the completion of executing tasks, or the arrival of jobs.

A place is an input to a transition if an arc exists from the place to the transition. If an arc exists from the a transition to a place, it is an output place of the transition. A transition is *enabled* when each of its input places contains at least one token. Enabled transitions can fire, by removing one token from each of input place and placing one token in each output place. Thus, the firing of a transition may cause a change of state (producing a different marking) of the PN. The *reachability set* is the set of markings that are reachable from a given initial marking. The reachability set together with arcs joining the marking indicating the transition that cause the change in marking is called the **reachability graph** of the net.

After the original conception, some extensions of PNs were proposed. *Inhibitor arcs* were introduced to increase the fundamental modeling or decision power of ordinary Petri nets. An inhibitor arc from a place to a transition has a circle rather than an arrowhead at the transition. The firing rule for the transition is changed such that the transition is disabled if there is at least one token present in the corresponding inhibiting input place.

In stochastic Petri nets, a random firing time elapses after a transition is enabled until it fires. Transitions which have nonzero firing times are called *timed transitions* and transitions with zero firing times are called *immediate transitions*. In MRSPN a timed transition can fires according to an exponential or any other general distribution function. Immediate transitions have priority to fire over timed transitions.

The markings of a stochastic Petri net can be classified into *vanishing markings* and *tangible markings*. In a vanishing marking at least one immediate transition is enabled and in a tangible marking no immediate transition is enabled. For stochastic Petri nets classes that avoid immediate transitions the analysis of the embedded stochastic process can start directly from the reachability graph. For instance, the reachability graph of an SPN can be mapped directly into a Markov chain [40] and then solved for transient and steady-state measures. However, before analysing the underlying stochastic process of an MRSPN we have an extra step after obtaining the reachability graph. The **reduced reachability graph** is obtained from the reachability graph by merging the vanishing markings into their successor tangible markings according some rules.[18] After constructing the reduced reachability graph we can start the analysis of the underlying stochastic process, which is going to be explored in the next section together with the developed examples.

11.5. PERFORMABILITY ANALYSIS APPLYING MARKOV RENEWAL THEORY

The use of Markov renewal theory for performability evaluation will be shown by its application to three examples of computer system architectures:

- series system with repair;

- parallel system with single, shared repair facility; and

- warm standby system with single, shared repair facility.

We start this section by describing each of the sample cases, followed by the identification of underlying stochastic processes, and concluding with the construction of kernel matrices using both approaches discussed (whenever applicable). Finally, the section is closed with the numerical solution of the resulting Markov renewal equations for measures of interest. Our emphasis in this chapter is on *synthesis of the kernel matrices* rather than on solution of the Volterra equations.

11.5.1. Series System with Repair

Consider a series system composed of two machines **a** and **b** with constant failures rates λ_a and λ_b. Upon failure of either machine, the system fails and is repaired with general repair-time distribution functions $G_a(t)$ and $G_b(t)$. We assume that machines cannot fail while the system is down, and that failure of one machine does not affect the operational status of the other.

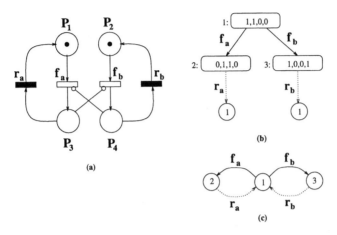

(a)

(b)

(c)

Figure 11.5: (a) Petri net of series system. (b) Reachability graph. (c) State transition diagram.

The overall behavior of the system can be easily understood from the MRSPN illustrated in Figure 11.5(a). Machine **a** is working whenever there is a token in place P_1. Transition f_a, firing according to an exponential distribution with parameter λ_a, represents the failure process of machine **a**. When machine **a** fails, a token is deposited in place P_3 and repair is immediately started. Transition r_a with a generally distributed firing function $G_a(t)$ represents the random duration of the repair procedure. A symmetrical set of places and transitions describes the behavior of machine **b**. The system has failed whenever a token is deposited in places P_3 or P_4. The two inhibitor arcs impose the restriction that no machine can fail while the system is undergoing repairs.

The reachability graph corresponding to the Petri net is shown in Figure 11.5(b). Each marking in the graph is a 4-tuple counting the number of tokens in places P_1 to P_4. Figure 11.5(b) also corresponds to the reduced reachability graph for the system since there are no vanishing markings. In the graph, solid arcs represent transitions firing according to exponential distribution functions, while dotted arcs denote state transitions firing according to general distributions.

Let a random variable Y_t be defined according to the operational condition of the system at any instant, i.e.,

$$Y_t = \begin{cases} 1 & \textit{if the system is working at time } t \\ 2 & \textit{if machine } \mathbf{a} \textit{ is being repaired at time } t \\ 3 & \textit{if machine } \mathbf{b} \textit{ is being repaired at time } t \end{cases}$$

Note that possible values of Y_t are the labels corresponding markings in Figure 11.5(b). We are interested in computing performability measures associated with the system. To do so, we need to determine the conditional transition probabilities $V_{i,j}(t)$ of $\{Y_t; t \in \mathcal{R}_+\}$.

We start the solution procedure with the identification of the type of stochastic process underlying the system behavior. From the reachability graph we can conclude that all state transitions correspond to Markov renewal moments $\mathbf{S} = \{S_n; n \in \mathcal{N}\}$, and, consequently, markings labeled 1, 2, and 3, define the embedded Markov chain $\mathbf{X} = \{X_n; n \in \mathcal{N}\}$, such that X_n is the state of the system at time S_{n+} (i.e., $X_n = Y_{S_{n+}}$).

If we assume that at the time origin the system has just entered a new state (i.e., $S_0 = 0$) then the bi-variate stochastic process $(\mathbf{X}, \mathbf{S})$ is an MRS, and consequently $\{Y_t; t \in \mathcal{R}_+\}$ is an SMP, since whenever the system changes state we identify a Markov renewal moment. Having identified Y_t, we prepare for its solution by constructing the kernel matrices $\mathbf{K}(t)$ and $\mathbf{E}(t)$. Note that since we are dealing with an SMP the construction of $\mathbf{E}(t)$ is immediate once $\mathbf{K}(t)$ is determined.

An additional step adopted before starting the construction of the kernel matrices was the construction of a simplified state transition diagram. Figure 11.5(c) shows a simplified version of the (reduced) reachability graph where the markings were replaced by the corresponding state indices. We preserved the convention for the arcs and extended the notation by representing states of the EMC by circles, and (eventually) others states by squares.

The only non-null elements in matrix $\mathbf{K}(t)$ correspond to the possible transitions in a single step. Consequently, we have the following structure of the matrix:

$$\mathbf{K}(t) = \begin{bmatrix} 0 & K_{1,2}(t) & K_{1,3}(t) \\ K_{2,1}(t) & 0 & 0 \\ K_{3,1}(t) & 0 & 0 \end{bmatrix}$$

The elements of the matrix can be constructed by induction from Figure 11.5(c):

$$
\begin{aligned}
K_{1,2}(t) &= Pr\{X_1 = 2, S_1 \le t \mid X_0 = 1\} \\
&= Pr\{the\ system\ fail\ up\ to\ time\ t\ and\ machine \\
&\quad \mathbf{a}\ is\ the\ cause\} \\
&= \frac{\lambda_a}{\lambda_a + \lambda_b}\left[1 - e^{-(\lambda_a+\lambda_b)t}\right]
\end{aligned}
$$

$$
\begin{aligned}
K_{1,3}(t) &= Pr\{X_1 = 3, S_1 \le t \mid X_0 = 1\} \\
&= Pr\{the\ system\ fail\ up\ to\ time\ t\ and\ machine \\
&\quad \mathbf{b}\ is\ the\ cause\} \\
&= \frac{\lambda_b}{\lambda_a + \lambda_b}\left[1 - e^{-(\lambda_a+\lambda_b)t}\right]
\end{aligned}
$$

$$
\begin{aligned}
K_{2,1}(t) &= Pr\{X_1 = 1, S_1 \le t \mid X_0 = 2\} \\
&= Pr\{repair\ of\ machine\ \mathbf{a}\ has\ completed\ by\ time\ t\} \\
&= G_a(t)
\end{aligned}
$$

$$
\begin{aligned}
K_{3,1}(t) &= Pr\{X_1 = 1, S_1 \le t \mid X_0 = 3\} \\
&= Pr\{repair\ of\ machine\ \mathbf{b}\ has\ completed\ by\ time\ t\} \\
&= G_b(t)
\end{aligned}
$$

The procedure to construct $K_{1,2}(t)$ and $K_{1,3}(t)$ deserves some further explanation. Since the reasoning is similar for both elements, we only detail the determination of $K_{1,2}(t)$. Let the random variables L_a and L_b be the respective time-to-failure of the two machines, we can compute $K_{1,2}(t)$ in the following way:

$$
\begin{aligned}
K_{1,2}(t) &= Pr\{X_1 = 2, S_1 \le t \mid X_0 = 1\} \\
&= Pr\{the\ system\ fail\ up\ to\ time\ t\ and\ machine\ \mathbf{a}
\end{aligned}
$$

$$
\begin{aligned}
&\textit{is the cause}\} \\
&= \; Pr\{L_a \le t \wedge L_b > L_a\} \\
&= \; \int_0^t \left[1 - \left(1 - e^{-\lambda_b \tau}\right)\right] d\left\{1 - e^{-\lambda_a \tau}\right\} \\
&= \; \int_0^t e^{-\lambda_b \tau} \lambda_a e^{-\lambda_a \tau} d\tau \\
&= \; \frac{\lambda_a}{\lambda_a + \lambda_b}\left[1 - e^{-(\lambda_a+\lambda_b)t}\right]
\end{aligned}
$$

We can then write the global kernel matrix as

$$
\mathbf{K}(t) =
\begin{bmatrix}
0 & \frac{\lambda_a}{\lambda_a+\lambda_b}\left[1 - e^{-(\lambda_a+\lambda_b)t}\right] & \frac{\lambda_b}{\lambda_a+\lambda_b}\left[1 - e^{-(\lambda_a+\lambda_b)t}\right] \\
G_a(t) & 0 & 0 \\
G_b(t) & 0 & 0
\end{bmatrix}
$$

We construct the local kernel matrix $\mathbf{E}(t)$ following a similar inductive procedure. In this case we are looking for the probability that the system will remain in a given state up to the next Markov renewal moment. This happens since $\{Y_t; t \in \mathcal{R}_+\}$ is an SMP, and there are no non-null elements in the main diagonal of matrix $\mathbf{K}(t)$. Therefore, elements of $\mathbf{E}(t)$ are the complementary sojourn distribution functions in each state:

$$
\mathbf{E}(t) =
\begin{bmatrix}
e^{-(\lambda_a+\lambda_b)t} & 0 & 0 \\
0 & 1 - G_a(t) & 0 \\
0 & 0 & 1 - G_b(t)
\end{bmatrix}
$$

We can always verify our answers by summing the elements in each row of both kernel matrices. Corresponding row-sums of the two matrices must add to unity, condition that is easily verified to hold in the example. Having completed the construction of the kernel matrices, we can solve a Markov renewal equation for the transient distribution of Y_t.

11.5.2. Parallel System with Single Repair Facility

Two machines (**a** and **b**) are working in a parallel configuration sharing a single repair facility working on an FCFS schedule. As in the previous case, we assume that both machines have exponential lifetime distributions with parameters λ_a and λ_b respectively. Whenever one of the machines fails it goes immediately to repair, unless the other machine is still undergoing repair. When the repair facility is busy and a second failure occurs, the second machine to fail waits in a repair queue until the first machine is put back into service.

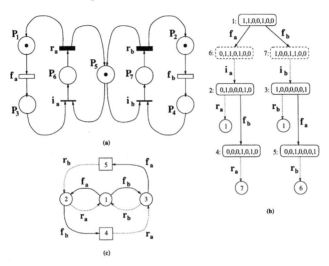

(a)

(b)

(c)

Figure 11.6: (a) Petri net of parallel system. (b) Reachability graph. (c) State transition diagram.

The procedure described in the last section can be repeated to solve this case. Figure 11.6(a) presents an appropriate MRSPN to describe the system behavior, and the corresponding reachability graph is reproduced in Figure 11.6(b). We observe in Figure 11.6(a) the same type of symmetry present in the series system. A token in place P_5 represents the availability of the single repair facility. Other extra places (P_6 and P_7) have been added to model the capture of the repair facility by the first machine to fail. We associate immediate transitions (i_a and i_b) to model the capture of the repair facility since we assume that starting a repair takes no time (if the facility is available). All the other places and transitions preserve the same semantics as in the series system.

Markings in Figure 11.6(b) are 7-tuples due to the addition of the three extra places. Another distinction from the previous system is that vanishing markings (enclosed by dashed ellipses in the diagram) also occur in the reachability graph. These markings are eliminated when the reduced reachability graph is constructed (not shown), and based on the reduced version we constructed the state transition diagram of Figure 11.6(c).

Define the stochastic process $\mathbf{Z} = \{Z_t; t \in \mathcal{R}_+\}$ to represent the system state at any instant, where

$$
Z_t = \begin{cases}
1 & \textit{if both machines are working at time } t \\
2 & \textit{if machine } \mathbf{a} \textit{ is under repair while machine } \mathbf{b} \textit{ is} \\
  & \textit{working at time } t \\
3 & \textit{if machine } \mathbf{b} \textit{ is under repair while machine } \mathbf{a} \textit{ is} \\
  & \textit{working at time } t \\
4 & \textit{if machine } \mathbf{a} \textit{ is under repair while machine } \mathbf{b} \textit{ is} \\
  & \textit{waiting for repair at time } t \\
5 & \textit{if machine } \mathbf{b} \textit{ is under repair while machine } \mathbf{a} \textit{ is} \\
  & \textit{waiting for repair at time } t
\end{cases}
$$

Analysis of the resultant (reduced) reachability graph shows that $\mathbf{Z}$ is an MRGP with an embedded Markov chain defined by the states 1, 2, and 3. We can observe that transitions to states 4 and 5 do not correspond to Markov renewal moments because they occur while timed transitions firing according non-exponential distributions are enabled. Furthermore, states 4 and 5 do not belong to the state space of the DTMC embedded in the process (EMC), therefore they are represented by squares in the state transition diagram to show this particular condition.

What makes this example particularly interesting is the fact that it allows us to demonstrate both techniques for the synthesis of the kernel matrices: the inductive and the deductive.

11.5.2.1. Inductive approach. Once identified as an MRGP, to find the distribution of $\mathbf{Z}$ we need to construct the kernel matrices. Starting with matrix $\mathbf{K}(t)$, we can identify its structure directly from Figure 11.6(c):

$$
\mathbf{K}(t) = \begin{bmatrix}
0 & K_{1,2}(t) & K_{1,3}(t) \\
K_{2,1}(t) & 0 & K_{2,3}(t) \\
K_{3,1}(t) & K_{3,2}(t) & 0
\end{bmatrix}
$$

The elements $K_{1,2}(t)$ and $K_{1,3}(t)$ are computed in a similar procedure as the correspondent elements in the series system case. Addition-
aly, since determination of elements $K_{2,1}(t)$ and $K_{2,3}(t)$ is quite alike,
so we will only show the procedure to construct $K_{2,1}(t)$. The third row
is completelly symmetrical to the second, so it can be easily undestood
once $K_{2,1}(t)$ is understood.

We need some auxiliary variables to help in the explanation of the
construction process of $K_{2,1}(t)$. Hence, we define the random variables
R_a and R_b to represent times necessary to repair machine **a** and **b**. The
distribution function of R_a (R_b) is G_a (G_b). Using this new variables
we can compute $K_{2,1}(t)$:

$$
\begin{aligned}
K_{2,1}(t) &= Pr\{X_1 = 1, S_1 \le t \mid X_0 = 2\} \\
&= Pr\{repair\ of\ \mathbf{a}\ is\ finished\ up\ to\ time\ t\ and\ \mathbf{b} \\
&\quad\quad has\ not\ failed\ during\ the\ repair\ of\ \mathbf{a}\} \\
&= Pr\{R_a \le t \wedge L_b > R_a\} \\
&= \int_0^t Pr\{L_b > \tau\} dG_a(\tau) \\
&= \int_0^t \left[1 - \left(1 - e^{-\lambda_b \tau}\right)\right] dG_a(\tau) \\
&= \int_0^t e^{-\lambda_b \tau} dG_a(\tau)
\end{aligned}
$$

The global kernel matrix inducted $\mathbf{K}(t)$ is

$$
\begin{bmatrix}
0 & \frac{\lambda_a}{\lambda_a+\lambda_b}\left[1 - e^{-(\lambda_a+\lambda_b)t}\right] & \frac{\lambda_b}{\lambda_a+\lambda_b}\left[1 - e^{-(\lambda_a+\lambda_b)t}\right] \\
\int_0^t e^{-\lambda_b \tau} dG_a(\tau) & 0 & \int_0^t \left(1 - e^{-\lambda_b \tau}\right) dG_a(\tau) \\
\int_0^t e^{-\lambda_a \tau} dG_b(\tau) & \int_0^t \left(1 - e^{-\lambda_a \tau}\right) dG_b(\tau) & 0
\end{bmatrix}
$$

Note that the global matrix is (and always is going to be) a square
matrix. In this case with dimensions 3×3, since we have 3 states
in the embedded Markov chain. However, the local kernel matrix not
necessary is a square matrix, since the cardinality of the state space of
Z can be larger than the cardinality of the state space of the embedded
Markov chain. This can be seen, for instance, in this system since

the embedded Markov chain has only 3 states while the system has 5
possible states.

The construction of the local kernel matrix for an MRGP requires
a more elaborate thinking process than for an SMP. This happens because, as explained, an MRGP can change states between two consecutive Markov renewal moments, and we need to capture these changes
through the $\mathbf{E}$ matrix. Careful analysis of Figure 11.6(c) reveals the
structure of the local kernel matrix:

$$\mathbf{E}(t) = \begin{bmatrix} E_{1,1}(t) & 0 & 0 & 0 & 0 \\ 0 & E_{2,2}(t) & 0 & E_{2,4}(t) & 0 \\ 0 & 0 & E_{3,3}(t) & 0 & E_{3,5}(t) \end{bmatrix}$$

$E_{1,1}$ should be similar to the series systems, since the system can
only go from state 1 to the other two states of the EMC exactly as in
the previous case. The difficulty comes with the induction of $E_{2,2}(t)$
and $E_{2,4}(t)$ (complement of $E_{2,2}(t)$). Once we solve for these, we have
the solution for the remaining components of the matrix due to the
symetry of the problem. Therefore, we explain the induction process
that leads to $E_{2,2}(t)$:

$$\begin{aligned} E_{2,2}(t) &= Pr\{Z_t = 2, S_1 > t \mid X_0 = 2\} \\ &= Pr\{repair\ of\ \mathbf{a}\ is\ not\ finished\ up\ to\ time\ t\ and\ \mathbf{b} \\ &\qquad has\ not\ failed\ until\ t\} \\ &= Pr\{repair\ of\ \mathbf{a}\ is\ not\ finished\ up\ to\ time\ t\} \times \\ &\qquad Pr\{\mathbf{b}\ has\ not\ failed\ until\ t\} \\ &= [1 - G_a(t)]e^{-\lambda_b t} \end{aligned}$$

We can now express the local kernel matrix as

$$\mathbf{E}(t) = \begin{bmatrix} \mathbf{E}_1(t) & \mathbf{E}_2(t) \end{bmatrix}$$

where

$$\mathbf{E}_1(t) = \begin{bmatrix} e^{-(\lambda_a + \lambda_b)t} & 0 & 0 \\ 0 & e^{-\lambda_b t} G_a^c(t) & 0 \\ 0 & 0 & e^{-\lambda_a t} G_b^c(t) \end{bmatrix}$$

$$\mathbf{E}_2(t) = \begin{bmatrix} 0 & 0 \\ \left(1 - e^{-\lambda_b t}\right) G_a^c(t) & 0 \\ 0 & \left(1 - e^{-\lambda_a t}\right) G_b^c(t) \end{bmatrix}$$

$$G_a^c(t) = 1 - G_a(t)$$

$$G_b^c(t) = 1 - G_b(t)$$

Both matrices can be verified using the procedure described in the end of the previous section. Once again, we verify that the answers attained satisfy the necessary requirement.

11.5.2.2. Deductive approach. With reference to the above discussion here we only evaluate the element of the kernel matrices related to the regenerative period starting from state 2, since there is no state transition during the subordinated process starting form state 1, and the subordinated starting from state 3 is symmetrical to the studied one.

The subordinated process starting from state 2 is a CTMC indeed, but to emphasize the generality of this approach we considered it as a SMP over the reduced state space of the subordinated process (i.e. state $2 \in \mathcal{R}$ and $4 \in \mathcal{R}$) with kernel $\mathbf{Q}(t)^*$:

$$\mathbf{Q}(t) = \begin{bmatrix} 0 & 1 - e^{-\lambda_b t} \\ 0 & 0 \end{bmatrix} \quad and \quad \mathbf{Q}^\sim(s) = \begin{bmatrix} 0 & \frac{\lambda_b}{s + \lambda_b} \\ 0 & 0 \end{bmatrix}$$

Since states 2 and 4 belongs to $\mathcal{R}$, i.e. the next regeneration can not be caused by a state transition out of $\mathcal{R}$, the matrix function $\mathbf{D}(t,w)$ does not play role (i.e. $D_{i,j}(t,w) = 0$, for $i,j \in \mathcal{E}$) in this case.

By applying equations (1) and (2) we have:

---

*For notational convenience we neglect the superscript 2 refer to the initial regeneration state in the subsequent derivations

$$(s+v)P_{22}^{\sim*}(s,v) = s/v - \lambda_b P_{22}^{\sim*}(s,v)$$

$$(s+v)P_{24}^{\sim*}(s,v) = -\lambda_b P_{24}^{\sim*}(s,v) + \lambda_b P_{44}^{\sim*}(s,v)$$

$$(s+v)P_{44}^{\sim*}(s,v) = s/v$$

Since $P_{44}^{\sim*}(s,v) = \frac{s/v}{s+v}$ we have:

$$P_{22}^{\sim*}(s,v) = \frac{s/v}{s+v+\lambda_b}$$

$$P_{24}^{\sim*}(s,v) = \frac{s/v}{s+v+\lambda_b} \frac{\lambda_b}{s+v}$$

The same steps results:

$$F_{22}^{\sim*}(s,v) = \frac{1}{s+v+\lambda_b}$$

$$F_{24}^{\sim*}(s,v) = \frac{1}{s+v+\lambda_b} \frac{\lambda_b}{s+v}$$

In time domain the sum of a the ith row of **F** plus the sum of a the ith row of **D** plus the sum of a the ith row of **P** has to equal to one for all t and w. In this double Laplace-Stieltjes and Laplace transform domain the same sum has to equal to $1/v$, which holds for $P_{22}^{\sim*}(s,v) + P_{24}^{\sim*}(s,v) + F_{22}^{\sim*}(s,v) + F_{24}^{\sim*}(s,v)$.

To implement equations (3) and (4) a symbolic inverse Laplace transformation is necessary with respect to v. Whenever the subordinated process is a CTMC with binary reward rates this step can be performed symbolically.[46]

The inverse Laplace transformation with respect to v results in:

$$P_{22}^{\sim}(s,w) = \frac{s}{s+\lambda_b}[1 - e^{-(s+\lambda_b)w}]$$

$$P_{24}^{\sim}(s,w) = \frac{\lambda_b}{s+\lambda_b} - e^{-sw} + \frac{s}{s+\lambda_b}e^{-(s+\lambda_b)w}$$

$$F_{22}^{\sim}(s,w) = e^{-(s+\lambda_b)w}$$

$$F_{24}^{\sim}(s,w) = e^{-sw} - e^{-(s+\lambda_b)w}$$

Hence by (3) and (4), the non-zero kernel elements are:

$$E_{22}^{\sim}(s) = \int_{w=0}^{\infty} P_{22}^{\sim}(s,w)dG_a(w)$$
$$= \frac{s}{s+\lambda_b}[1 - G_a^{\sim}(s+\lambda_b)]$$

$$E_{24}^{\sim}(s) = \int_{w=0}^{\infty} P_{24}^{\sim}(s,w)dG_a(w)$$
$$= \frac{\lambda_b}{s+\lambda_b} - G_a^{\sim}(s) + \frac{s}{s+\lambda_b}G_a^{\sim}(s+\lambda_b)$$

$$K_{21}^{\sim}(s) = \int_{w=0}^{\infty} F_{22}^{\sim}(s,w)dG_a(w)$$
$$= G_a^{\sim}(s+\lambda_b)$$

$$K_{23}^{\sim}(s) = \int_{w=0}^{\infty} F_{24}^{\sim}(s,w)dG_a(w)$$
$$= G_a^{\sim}(s) - G_a^{\sim}(s+\lambda_b)$$

The Laplace transform of the relevant entries of $\mathbf{E}(t)$ and $\mathbf{K}(t)$ reached by the inductive method results in the same expressions. Finally the LST domain description of the kernel matrices are:

$$\mathbf{K}^{\sim}(s) = \begin{bmatrix} 0 & \frac{\lambda_a}{s+\lambda_a+\lambda_b} & \frac{\lambda_b}{s+\lambda_a+\lambda_b} \\ G_a^{\sim}(s+\lambda_b) & 0 & G_a^{\sim}(s) - G_a^{\sim}(s+\lambda_b) \\ G_b^{\sim}(s+\lambda_a) & G_b^{\sim}(s) - G_b^{\sim}(s+\lambda_a) & 0 \end{bmatrix}$$

$$\mathbf{E}^{\sim}(s) = \begin{bmatrix} \mathbf{E_1}^{\sim}(s) & \mathbf{E_2}^{\sim}(s) \end{bmatrix}$$

where

$$\mathbf{E_1}^{\sim}(s) = \begin{bmatrix} \frac{s}{s+\lambda_a+\lambda_b} & 0 & 0 \\ 0 & E_{22}^{\sim}(s) & 0 \\ 0 & 0 & \frac{s}{s+\lambda_a}[1 - G_b^{\sim}(s+\lambda_a)] \end{bmatrix}$$

and

$$\mathbf{E_2}^{\sim}(s) = \left[\begin{array}{cc} 0 & 0 \\ E_{24}^{\sim}(s) & 0 \\ 0 & \frac{\lambda_a}{s+\lambda_a} - G_b^{\sim}(s) + \frac{s}{s+\lambda_a}G_b^{\sim}(s+\lambda_a) \end{array} \right]$$

11.5.3. Warm Standby with Single Repair Facility

Two statistically identical machines ("X" and "Y") are working in a warm standby configuration sharing a single repair facility working on an FCFS schedule. If both machines are available, one of the is active on-line, while the other one is active off-line (spare). Machine "X" is the active one and "Y" the spare on the initial condition of the system. An active machine has constant failure rate λ_a, while the machine acting as spare has constant failure rate λ_b (usually $\lambda_a \leq \lambda_b$). If the on-line (off-line) machine fails, its repair begins immediately and completely restores it during a random repair time having an arbitrary distribution function G_a (G_b), and the other component continues to work on-line. We assume that the switchover from the active to the spare machine takes no time. Similarly to the parallel case, when the repair facility is busy and a second failure occurs, the actions on the last machine to fail are postponed until the other machine is put back into service.

The MRSPN on Figure 11.7(a) describes the expected system behavior. We can then construct the correspondent reachability graph, which is reproduced in Figure 11.7(b). A token in place P_1 represents that the machine working as active is in operational condition. When the active machine fails a token is placed in P_3, and then repairs begin immediately in the failed machine while a switchover to the spare machine is executed. A token in place P_2 indicates that the spare machine is available for switchover, but since we assume that the spare machine can also fail, we included place P_4 to capture this situation. Place P_5 has a token whenever a switchover has just ocurred and the failed machine (previous active machine) is undergoing repairs. This place has been included to capture the difference in distribution functions associated with repair of active and spare machines.

Similarly to the previous case, we observe the occurrence of vanishing markings (enclosed by dashed ellipses in the diagram). This marking occurs because of the zero time switchover, and is eliminated

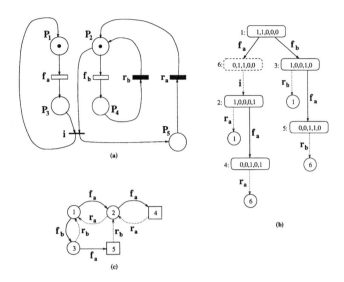

Figure 11.7: (a) Petri net of warm standby system. (b) Reachability graph. (c) State transition diagram.

when the reduced reachability graph is constructed. Based on the reduced reachability graph we constructed the state transition diagram of Figure 11.7(c).

Define the random sequence $\mathbf{Z} = \{Z_t; t \in \mathcal{R}_+\}$ to represent the system state at any instant, where

$$
Z_t = \begin{cases}
1 & \text{if active and spare are working at time } t \\
2 & \text{if previous active is under repair while spare is} \\
  & \text{working at time } t \\
3 & \text{if spare is under repair while active is working} \\
  & \text{at time } t \\
4 & \text{if active has failed while the previous active is} \\
  & \text{under repair at time } t \\
5 & \text{if active has failed while the spare is under repair} \\
  & \text{at time } t
\end{cases}
$$

Analysis of the resultant (reduced) reachability graph shows that $\mathbf{Z}$ is an MRGP with an embedded Markov chain defined by the states 1,

2, and 3. We can observe that transitions to states 4 and 5 do not correspond to Markov renewal moments, therefore they were represented by squares in the state transition diagram. Markings $< 0, 0, 1, 0, 1 >$ and $< 0, 0, 1, 1, 0 >$ (states 4 and 5 in the transition diagram) represent the failure states of the system: one machine has failed when the other is still undergoing repair.

Once identified as an MRGP, we need to construct the kernel matrices to find the transition probability distributions of $\mathbf{Z}$. Starting with matrix $\mathbf{K}(t)$, we can identify its structure directly from Figure 11.7(c):

$$\mathbf{K}(t) = \begin{bmatrix} 0 & K_{1,2}(t) & K_{1,3}(t) \\ K_{2,1}(t) & K_{2,2}(t) & 0 \\ K_{3,1}(t) & K_{3,2}(t) & 0 \end{bmatrix}$$

The computation of all the non-zero elements of the global kernel matrix proceeds similarly to the series and parallel system. Therefore, we can induce the following global kernel matrix $\mathbf{K}(t)$:

$$\begin{bmatrix} 0 & \frac{\lambda_a}{\lambda_a + \lambda_b}\left[1 - e^{-(\lambda_a + \lambda_b)t}\right] & \frac{\lambda_b}{\lambda_a + \lambda_b}\left[1 - e^{-(\lambda_a + \lambda_b)t}\right] \\ \int_0^t e^{-\lambda_a \tau} dG_a(\tau) & \int_0^t \left(1 - e^{-\lambda_a \tau}\right) dG_a(\tau) & 0 \\ \int_0^t e^{-\lambda_a \tau} dG_b(\tau) & \int_0^t \left(1 - e^{-\lambda_a \tau}\right) dG_b(\tau) & 0 \end{bmatrix}$$

Likewise, we can express the local kernel matrix as

$$\mathbf{E}(t) \begin{bmatrix} \mathbf{E}_1(t) & \mathbf{E}_2(t) \end{bmatrix}$$

where

$$\mathbf{E}_1(t) = \begin{bmatrix} e^{-(\lambda_a + \lambda_b)t} & 0 & 0 \\ 0 & e^{-\lambda_a t} G_a^c(t) & 0 \\ 0 & 0 & e^{-\lambda_a t} G_b^c(t) \end{bmatrix}$$

$$\mathbf{E}_2(t) = \begin{bmatrix} 0 & 0 \\ \left(1 - e^{-\lambda_a t}\right) G_a^c(t) & 0 \\ 0 & \left(1 - e^{-\lambda_a t}\right) G_b^c(t) \end{bmatrix}$$

$$G_a^c(t) = 1 - G_a(t)$$

$$G_b^c(t) = 1 - G_b(t)$$

The subordinated process starting from state 3 is similar to the parallel system example just discussed. The subordinated process starting from state 2 differs a bit because the failure intensity during the repair of component a is λ_a while it was λ_b in the parallel system, hence we can reach the elements (and all the derivation) of the 2nd row of matrices $\mathbf{E}(t)$ and $\mathbf{K}(t)$ by substituting λ_b by λ_a in the results (derivations) of the previous section.

11.5.4. Numerical Results

For completeness of our analysis, the Markov renewal equations corresponding to the selected examples were solved for numerical values. Deterministic repair-time distribution functions were considered in all three examples, i.e.,

$$G_a(t) = u(t - \mu_a), \qquad \mu_a > 0$$

$$G_b(t) = u(t - \mu_b), \qquad \mu_b > 0$$

where $u(t)$ is the unitary step function. Table 1 summarizes the numerical values for parameters used in the computations. The units are hours for repair-time (parameters μ_a and μ_b) and hour^{-1} for the failure rates (parameters λ_a and λ_b). In the standby case, the failure rate of the spare unit was made lower than the failure rate of the active unit to characterize the warm standby situation.

A Laplace-Stieltjes transform method was adopted to solve the Markov renewal equation, which in LST domain becomes

$$\mathbf{V}^\sim(s) = \mathbf{E}^\sim(s) + \mathbf{K}^\sim(s)\mathbf{V}^\sim(s)$$

The time domain probabilities were calculated by first deriving the matrix $\mathbf{V}^\sim(s)$ using a standard package for symbolic analysis (e.g., MATHEMATICA), and then numerically inverting the resulting LST expressions resorting to the Jagerman's method.[47]

Table 11.1: Parameters used in the numerical solutions.

example	λ_a	λ_b	μ_a	μ_b
Series System	.01	.01	5	5
Parallel System	.01	.01	5	5
Standby System	.01	.001	5	5

Figures 8, 9, and 10 report availability and performability results for all examples under the parameters established. Following the approach used in [48], we also ploted corresponding Markovian system results, where each deterministic firing transition was replaced by an equivalent 25-stage Erlang distribution. The Markovian models were solved using the Stochastic Petri Net Package (SPNP) introduced in [49].

As expected the plots reflect better availability for the warm standby system, followed by the parallel system. However, when considered from the interval power available, the situation reverses. The series system with repair provides more available power during a given interval than the parallel or warm standby systems.

11.6. CONCLUSIONS

An overview of Markov renewal theory was presented to introduce a promising alternative for the performability analysis of non-Markovian models. Our emphasis was to clarify the distinction between semi-Markov and Markov regenerative processes, and to establish a methodical approach on how to identify and prepare for the solution of problems involving the mentioned stochastic processes.

Although the development of adequate numerical approaches for the analysis of these models still require further efforts, we studied two approaches for the analytical formulation of systems behavior, and two methods for their analysis.

The major contribution of this chapter is the didactic structure adopted to present and discuss performability analysis in the context of non-Markovian systems. Essential examples of performability analysis of series, parallel and warm standby systems were elaborated to show the phases of applications of the introduced theoretical results.

The whole solution process associated with each of the examples was described in detail aiming to suggest a methodological approach when dealing with Markov renewal theory. Stochastic Petri nets were used to support the analyses of the examples and facilitate their understanding.

REFERENCES

1. J.F. MEYER, "Performability: a retrospective and some pointers to the future," Performance Evaluation, **14**, 139–156 (1992).

2. J. GRAY AND D.P. SIEWIOREK, "High-Availability Computer Systems," Computer, **24**, 39–48 (1991).

3. M. BEAUDRY, "Performance related reliability for computer systems," IEEE Transactions on Computers, **C-27**, 540–547 (1978).

4. J.F. MEYER, "On evaluating the performability of degradable computer systems," IEEE Transactions on Computers, **C-29**, 720–731 (1980).

5. J.K. MUPPALA, S. WOOLET, AND K.S. TRIVEDI, "Real-Time Systems Performance in the Presence of Failures," Computer, **24**, 37–47 (1991).

6. K.S. TRIVEDI, Probability and Statistics with Reliability, Queuing, and Computer Science Applications (Prentice-Hall, Englewood-Cliffs, 1982).

7. D.P. SIEWIOREK, "Architecture of Fault–Tolerant Computers: An Historical Perspective," Procedings of the IEEE, **79**, 1710–1734 (1991).

8. K.S. TRIVEDI, J.K. MUPPALA, S.P. WOOLET, AND B.R. HAVERKORT, "Composite performance and dependability analysis," Performance Evaluation, **14**, 197–215 (1992).

9. S. KARLIN AND H.M. TAYLOR, A First Course in Stochastic Processes (Academic Press, San Diego, 2nd. ed., 1975).

10. R.F. BOTTA, C.M. HARRIS, AND W.G. MARCHAL, "Characterizations of Generalized Hyperexponential Distribution Functions," Communications in Statistics - Stochastic Models, **3**, 115–148 (1987).

11. M.F. NEUTS, "Renewal Processes of Phase Type," Naval Research Logistics Quarterly, **25**, 445–454 (1978).

12. D.R. COX, "The analysis of non–markovian stochastic processes by the inclusion of supplementary variables," Proceedings of the Cambridge Phylosophical Society, **51**, 433–440 (1955).

13. P. FRANKEN, D. KONIG, U. ARNDT, AND V. SCHMIDT, Queues and Point Processes (Akademie-Verlag, Berlin, 1981).

14. T. ROLSKI, "Stationary random processes associated with point processes," Lecture Notes in Statistics (Springer–Verlag, 1981), **5**.

15. V.S. KOROLYUK, "Markov Renewal Sequences in Reliability Analysis," in Semi–Markov Models. Theory and Applications, edited by Jacques Jansen (Plenum Press, New York, 1986), 217–230.

16. P. FRANKEN AND A. STRELLER, "Stochastic Processes with an Embedded Point Process and their Application to System Reliability Analysis," in Semi-Markov Models. Theory and Applications, edited by Jacques Jansen (Plenum Press, New York, 1986) 253–279.

17. D.R. COX, Renewal Theory (Methuen & Co., London, 1970).

18. H. CHOI, V.G. KULKARNI, AND K.S. TRIVEDI, "Markov Regenerative Stochastic Petri Nets," Performance Evaluation, **20**, 337–357 (1994).

19. E. ÇINLAR, "Markov Renewal Theory," Adv. Appl. Prob., **1**, 123–187 (1969).

20. E. ÇINLAR, Introduction to Stochastic Processes (Prentice-Hall, Englewood Cliffs, 1975).

21. V.G. KULKARNI, Modeling and Analysis of Stochastic Systems (Chapman & Hall, London, 1995).

22. W. FELLER, An Introduction to Probability Theory and its Applications. Vol II (John Wiley & Sons, 2nd. ed., 1966).

23. W.L. SIMTH, "Renewal Theory and its Ramifications," J. Roy. Statist. Soc. - Ser B, **20**, 243–302 (1958).

24. W.L. SIMTH, 'Regenerative Stochastic Processes," Proc. Roy. Soc. London - Ser A, **232**, 6–31 (1955).

25. W.L. SIMTH, "Remarks on the paper "Regenerative Stochastic Processes," Proc. Roy. Soc. London - Ser A, **256**, 496–501 (1960).

26. P. LÉVY, "Systèmes Semi–Markoviens à au plus une infinité dénombrable d'états possibles," in Proc. Int. Congr. Math. (Amsterdam, 1954), **2**, 294.

27. P. LÉVY, "Processus semi–Markoviens," in Proc. Int. Congr. Math. (Amsterdam, 1954), **3**, 416–426.

28. L. TAKÁCS, "Some Investigations Concerning Recurrent Stochastic Processes of a Certain Type," Magyar Tud. Akad. Mat. Kutató Int. Közl, 115–128 (1954).

29. R. PYKE, "Markov Renewal Sequencees: Definitions and Preliminary Properties," Ann. Math. Statist., **32**, 1231–1242 (1961).

30. R. PYKE, "Markov Renewal Sequences with Finitely Many States," Ann. Math. Statist., **32**, 1243–1259 (1961).

31. R. PYKE, AND R. SCHAUFELE, "The Existence and Uniqueness of Stationary Measures for Markov Renewal Sequences," Ann. Math. Statist., **37**, 1439–1462 (1966).

32. MIKLÓS TELEK, Some advanced reliability modelling techniques, Phd Thesis (Hungarian Academy of Science, 1994).

33. R. GERMAN AND C. LINDEMANN, "Analysis of deterministic and stochastic Petri nets by the method of supplementary variables," Performance Evaluation, **20**, 317–335 (1994).

34. A. BOBBIO AND M. TELEK, "Markov regenerative SPN with non-overlapping activity cycles," in <u>International Computer Performance and Dependability Symposium - IPDS95</u> (1995).

35. G. CIARDO, R. GERMAN, AND C. LINDEMANN, "A characterization of the stochastic process underlying a stochastic Petri net," <u>IEEE Transactions on Software Engineering</u>, **20**, 506–515 (1994).

36. A. BOBBIO, V.G. KULKARNI, A. PULIAFITO, M. TELEK, AND K.S. TRIVEDI, "Preemptive repeat identical transitions in Markov regenerative stochastic Petri nets," in <u>Petri Net Performance Models '95</u> (1995).

37. C. FRÖBERG, <u>Introduction to Numerical Analysis</u> (Addison-Wesley, Reading, 2nd. ed., 1969).

38. R. GERMAN, D. LOGOTHETIS, AND K. TRIVEDI, "Transient analysis of Markov Regenerative Stochastic Petri Nets: A Comparison of Approaches," in <u>Petri Net Performance Models '95</u> (1995).

39. R. GERMAN, "Transient Analysis of deterministic and stochastic Petri nets by the method of supplementary variables," in <u>MASCOT'95</u> (1995).

40. M.K. MOLLOY, "Performance Analysis using Stochastic Petri Nets," <u>IEEE Trans. Comput.</u>, **C-31**, 913–917 (1982).

41. M. AJMONE MARSAN, G. CONTE, AND G. BALBO, "A Class of Generalized Stochastic Petri Net for the Performance Evaluation of Multiprocessor Systems," <u>ACM Trans. Comput. Syst.</u>, **2**, 93–122 (1984).

42. J.B. DUNGAN, K.S. TRIVEDI, R.M. GEIST, AND V.F. NICOLA, "Extended Stochastic Petri Nets: Applications and Analysis," in <u>Performance'84</u>, edited by E. Gelembe (Elsevier Science Publishers B.V., Amsterdam, 1985), 507–519.

43. M. AJMONE MARSAN AND G. CHIOLA, "On Petri nets with deterministic and exponentially distributed firing times," <u>Lecture Notes in Computer Science</u>, **266**, 132–145 (1987).

44. J.L. PETERSON, Petri Net Theory and the Modeling of Systems (Prentice-Hall, Englewood Cliffs, 1981).

45. J.L. PETERSON, "Petri Nets," Computing Surveys, **9**, 223–252 (1977).

46. M. TELEK, A. BOBBIO, L. JEREB, A. PULIAFITO, AND K.S. TRIVEDI, "Steady state analysis of Markov Regenerative SPN with age memory policy," in MMB '95 (1995).

47. D.L. JAGERMAN, "An Inversion Technique for the Laplace Transform," The Bell System Technical Journal, **61**, 1995–2002 (1986).

48. D. LOGOTHETIS AND K.S TRIVEDI, "Time–Dependent Behavior of Redundant Systems with Deterministic Repair," in Computations with Markov Chains, edited by W.J. Stewart (Kluwer Academic Publishers, Norwell, 1995), 135–150.

49. G. CIARDO, J. MUPPALA, AND K.S. TRIVEDI, "SPNP: Stochastic Petri net Package," in Proc. Int. Workshop on Petri Nets and Perf. Models, (IEEE Computer Society Press, Los Alamos, 1989), 142–150.

SPNP results:

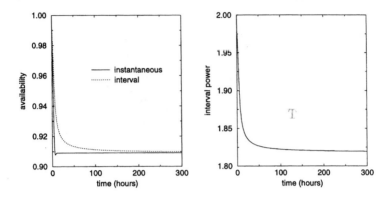

LST results:

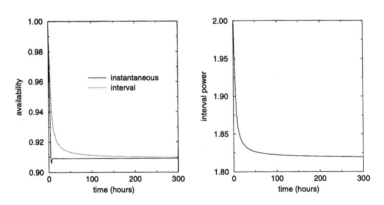

Figure 11. 8 - Numerical results for the series system.

SPNP results:

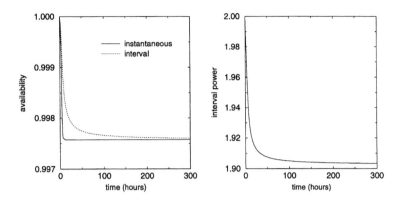

LST results:

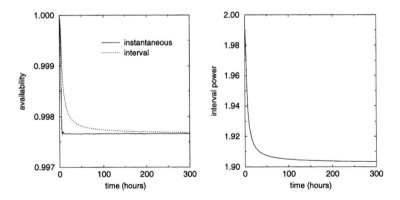

Figure 11. 9 - Numerical results for the parallel system with single repair.

SPNP results:

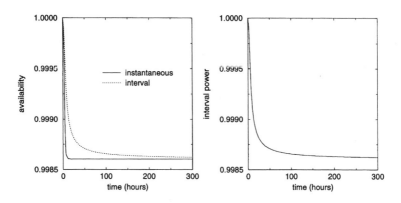

LST results:

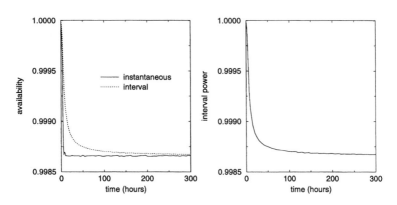

Figure 11. 10 - Numerical results for the warm standby system with single
repair.

CHAPTER 12

MODELING AND DISTRIBUTED SIMULATION TECHNIQUES FOR SYNTHETIC TRAINING ENVIRONMENTS

David B. Cavitt, C. Michael Overstreet, and Kurt J. Maly

Synthetic Training Environments (STE) can be used to teach people to function within complex systems without the real-world limitations of safety, cost, training areas, or personnel. A cost-effective technique for creating these environments is to integrate a distributed system of computer simulations, virtual environments, and live participants. This chapter characterizes the distributed simulation component of a synthetic training environment. It identifies salient issues for modeling and simulation for a distributed environment and discusses how this technology is currently used in synthetic training environments. Distributed simulations for the training environment require modeling of physical systems, environments, and human behaviors. In addition to the system models, a successful distributed simulation will have many specialized components, including user interfaces, graphics, networking, databases, and simulation management. Software design and implementation is complicated by issues such as complex interactions among models, real-time man-in-loop requirements, and transparently integrating real systems with virtual components so the STE presents a consistent and realistic virtual environment. One successful application of a simulation training tool is ModSAF, built by Loral Advanced Distributed Simulation. It is a Distributed Interactive Simulation (DIS) used for military training and combat doctrine development. ModSAF simulates the hierarchy of military units and their associated behaviors, combat vehicles, and weapons systems. The design provides an open, extensible software architecture, has proven to be scalable, provides fault tolerance, exhibits good transparency, and successfully allows for man-in-loop interactions to provide supervisory control of the situation being simulated. ModSAF provides a useful case study to examine key issues in using distributed simulation for training.

12.1. INTRODUCTION

Training people to function within complex systems has necessitated the use of computer systems to create synthetic training environments. STE provide realistic training environments that can reduce training costs, control personnel and training area requirements, and in potentially hazardous training environments increase safety. Synthetic training environments have been successfully used in many application domains. Examples include training personnel and developing tactical plans for the extraction and rescue of hostages, training astronauts to operate equipment and work in a weightless environment (space), and military combat training and doctrine development. STE consist of humans interacting with a virtual environment for the purpose of experimentation, study, or evaluation. Some STE rely solely on manned simulators or mock-ups to create the virtual environment. For some applications, having real-world entities (e.g., humans, animals, automobiles) participate in or contribute to the virtual environment is feasible and adds to the effectiveness of the training environment. For STE that need many entities, a cost-effective technique is to rely on computer simulations to create and populate the virtual environment. Many STE incorporate all three components; virtual simulators (mock-ups and manned simulators), live participants, and computer simulations. Although technical issues and limitations still exist, the increased performance and reliability of computers, local-area networks (LANs), and wide-area networks (WANs), allows these components to be geographically dispersed, sometimes across continents, and still participate in the STE.

The technology used to create virtual environments is still emerging and as people create more complex, higher fidelity environments with more entities, hardware and software limitations become restrictive. Manned simulators are typically big and expensive, limiting their effectiveness for large-scale training environments. For training exercises that require many live participants the logistics of including the personnel can be significant. Simulations provide the capability to consistently and accurately reproduce training exercises for the purposes of experimentation, evaluation, and analysis. When computer simulations are used in STE, the simulation processing requirements are frequently partitioned among many independent simulation nodes resulting in what is called *Distributed Simulation*. A significant benefit of using distributed simulations in STE is its ability to enhance realism by populating the STE with simulated entities and by implementing selective model fidelity defining and controlling the faithfulness with which real-world objects are represented. Distributed simulations must include models that provide the trainee with a perception of the real-world system at a level of realism sufficient for the goals of the training exercise.

Physical models in distributed simulation represent real-world entities, objects, or subsystems. A physical model has a state that represents real-world properties and where applicable defines an interface for interaction with other physical models. Consider an STE consisting of a virtual battlefield-simulation. The virtual battlefield simulates tanks (real-world entities) and specifies their sizes, traveling speeds, and armaments (state and properties). Each tank model has weapons and sensor interfaces that allow these subsystem states to be used to make decisions about when detections and engagements with enemy vehicles occur (interactions with another physical model). Behavioral models for STE are required to simulate collective or individual human behaviors that control the STE physical models. These behaviors may be responses to some change in state of the virtual environment. In the above example, the execution of a behavioral model simulating the engagement of an enemy vehicle is a response to a simulation event detecting that vehicle. Since most real-world systems are not closed systems, distributed simulations used in STE will typically provide some form of environmental models to enhance realism. Again using the virtual battlefield-simulation example, including environmental models is necessary because in a real-world battlefield smoke, darkness, clouds, and dust contribute significantly to the effectiveness of sensor systems, weapons systems, and vehicle movement, as well as effecting human perception and performance. These physical, behavioral, and environmental models must provide an adequate representation of the real-world system with properties at the correct fidelity level and allow realistic perception, interaction, and interpretation by the trainees operating within the STE.

Aside from model design and implementation, many technical issues exist with distributed simulation software infrastructure. Many of these are driven by the requirements for real-time man-in-loop capabilities for geographically dispersed players and valid interactions among the live, virtual, and simulation components of the STE. Design decisions for the many components (networking, databases, parametric data, timing and coordination, simulation management and control, graphics and user interfaces, tracing and data logging, and security and protection) affect performance, reliability, scalability, and other important aspects of the system. Additionally, the design and implementation must incorporate the characteristics that define good distributed systems software. These characteristics include open hardware and software architectures, concurrency and performance, scalability, fault tolerance and availability, and transparency.

The purpose of this chapter is to identify issues surrounding modeling and simulation techniques for distributed simulations in STE and illustrate how those techniques are used in a real application. Since many diverse yet interrelated modeling, design, and implementation issues exist, for this discussion it is useful to classify and organize them into two taxonomies. These taxonomies are not inclusive of all issues that are considered and are not sufficient for a complete and detailed study. However this chapter is a survey and the taxonomies provide a framework for our discussion. Figure 12.1 shows a taxonomy of the primary aspects of modeling that are discussed in this chapter. In Section 12.2 we discuss the issues relevant to model realism, fidelity, and validation. This introduction includes definitions of model types and Section 12.2 discusses aspects of behavioral models. Section 12.4.4, the case study, provides examples of physical, behavioral, and environmental model types. This chapter's discussion on distributed simulation design and implementation is outlined by Figure 12.2. Section 12.3 considers the networking, database, and graphics portions of the taxonomy with examples in Sections 12.4.2 and 12.4.4. Timing and coordination, and supervisory control are discussed throughout the chapter.

As mentioned, Section 12.4 provides a case study and illustrates how these technologies are applied in ModSAF, a Distributed Interactive Simulation (DIS) used in military synthetic training environments. ModSAF has been successfully used on an international wide-area network (WAN) interconnecting hundreds of UNIX workstations, manned simulators, and live military units (e.g., battalions of ground troops and

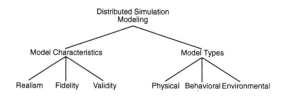

FIGURE 12.1. Distributed Simulation Modeling Taxonomy

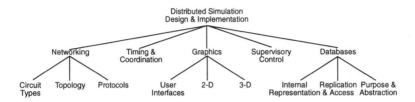

FIGURE 12.2. Distributed Simulation Design & Implementation Taxonomy

carrier battlegroups). During actual military training and evaluation exercises, ModSAF has simulated up to 5000 military combat vehicles and their associated hierarchy of command and control units. On-going development of ModSAF and open research issues are discussed in Sections 12.4.5 and 12.5. A chapter summary is presented in Section 12.6.

12.2. MODEL REALISM, FIDELITY, AND VALIDITY

Realism is the trainee's impression of how closely the model replicates the real-world system; model fidelity is the accuracy and correctness of the representation. Validation is the process of determining if the fidelity provided by the model adequately represents the real-world system for the purpose of the simulation. An important aspect of distributed simulation is determining what level of model fidelity is adequate to meet the objectives of an exercise. The level of fidelity achieved must be determined based on a trade-off in the simulation's performance and the effectiveness of the simulation in achieving the training goals. Proposals for various methodologies used to determine model fidelity are in Foster[9,10], Prasad[26], and Harvey[27]. A component of STE and simulation models that contributes to model realism and fidelity is equipment cues that give a real-world look and feel from an operator's viewpoint. Examples of equipment cues are the tactile feedback of an aircraft control stick or the presentation of instrument dials on a virtual cockpit interface. Environmental cues provide duplication of real-world environments including visual and motion sensation such as seeing clouds and rain in a virtual scene of the atmosphere or the sensation of banking when an aircraft changes direction.

Model fidelity from an objective viewpoint describes the model in terms of its ability to duplicate reality. Perceptual fidelity considers the simulation from the trainee's view and how well the model represents the real-world system. Both perceptual and objective fidelity are used to establish criteria to evaluate fidelity and are based on both quantitative and qualitative aspects of the model. Examples of quantitative aspects are timing delays affecting model interaction, consistency of model data with empirical data from the real-world system, and static and dynamic characteristics of the model representation. Examples of qualitative criteria are the trainee's response to the system and the level of immersion that the trainee experiences while in the STE. Defining fidelity criteria requires a very careful distinction between the different uses of the simulation be it for training, research, evaluation, or acquisition.

Modeling realistic behaviors is done in many ways; aggregating the effects of the collective behaviors of many entities using probabilistic methods or simulating entity-level behaviors and using them in a more deterministic way to effect the overall simulation state. Behavioral models in distributed simulation generally refer to human behaviors, but can also be considered activities associated with any actions that affect changes to entity state. The inevitable trade-offs in the cost of implementation and performance require a variable level of automation to control entity behaviors. The level of control ranges from semi-automated behaviors requiring some degree of human intervention to a fully-automated behavior that is completely controlled by the computer simulation. The benefits of fully-automated control can be significant in an STE populated with many entities. Current research by the AI community includes the use of SOAR intelligent agents to create and manage fully-automated entity behaviors as discussed in Tambe[15]. The benefit of implementing SOAR in distributed simulations, for example, allows a simulated aircraft to be assigned a mission and to completely carry out that mission without any intervention from a person controlling the STE.

Model validation is difficult and many paradigms are used to assess STE representations of reality. Timing and coordination requirements of distributed simulations add to model complexity and make validation more difficult. A methodology for determining valid entity interactions is discussed by Harvey[27] and is based on a comparison of a model's functional requirements and the outputs from knowledge acquisition and knowledge engineering processes. A low-level analysis proposed by Foster[9,10] develops a model to determine allowable error rates for transmitting entity state information to assure valid model interactions.

12.3. DISTRIBUTED SIMULATION ARCHITECTURE AND DESIGN

The software architecture of a distributed simulation must be carefully designed. Particularly for simulations that model large space and time components of real-world systems. Some synthetic training environments have real-time processing requirements which increase the complexity of distributed simulation architecture and design.

Local-area, wide-area, and long-haul networks and their reliability, throughput, packet loss rates, and message latencies affect the design of the distributed simulation components. Many distributed simulations operate in their own dedicated network to avoid resource contention and provide the real-time performance required for realistic STE. Figure 12.3 shows the Defense Simulation Internet (DSI), an integrated long-haul network designed to support real-time, distributed interactive simulation and funded by the U.S. Department of Defense (DoD).

The DSI backbone is connected by hubs that allow different simulation sites (LANs) to connect to the DSI. The backbone circuit technology uses multiple T1 lines to achieve aggregate bandwidths of around 6 Mbps. The T1 lines are to be upgraded to T3 (45 Mbps) in the near future. The near-term goal of the Department of Defense is for the network to support distributed simulations for training exercises using hundreds of UNIX workstations and simulating up to 50,000 dynamic, interacting entities (e.g., tanks, aircraft, infantry). On-going research is exploring use of fiber-optics for the backbone circuits. Lower-level communications protocols used on the DSI include UDP, TCP, Ethernet, and ATM. Distributed simulations typically define their own higher-level communications protocols to share simulation data such as entity information (vehicle positions and orientation), entity interaction information (notification of weapons detonation), environment information (rain on the horizon), and simulation control information (request to simulate a vehicle). The Distributed Interactive Simulation (DIS) protocol used by nodes on the DSI network is discussed in IEEE standard 1278-1993.[1]

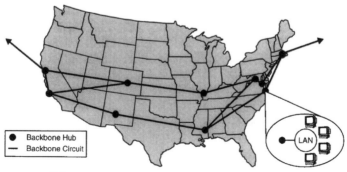

FIGURE 12.3. Defense Simulation Internet (DSI)

STE require large databases of information that must be accessed frequently. To reduce access latencies distributed simulations typically replicate these databases, requiring frequent updates by all the simulation nodes to maintain a consistent virtual environment. Dynamic characteristics of the simulation such as frequency of access have a dramatic effect on simulation performance. The internal representation also effects the utility and performance of the distributed simulation's databases. For many STE the largest and most complex databases are those that model real-world space and environment such as terrain or atmospheric models. Different representations attempt to balance differing levels of fidelity and resolution with factors affecting the speed of database searches, memory requirements, and storage requirements. Terrain databases used primarily to create graphical visualizations (such as in manned simulators) use polygonal representations that are optimized for quick rendering and display of two-dimensional and three-dimensional terrain representations. However, in distributed simulations where entities are continually interacting with their surroundings, alternative representations must support data abstractions at differing levels of resolution, be organized spatially to reduce database search costs, and be expandable to allow new static and dynamic objects to be included in the representation. The representation must not, however, result in conflicting views of the virtual environment among interacting entities. Quadtree representations and Compact Terrain Database (CTDB) representations discussed in Stanzione,[23] and Smith,[24] provide examples.

Other types of database abstractions consist of parametric data that provide a means of altering the run-time characteristics of distributed simulations without altering the simulation's implementation and infrastructure. Data-driven execution allows for dynamic reparameterization of simulation entity characteristics and behaviors which is important when common models are reused for training and evaluation.

Graphics, user interfaces, and data presentation contribute significantly to the success of distributed simulations in achieving an adequate perception of reality. Maintaining the graphics displays can be a computationally expensive portion of the STE. Two-dimensional and three-dimensional visual environments are used depending on the requirements for human interaction. Presenting data as meaningful information for the trainee and doing it within the constraints of a real-time system can be challenging to design and implement. Stytz[20] presents a 3-D visualization environment for immersing a human operator within a virtual battlefield-simulation, allowing free or tethered (attached to simulation objects) movement within the virtual environment.

Other software design and implementation issues must be considered for distributed simulations in STE. Timing and coordination aspects of distributed simulation are significant. Distributed simulations typically exhibit high-degrees of concurrency and entity dependencies and interactions require proper synchronization of simulation events to duplicate the real-world ordering of actions and responses. Absolute time-stamps remove inconsistencies between the perceived virtual environments of distributed simulations. Katz[14] proposes an empirical approach for determining the accuracy of timestamps to correlate events among simulations nodes. Simulation management and control functions are responsible for the proper execution of the simulation. This includes proper configuration of the simulation models and STE interfaces. Cleveland[28] discusses a mechanism for implementing control of entities intentionally leaving and entering a training exercise. These intentional connects and disconnects from a DIS exercise under the supervisory control of simulation manager must be considered in a realistic training environment that includes live participants. Tracing and data logging is important because it allows analysts and STE users to characterize and assess the performance of the distributed simulation as well as the performance of the trainee. Since large amounts of data can be generated, distributed simulations must be able to gather and store measured data and where required aggregate the data and present it as meaningful information for analysis.

12.4.   CASE STUDY: MODSAF DISTRIBUTED INTERACTIVE SIMULATION

12.4.1. Background

Modular Semi-Automated Forces (ModSAF) is a commercially developed distributed simulation used by the military for combat training and for tactics and military doctrine development. ModSAF uses a synthetic battlefield-simulation environment based on Distributed Interactive Simulation (DIS) technology which is presented in DIS Steering Committee[18]. This technology utilizes a network of independent simulation nodes communicating with each other using the DIS protocol. ModSAF is used to create computer-generated forces within the synthetic training environment which also incorporates live participants and virtual training simulators. The Advanced Research Project Agency (ARPA) is providing much of the guidance and funding for research in DIS technology. In the late 1980s, in conjunction with the Army, ARPA successfully demonstrated the capabilities of DIS in synthetic training environments during the development of SIMNET, a technology demonstration that populated a virtual battlefield with up to 1000 entities and military units.

To create a realistic synthetic training environment the virtual battlefield must be populated with many individual combatants and military units. ModSAF's computer-generated forces provide this capability, only simulating the external behavior of military units and their component vehicle and weapon systems to a level of realism sufficient to meet the goals of the training exercise. ModSAF provides entity-level simulation of military combat units (e.g., tanks, aircraft, dismounted infantry) as well as aggregate-level simulation of higher-level military units (e.g., command and control forces, theater-level forces). In ModSAF each entity, once assigned a mission, is able to act autonomously, moving, sensing, and interacting with other entities. However, entities' abilities to completely duplicate real-world behaviors are limited, especially in a complex dynamic battlefield environment. For this reason low-level control over the entities can be provided by human intervention. People can also interact with ModSAF to provide supervisory control for the simulation of higher-level military operations and missions. This capability (and requirement) of human control over the entities is the reason the entities are called *semi-automated forces* or SAF. *Intelligent Forces* (fully-automated intelligent agents or IFORS) are being incorporated into the ModSAF architecture but their use is currently limited by both large computational requirements and the knowledge acquisition requirements.

12.4.2. ModSAF Architecture and the DIS Environment

ModSAF, while still evolving, illustrates one set of decisions for many of the issues discussed in Sections 12.2 and 12.3. The ModSAF architecture has four primary functional components: supervisory control, behavioral modeling, physical systems modeling, and simulation infrastructure. Supervisory control provides functionality to create, delete, and modify computer-generated forces (CGF) and their associated tasks and missions, control and monitor the battlefield environment, and control and monitor the execution of ModSAF within a DIS training exercise. The behavioral models in ModSAF exhibit both collective and individual entity behaviors. Individual behaviors are the entity-level simulations necessary to duplicate outward behavior of humans or control systems that guide real-world actions of entities. An example of an individual behavior is a soldier marching on a road. Collective behaviors are the aggregate-level simulations that duplicate outward behavior of real-world actions of a group of entities. An example of a collective behavior is a section of fixed-wing aircraft rendezvousing at a waypoint before attacking a ground target. ModSAF's physical models are the systems and subsystems that are effected by and constrain entities' behaviors. These models include vehicle kinematics, weapons, sensors, and communications systems. The simulation infrastructure consists of functional software components that are required to support the execution of DIS. This includes software for networking and communications, event scheduling and time management, mathematical routines, etc.

The functional components described above are combined to make ModSAF applications that may be used differently during a DIS exercise. ModSAF can be executed as a graphics-only application called a *SAFStation* or as a simulation-only application called a *SIMStation*. This functionality can be controlled by compilation directives and an extensive set of command-line options. A SAFStation acts as a front-end to the simulation nodes, providing human interaction and supervisory control during the training exercise. A SIMStation is the simulation engine, executing the behavioral and physical models, maintaining the state of the virtual battlefield, and communicating any required state data to other simulation nodes participating in the DIS exercise. Partitioning ModSAF into different functional STE stations gives STE configuration planners control over the workload characterization. For example, if a training exercise requires limited supervisory control, fewer SAFStations than SIMStations can be used in the STE configuration reducing the cost of keeping graphical displays updated and increasing the number of compute cycles available for model execution. Additionally, ModSAF may be configured as a SAFStation and a SIMStation, referred to as a *pocket system*, providing capabilities for both human interaction and simulation, albeit at reduced performance. A trace history of the training exercise can be recorded by a *SAFLogger* application. The SAFLogger application reuses software from the ModSAF simulation infrastructure to control, monitor, and capture the packet data on the DIS network. The data can be used for postmortem analysis or recreation of the exercise at slower-than-real-time, real-time, and faster-than-real-time speed.

The ModSAF SAFStations, SIMStations, and SAFLoggers are all connected to local-area networks (LANs) and wide-area networks (WANs) that use Ethernet and ATM transmission protocols and can utilize T1, fiber-optic, and co-axial transmission media. Live participants are able to link up to a DIS training exercise using computer systems that convert their tactical data link protocols to data packets that can be transmitted on the DIS network. Manned training simulators (mock-ups) are similarly linked to the DIS network. The similarity of the information passed between

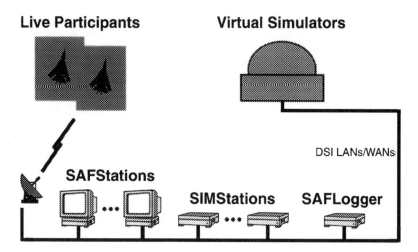

Figure 12.4.   DIS Synthetic Training Environment

actual systems used by live participants, manned simulators, and DIS
systems makes incorporating hardware and software components of real
systems into a DIS environment feasible. Additional DIS systems provide
synthetic generation of real-world environments (e.g., rain, clouds, dust)
and ordinance services with highly accurate models of weapons systems
and other kinematic models. These combined systems make up the
synthetic DIS training environment illustrated in Figure 12.4. The DIS
protocol allows all the systems to interact within the same training
environment and lets dissimilar simulations perceive a common and
consistent virtual battlefield-simulation. For each training exercise the
protocol specifies an *exercise id* as part of the DIS Protocol Data Unit
(PDU) transmitted throughout the DIS network. Systems using the same
exercise id see the same virtual battlefield-simulation. The PDU is the basic
packet of DIS information that communicates data on entity state,
simulation events, the synthetic environment, and the virtual battlefield.

ModSAF maintains complete information about the DIS
environment by using database abstractions to store entity and battlefield
state information, behavioral information, Command and Control (C2)
information, and supervisory control information. The two database
abstractions are referred to as the DIS database and the Persistent Object
(PO) database. The DIS database contains information about battlefield
state, entity state, and events modifying those states. Entities are simulated
entirely within a single process and are considered *local entities* on the

SIMStation which simulates them. On each SIMStation local entities are considered to have *ground truth* data, the most accurate and up-to-date state information on that entity anywhere within the DIS network. The state information that a SIMStation has on entities it is not simulating is the *perceived state* data and the associated entity is considered to be a *remote entity*. The DIS database contains enough state data on remote entities to allow valid interactions between the remote and locally simulated entities. Entity interaction within the context of ModSAF is the ability for an entity to observe a change in another entity's state and initiate its own state changes based on the behavior of the other entity. The exchange of state information through the DIS protocol and ModSAF's DIS database abstraction are the mechanisms for achieving interaction among remote and local entities within the DIS environment.

The PO database abstraction contains information about the military units' command hierarchy, unit and vehicle tasks and missions, and the status of those entities in executing those behaviors. It also contains control information on the simulation exercise and world-view information about the virtual battlefield-simulation. This database is replicated on each ModSAF simulator participating in the training exercise by using a PO protocol. This provides a fault-tolerance capability if a simulator node drops out of the exercise, allowing other simulation nodes to assume responsibility for its workload without losing data, thus the use of *persistent* in describing the database abstraction. The PO database is used to communicate commands from SAFStations to SIMStations, facilitating the requirement to allow human control over the entity and simulation exercise. It also provides information used for load-balancing across the different computers running ModSAF within the same DIS training exercise. Both the DIS and PO protocols have defined periodic update rates, providing a consistent view of the DIS by all ModSAF applications in the network.

The user interface is a key component to any synthetic training environment. ModSAF's Graphical User Interface (GUI) presents an effective interface for interacting with a dynamic virtual battlefield-simulation. It allows for free-play man-in-loop interactions with the SAF used in the DIS environment. Figure 12.5 shows the GUI and its 3 primary components. The palette of buttons (label A) contains a *Select* button for selecting an object from the tactical map, a set of *Editor* buttons that allow the user to interact with the various run-time editors for supervisory control of the simulation, and a set of *Map* buttons that adjust the tactical map and obtain information about vehicles and terrain in the virtual battlefield. The editor area (label B) displays the editor menus that present information on existing or new entities (e.g., vehicles, units, routes lines, targets). The

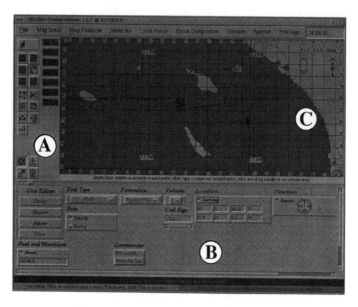

Figure 12.5. ModSAF Graphical User Interface

editors also provide dynamic control over vehicle and unit behaviors and provide a visual representation of selected military units, their hierarchy, and their behaviors. The figure shows the Unit Editor used to create military units and modify their properties. The virtual battlefield is displayed two-dimensionally in the Plan View Display (PVD). The PVD (label C) displays the battlefield's terrain features, vehicle and unit icons, geometry (e.g., routes, areas, lines, points) and dynamic simulation events such as the direct and indirect fire of weapons rounds. The operator has control over the editor and PVD areas of the GUI, by scaling, panning, zooming, and scrolling based on the area of interest. The horizontal menu bar at the top of the GUI provides additional supervisory control with capabilities for example to control the operator privileges to interact with the simulation depending on whether they are a *Battlemaster, a System Operator,* or a *Commander.* For example, while in *System Operator* or *Commander* mode the ability to create units and load scenarios are disabled.

The GUI software architecture is designed to be flexible and extensible. The flexibility comes from a data-driven interface specification which allows the presentation of data to be modified or specialized without recompiling ModSAF. The GUI is configured automatically at load-time using the interface specification and the data are presented at a consistent level of detail restricting the form and content of what is usable and modifiable by the trainee/operator during the DIS exercise. Adding new functionality to the interface is possible because of the layered architecture discussed below.

12.4.3. ModSAF Design Goals and Implementation Features

A primary design goal of ModSAF is to have an open software architecture with the ability to freely add and remove models and functional components without extensive modifications to the simulation's program structure or code. ModSAF's design uses four techniques to achieve this goal: layering, object-based programming, well-defined interface specifications, and a data-driven execution. Layers can only use functions provided by lower layered components. This simplifies design and isolates potential dependencies. It also allows for subsystems to be removed and replaced and promotes reuse of existing software components from other systems. The ModSAF implementation layers the subsystems according to the services they provide and then implements a system of callbacks and periodic polling to deal with data flow among the different services.

Using an object-oriented approach for the design and implementation of ModSAF allows entity state, entity behaviors, and entity functions to be encapsulated and used only in their proper context. ModSAF implements classes by associating class data and functions with the DIS and PO database abstractions, assigning handles to different objects in the database and using those handles to access the associated data. In ModSAF the two basic classes are *DIS DB Object Classes* and *C2 Object Classes*, corresponding to the DIS and PO databases, respectively. Following the object-based paradigm, subsystems and their associated software implementations have public and private data accessed only through the provided software functions.

ModSAF provides two automated tools to check for consistent use of interfaces among modules, *Interck* and *Interdoc*. ModSAF also provides rigorous programmer guidelines for the development of software components. The run-time characteristics of ModSAF entities are largely dependent upon detailed characteristics and behavior specifications found in data input files. ModSAF's data-driven approach for execution is important for experimentation and use within the training environment. It allows for an iterative, "what-if" approach without having to recompile. The data input files are used to reparameterize ModSAF objects and models including the physical characteristics of SAF vehicles and units, military icons shown on the PVD, and individual and collective vehicle and unit behaviors.

Other aspects of ModSAF design and implementation include the ability to execute subsystems on different platforms, and efficient scheduling and time management paradigms to meet the timing requirements of a DIS environment. As discussed earlier, the replication of the DIS and PO database abstractions support the execution of ModSAF subsystems across separate computers. Use of different computers for SAFStations, SIMStations, SAFLoggers, and Ordinance Servers identifies the need for this capability as well as fault-tolerance for node and network failures. Typically, DIS exercises are long running and require ModSAF to schedule and manage many events, service, and resource requests. The ModSAF schedular efficiently polls for periodic services as well as invokes non-periodic events. The internal clocks of ModSAF provide real-time millisecond resolution, faster- and slower-than-real-time resolution, and *shared simulation* millisecond resolution for the synchronization of independent simulation nodes participating in the DIS exercise. ModSAF's modular structure and well-defined interfaces support hardware and language independence. Currently ModSAF (version 1.5.1) consists of 355 object code libraries which includes over 800,000 lines of source code and 120,000 lines of parametric data. ModSAF runs on Sun, SGI, MIPS and other common UNIX workstations. Efforts are currently underway to port ModSAF to different UNIX workstations, PC platforms, and massively parallel machines. ModSAF is written using standard K&R C, X Windows, and the Motif widget set.

12.4.4. ModSAF Modeling

ModSAF's architecture incorporates models of physical, behavioral, and environmental systems. The overriding factor in determining the level of fidelity of each model is externally observable features significant to other ModSAF models. For example, the movement of a tank along a road is simulated by using a speed and direction, as opposed to simulating the rate and rotation of the tank's wheels and tracks. ModSAF's design and implementation allows models to be readily added and deleted, dynamically reconfigured, and used in the composition of more complex models. Physical models include simulations for hulls, turrets, sensors, and weapons. Additional common support models simulate detonations, fire control systems, damage, collisions, communications, and supplies.

ModSAF behavioral models are referred to as *tasks*. These models simulate human behavior, and command and control operations of military units and individuals on the battlefield. ModSAF has five task types: *unit tasks* perform activities associated with units that have roles commanding and supervising lower-level tasks of subordinate units and individual vehicles, *individual tasks* perform activities associated with individual vehicles and typically control processes and actuators in ModSAF's physical models, *reactive tasks* perform activities required for response to battlefield-simulation events, *enabling tasks* act as triggers initiating new tasks in response to some specified condition or simulation state, and *arbitration tasks* are internal tasks used by ModSAF to decide which one of multiple and potentially conflicting task recommendations should be executed. Multiple tasks that must execute together to accomplish a certain battlefield event are combined into a *task frame*. Each task frame represents a specific phase of some defined *mission*, a collection of task frames that simulates a sequence of activities used to achieve some objective in the virtual battlefield-simulation.

ModSAF implements tasks as *Augmented Asynchronous Finite State Machines* (AAFSM). The finite state machine defines a set of low-level actions, task input and outputs, and a set of functions that act as transitions between different task states. The AAFSM is augmented because it can use and modify program variables other than its state variables and it is asynchronous because the task can execute and generate outputs in response to simulation events as well as executing at a periodic rate. The implementation of the AAFSM is referred to as the task model. The task model classifies its data structures as either shared or local, and either public or private, depending on the use of the task state and data by other ModSAF components or simulation nodes in the DIS environment. Those aspects of the task model and its execution that must be shared are maintained in the PO database, making them available to all ModSAF simulations participating in the exercise. A *task manager* is responsible for maintaining the task frame hierarchy (military command and control architecture). It uses a stack to manage the task frames and for determining the execution order.

An important aspect of the design of the task manager is *task arbitration* which deals with the execution of competing objectives within the behavioral models. The arbitration tasks take multiple recommendations from groups of tasks and combine them into one output used by either another task or by some actuator of a physical subsystem. Different arbitration tasks control movement, weapons, and sensors models and the recommendations of each arbitrator are prioritized to determine which commands are actually used and when.

ModSAF's synthetic environment models add realism to the virtual battlefield-simulation. The models are under continual development and are discussed in Birkel[21]. They include representations for Dynamic Virtual Worlds (DVW), Dynamic Terrain and Objects (DTO), Weather in DIS (WINDS), Total Atmosphere-Ocean Server (TAOS), and Compact

Terrain Database (CTDB). DVW representations include natural illuminations from the sun and moon (ephemeris models), inherent contrast between foreground and background objects, atmospheric transmission models (i.e., transmittance, attenuation), battlefield obscurants (e.g., smoke, dust), and flares (e.g., illumination and signals). DTO provides representations for [explosion] craters, damaged bridges and buildings, and destroyed vehicles. WINDS and TAOS provide an integrated, high-resolution representation of base weather phenomenology (storms, clouds, currents) and the dynamics of the combined atmosphere and ocean regimes. The CTDB represents the terrain and terrain features that are used in the virtual battlefield-simulation. The terrain information includes elevation and soil type data. Feature information includes buildings, trees, roads, and rivers as well as *abstract* terrain features such as footprints of tree canopies and political boundaries. ModSAF uses the CTDB when simulating the terrain reasoning component of military mission planning and C2 operations during the DIS training exercise. Terrain reasoning is used for low-level entity control (e.g., near-term movement and obstacle avoidance) and for higher-level C2 operations (e.g, route planning and unit coordination). A detailed discussion of the ModSAF terrain database is found in Stanzione[23] and Smith[24]. The terrain database, weather models, and other synthetic environment models each interact to provide a more realistic and complete synthetic training environment.

12.4.5. ModSAF Assessment and Future Goals

The hardware and software technology used by ModSAF has been demonstrated in real-life training exercises, engineering, and technology demonstrations. The design and implementation techniques used to develop ModSAF have proven successful by allowing DIS researchers and simulation developers to integrate and test different simulation models, software components, and algorithms to support research, training, and development projects. However there is concern over ModSAF's capabilities to scale and interoperate in the synthetic training environments of the future. Limitations are discussed in White[25] and are related to ModSAF architecture. These include the task frame representation of behaviors not being suited for different kinds of simulation engines, no standard approach for making requests for remote services, no standard approach for integrating with other simulators, and scaling capabilities being limited to algorithmic tuning and processing reductions in model and behavior software.

ARPA has taken action to address these limitations and continues to evolve and demonstrate DIS technology. On-going ModSAF development

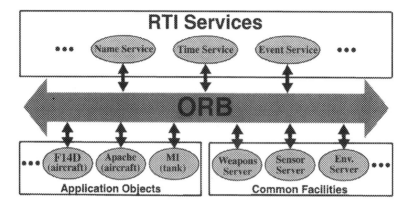

Figure 12.6.   Proposed HLA/RTI and OMA Architecture

efforts are based on the goals of an Advanced Technology Demonstration
called Simulated Theater of War '97 (STOW-97). The goals are to show
the capabilities of DIS technology in a combat development and training
exercise that will involve up to 50,000 entities, most of which will be CGF
(SAF and IFORS) simulated by ModSAF (or variants of ModSAF). The
participating simulation nodes will be connected by LANs and WANs
located throughout the United States and the United Kingdom. To meet the
goals and requirements of STOW-97 (and future DIS exercises), an attempt
is being made to re-engineer ModSAF to be compliant with a High-Level
Architecture (HLA) standard proposed by a consortium of government,
civilian, and academic researchers and simulation developers. HLA defines
a functional architecture that addresses the problem of allowing a diverse
set of hardware platforms and simulations to validly interoperate in DIS
exercises. HLA establishes a distinction between "simulation" and
"common infrastructure", functionally separating model entities, attributes,
and behaviors from the software infrastructure that provides services to
facilitate their simulation. HLA defines Run-Time Infrastructure (RTI)
services that support interaction among simulators participating in training
exercises. Reverse engineering and analysis has been done on the more
than 800,000 lines of code and 120,000 lines of parametric data in
ModSAF to identify the common models and simulation infrastructure.

    Additional changes propose an Object Management Architecture
(OMA) that describes a software architecture for the simulation
infrastructure. It incorporates object-oriented design and implementation
using the Object Request Broker (ORB) model, Common Services,
Common Facilities, and an Interface Definition Language (IDL). The IDL
maps the HLA RTI services to the application objects and common

facilities of the ModSAF implementation, using the ORB for their direct invocation. These core changes are an attempt to increase the performance and efficiency of the synthetic training environment by increasing concurrency and scaling of ModSAF's CGF and improving interoperability with other platforms in the DIS environment. Figure 12.6 illustrates the proposed architecture which is justified and discussed in White[25].

12.5. RESEARCH ISSUES

Successfully integrating distributed simulations into synthetic training environments requires the use of emerging hardware and software technology. Open research issues include:
- the design, development, and standardization of distributed simulation protocols and networking interfaces for high-performance and interoperability of STE components.
- design and implementation techniques for modeling realistic synthetic environments such as terrain and atmosphere.
- performance models to analyze and articulate distributed simulation resource and service utilization and to predict service and resource requirements to achieve training and experimentation goals.
- effective graphical interfaces for human interaction and supervisory control.
- verification, validation, and testing of models and their interactions to assess realism and accuracy of distributed simulations.
- standards for the interchange of data (e.g., terrain representations, data logging) for reuse and interoperability of distributed simulations with other systems and components used in an STE.

12.6. SUMMARY

This chapter provides an overview of distributed simulations in synthetic training environments. Issues associated with the design and implementation of realistic simulation models are discussed and supported by examples. Technical issues associated with the design and implementation of networks and protocols and an example of a network successfully used for distributed interactive simulations of a virtual battlefield are presented along with technical issues such as the use of databases, graphical interfaces, and other software design and implementation issues. The detailed case study of ModSAF presented in this chapter illustrates how current distributed simulation technology has been successfully implemented and used in a synthetic environment designed for military combat training, doctrine development, and systems' evaluation.

The design and development of ModSAF, as well as its use in real training exercises and technology demonstrations, reveals several facts about the use of distributed simulations in STE: whatever current technology provides in terms of capabilities and performance, an insatiable demand for more will continue (e.g., simulate more entities with greater fidelity and better interoperability). For the foreseeable future, technology will continue to limit the capabilities of distributed simulations and STE and because of these limitations a need for better designs and implementation techniques will persist. Distributed simulations will continue to leverage off emerging technologies and will be just adequate to meet STE requirements and goals. This chapter presented some limitations, future goals, and research issues for distributed simulation in STE.

ACKNOWLEDGEMENTS

Thanks to Ed Harvey, Jack McGinn, Bill Edmonds, and Mark Checchio, at BMH Associates, Inc. who continue to provide support in understanding the many aspects of military systems and doctrine development within DIS and synthetic training environments. Acknowledgments also go to CDR P.A. Feldmann, USN, the ARPA Information Systems Office Synthetic Forces Program Manager, for her guidance and support for this research. This research was funded by BMH Associates, Inc., Norfolk, VA, under grant number BMH-01N61339-95-C-0030.

REFERENCES

1. IEEE STANDARDS BOARD. 1993, IEEE Standard for Information Technology-Protocols for Distributed Interactive Simulation Applications, Technical Report IEEE-Std-1278-1993 (Institute for Electrical and Electronics Engineers, Washington, D.C.).

2. E. WHITE, ModSAF 1.4 Reverse Engineering Report (Applied Research Laboratories, The University of Texas at Austin, 28 April 1995).

3. INSTITUTE FOR SIMULATION AND TRAINING, Enumeration and bit Encoded Values for Use With Protocols for Distributed Interactive Simulation Applications (Institute for Simulation and Training, UCF, Orlando, FL, 15 June 1993), Section 7, p 147.

4. LADS, ModSAF Software Architecture Design and Overview Document (SADOD) (Loral Advanced Distributed Simulation, LADS Document Number 94070 v1.0, 14 April 1995).

5. K. DORIS, M. LOBER, "DIS Network Traffic Analysis Estimation Techniques", Proceedings from the 15th I/ITSEC (1993).

6. G. COULOURIS, J. DOLLIMORE, T. KINDBERG, Distributed Systems, Concepts and Design (Addison-Wesley Publishing Co., 1994).

7. P. VERISSIMO, H. KOPETZ, "Design of Distributed Real-Time Systems", Distributed Systems (Addison-Wesley Publishing Co., ACM Press, New York, 1993), 511-530.

8. INSTITUTE FOR SIMULATION AND TRAINING, Rationale Document-Entity Information and Entity Interaction in a Distributed Interactive Simulation (Institute for Simulation and Training, UCF, Orlando, FL, January 1992).

9. L. FOSTER, P. MAASSEL, D. MCBRIDE, "The Characterization of Entity State Error and Update Rate for Distributed Interactive Simulation", 11th DIS Workshop on Standards for the Interoperability of Distributed Simulations (Institute for Simulation and Training, UCF, Orlando, FL, September 1994), 61-73.

10. L. FOSTER, P. FELDMANN, "The Limitations of Interactive Behavior for Valid Distributed Interactive Simulation", 13th DIS Workshop on Standards for the Interoperability of Distributed Simulations (Institute for Simulation and Training, UCF, Orlando, FL, September 1995).

11. J. CALVIN, D. VAN HOOK, "AGENTS: An Architectural Construct to Support Distributed Simulation", 11th DIS Workshop on Standards for the Interoperability of Distributed Simulations (Institute for Simulation and Training, UCF, Orlando, FL, September 1994), 357-362.

12. J. PALMORE, "Conceptual Models for Verification, Validation, and Analysis in Distributed Interactive Simulations", 11th DIS Workshop on Standards for the Interoperability of Distributed Simulations (Institute for Simulation and Training, UCF, Orlando, FL, September 1994), 3-8.

13. E. FEUSTEL, "A Constructive Definition of Fidelity", 11th DIS Workshop on Standards for the Interoperability of Distributed Simulations (Institute for Simulation and Training, UCF, Orlando, FL, September 1994), 49-54.

14. A. KATZ, "Synchronization of Network Simulators", 11th DIS Workshop on Standards for the Interoperability of Distributed Simulations (Institute for Simulation and Training, UCF, Orlando, FL, September 1994), 81-87.

15. M. TAMBE, L. JOHNSON, R. JONES, F. KOSS, J. LAIRD, P. ROSENBLOOM, K. SCHWAMB, "Intelligent Agents for Interactive Simulation Environments", AI Magazine, 16, 15-39 (Spring 1995).

16. E. HARVEY, P. FELDMANN, "Air Synthetic Force Development", Position Paper, Engineering Demonstration 1 (ED1), October, 1995.

17. T. NEUBERGER, O. MALMIN, "Applying Distributed Interactive Technology to Operation Training: A Perspective From Navy STOW-E", Center for Naval Analysis (1995).

18. DIS STEERING COMMITTEE. 1994, "The DIS Vision: A Map to the Future of Distributed Interactive Simulation", Technical Report IST-SP-94-01 (Institute for Simulation and Training, UCF, Orlando, FL).

19. A. CERANOWICZ, "ModSAF and Command and Control", Modular Semi-Automated Forces: Recent and Historical Publications (Loral Advanced Distributed Simulation, LADS Document Number 94007 v. 1.0, 13 May, 1994).

20. M.R. STYTZ, E.G. BLOCK, B.B. SOLTZ, K. WILSON, "The Synthetic BattleBridge: A Tool for Large-Scale VEs", IEEE Computer Graphics and Applications, 16, 16-26 (January 1996).

21. P. BIRKEL, "Synthetic Environments Program Summary Brief", Presented at ALLSAF 2 Conference (Reno, NV, 10 January 1996).

22. R.L. SCHAFFER, "Environmental Extensions to ModSAF", Modular Semi-Automated Forces: Recent and Historical Publications (Loral Advanced Distributed Simulation, LADS Document Number 94007 v. 1.0, 13 May, 1994).

23. T. STANZIONE, "Terrain Reasoning in the SIMNET Semi-Automated Forces System", Modular Semi-Automated Forces: Recent and Historical Publications (Loral Advanced Distributed Simulation, LADS Document Number 94007 v. 1.0, 13 May, 1994).

24. J.E. SMITH, Compact Terrain DataBase Library, User Manual and Report (Loral Advanced Distributed Simulation, Inc., November 1994).

25. E. WHITE, "Synthetic Forces Architectural Trade Study", Presented at ALLSAF 2 Conference (Reno, NV, 10 January 1996).

26. J.V.R. PRASAD, D.P. SCIIRAGE, W.D. LEWIS, D. WOLFE, "Performance and Handling Qualities Criteria For Low Cost Real-Time Rotorcraft Simulators-A Methodology Development", Presented with "A Systems Approach to Quantatative and Qualitative Determination of Fidelity Levels for Simulators", (Georgia Tech, CERWAT, 1991).

27. E. HARVEY, "Synthetic Force Simulation Fidelity", Presented at Engineering Demonstration 1 for ARPA STOW-97 (20 October 1995).

28. P.H. CLEVELAND, "Intentional Disconnects From A DIS Network", 11th DIS Workshop on Standards for the Interoperability of Distributed Simulations (Institute for Simulation and Training, UCF, Orlando, FL, September 1994), 75-79.

29. G. BATE, D. CARVER, "Network Performance Simulation For Distributed Interactive Simulations", 11th DIS Workshop on Standards for the Interoperability of Distributed Simulations (Institute for Simulation and Training, UCF, Orlando, FL, September 1994), 133-137.

CHAPTER 13

A Model-based Study of CASE Adoption and Diffusion

Kallol Bagchi

13.1. INTRODUCTION

CASE (Computer Aided Software Engineering) is a technology designed to automate various software design and development processes [1,2]. The primary advantages of CASE tools are increased productivity and quality improvement, reduced development and maintenance costs, faster delivery and improved documentation. CASE tools are of essentially three types: productivity back-end tools that aid in programming/project, development support tools that support system development at all stages of a system life cycle, and development tools that enforce a system development methodology at all stages of a system life cycle. CASE can provide an incremental approach to system design with graphical user interfaces. Data definitions can proceed simultaneously with diagrams. Changes in design can be made comparatively easily. One implementor notes a 15% increase in productivity, improved communications with the clients, simultaneous work on a common data model, reduced management and secretarial works, better error-checking etc., [p. 13] [1]. Others cite a factor of 30-300% gain in productivity [p. 11] [1].

CASE products exist at various levels and for different purposes, such as requirement definition (Excelerator/ Analyst ToolKit) , analysis and design-aids (Teamwork, Maestro) , full software engineering life cycle (IEW/IEF, APS) , application code generation (Pacbase, Telon). Many of these tools were based on design methodologies of Yordon-DeMarco, Gene-Sarson , Jackson etc.[1] Some later tools incorporated techniques like OO and AI, such as Booch OO-based tool which has become one of the popular CASE tools in recent years.[16]

In this chapter, the adoption and diffusion process of CASE technology will be investigated.

13.2. CASE AS A TECHNICAL INNOVATION

Among the recent information technologies, CASE has one of the most inter esting histories. Experts were raving about this new technology that promised to solve the software design crisis by improved and clean productivity and quality procedure , provably correct design and improved performance, ease of alteration, better communication etc., among other things[1,2, 22-23]. Thus, "CASE tools are regarded as one of the potential directions to confront the software crisis. Many authors heralded CASE tools as a miracle solution...."[21], [p. 11]. It was claimed that CASE "..is a whole new approach which in time will move data processing from a software crafting approach to a software engineering discipline. What this statement truly means will become an important agenda for interpretation for the 1990's and beyond " [21] [p. 18]. Many believed that "compared to the expected future usage of other tools, ..CASE tools are among the most popular tools available..." [21] [p. 9]. International Conferences like International Workshop on CASE [21] as well as special issues of academic journals were devoted to the cause of this technology. Experts predicted success of this technology in industry. It seemed that CASE was all set for a big IT market segment.

Thus it can be said that CASE technology, with its introduction, has made quite an impact and thus can be termed as a technological innovation. The significance of change can be noted further, as described below. Some called it a "software industrial revolution" , others termed it as a "miracle solution " , a "direction to confront the software crisis", "a whole new approach" etc. Many of the advantages of such tools, as perceived by the experts over the-then existing technology , have been discussed above. Software implementors note, " the complexity of information engineering is simply too great to do by hand....(it) requires recourse to CASE tools" [p. 24] [1] or " On this project the Oracle CASE tool provided definite benefits in terms of timescale, cost and quality of deliverables," [p. 16] [1] or " with ever increasing power and functionality the CASE tools are providing, it is believed that they can help provide the means by which these problems (of developing integrated business systems which have distributed operational environment) will be met [1] [pp. 25-26] " and later the same author notes, " we have shown that CASE tools CAN be used to develop significant business system configurations" [1] [p. 41]. These remarks from designers and implementors, no doubt consolidate the fact that CASE technology provided critical departure from the traditional way of software design and appeared to provide superior advantages over the existing software technology.

The importance of studying CASE adoption and diffusion is next discussed. There are several reasons for such studies. First, as one of the emerging information technologies, CASE tools started appearing in the early 1980's. By 1990, the number of CASE tools had grown to over 1000 [p. 214] [1]. Later, conflicting claims appeared in literature regarding the success of this technology. Orlikowski mentions that studies reported increased productivity using the CASE tools as well as elusive productivity gains. [3] This may have affected the diffusion process, via the channels of communication. So the study of the diffusion process of this technological innovation could be interesting. Second, the innovation and diffusion research in IS is growing and although CASE is an important IT innovation, its growth has not yet been studied from an innovation diffusion perspective. Third, the benefits for any organization, as mentioned above , could be real and impressive, if the right tools are adopted at the right time in the right manner. It makes sense for IS and other managers of any organization to get a clear and detailed picture of the adoption of this technology. Fourth, many previous adoption studies are based on the number of organizations actually "bought" or "installed" the new technology. However, for many new ITs, buying or installation do not necessarily imply adoption by an organization. As Iivari [30] and several other researchers note, in the case of CASE, many organizations failed to adopt the technology after buying it.

An adoption study based on IS job advertisements perhaps may be more appropriate. This is because many companies will advertise for professionals , when they are thinking seriously in terms of the usage of the technology. Similarly third party contractors and head hunters usually advertise for professionals only when there is a need for using the technology in one or more companies. In this line of logic, it is believed that a study based on actual advertisement could yield a more realistic picture of the diffusion and adoption of CASE technology. .

13.3. THE DIFFUSION MODELS

The diffusion models are broadly of three types: Internal Influence (communication by word-of-mouth), External Influence (communication by mass-media) and Mixed Influence (communication by a combination of internal and external influences). Different adoption models have been suggested in literature for various IT products.

The internal influence model as described in the diffusion literature is also known as the imitation model. Here the emulation of prior adopters by potential adopters determine the nature of diffusion. The diffusion takes place through specific channels of communication (interpersonal or interorganizational within the society) within a specific community or social systems. In the external influence model, diffusion takes place through specific channels of communication that is external to the social system. Here no assumptions on the interaction between prior and potential adopters are made; rather the rate of adoption is dependent on the potential number of adopters who are present in the social system at a particular point in time. The members of the social system could be isolated or do not spread information about the product/technology through interpersonal or interorganizational communications, but through an outside communication mass medium like newspaper, magazine etc. The mixed influence model is a combination of internal and external influences like media and early adopters.

Previous IS adoption research has shown that internal influence was instrumental among late adopters [4], early adopters rely on external channels [4], external channels are responsible for diffusion of software practices [5] but sometimes have limited effect on software tools [15]. Diffusion models for IT outsourcing have been suggested and appeared in the literature [7, 8]. Chow [9] has a dynamic diffusion model on demands of computers, where the constant adoption population has been relaxed. Gurbaxani and Medelson have suggested price-adjusted S-curve models for IS Spending growth [26], to take care of the effect of price on demand of computing. Details on various types of S-curves have appeared in literature, that can be used for MIS studies [6-8, 10-11].

The diffusion model can be characterized by two parameters--its point of inflection, where the maximum rate of diffusion is reached and the symmetry around the point of inflection. Next, a few theoretical models of diffusion is described, which will be used for analyzing the diffusion process of CASE tools.

The Exponential Model

This model is based on the exponential curve, shown after a logarithmic transformation as :

$$\log (Y) = A + BT \ ,$$

where A and B are suitable constants, T denotes the year and Y the estimate. The exponential model is useful for modeling the diffusion , when the innovation is at an early stage.

The Internal Influence Gompertz Model.

This model is based on the Gompertz curve, which is given by:
$$Y = KA^{**}B^T \ ,$$
where A and B are constants and $0 <= A, B <= 1$, B is the coefficient of internal influence, K is a constant. Y, the number of existing subscribers, reaches maximum at the value K/e. The Gompertz curve is non-symmetric, its point of inflection is at .37 and it has a constant coefficient of internal influence. It has been used in modeling diffusion of consumer durable goods, agricultural innovations.[10] The Gompertz curve attains a maximum rate of growth at an earlier stage and exhibits a near constant rate of growth near the end.

The Internal Influence Logistic Model

Next, the model based on the logistic curve is considered. The equation is given by:
$$Y = 1/(K + Ab^T),$$
where $A > 0$, $0 < b < 1$, K are constants as above, Y reaches the value 1/K, when T approaches infinity. The Logistic curve is symmetric, its point of inflection is at .5 and it has constant coefficient of internal influence. It has been used in modeling diffusion of industrial, high technology and administrative innovations.[10]

The External Influence Model

The equation for external influence model is given by:

$$Y = K(1 - e^{-pt}), \ p > 0, \ K > 0$$

where p is the coefficient of external influence, K is the number of potential adopters and Y is the total number of adopters of the innovation. It results in a decaying or modified exponential diffusion curve. It has been used to in modeling of a new drug, innovation data consisting of labor strikes and political assassinations in developing nations.[34]

The Mixed Influence Model

This mixed-influence model has been used in [7], and has been shown to perform better than ordinary least square and maximum likelihood estimation models. It is given by the following equation:

$$Y=K[(1-e^{-(p+q)t})/(1+(q/p)e^{-(p+q)t})) -(1-e^{-(p+q)(t-1)})/(1+(q/p)e^{-(p+q)(t-1)})],$$

where p, q are coefficients of external and internal influences respectively. The mixed influence models have been used in modeling IT outsourcing. [7, 8]

The S-curves discussed in this article are based on Internal (Logistic and Gompertz), External and Mixed models.

13. 4. Research Questions for CASE Adoption

In page 74 of [6], for example, Gurbaxani notes while observing that BITNET adoption model is a S-curve-based one ," A similar argument also applies to the adoption of new technical practices--such as the use of CASE methodologies by software development groups..". This is an interesting research observation that needs to be verified. So an S-curve based model of CASE adoption which may have an external adoption factor and a predominant internal adoption factor is proposed in this article and is explained next.

Complexity of CASE tools was less in the initial stages. However, the complexity has grown quite rapidly in recent years, with increased functionality. Thus one implementor notes, "many of the early CASE tools had very easy to learn graphic user interfaces....Users could draw diagrams and collect information easily enough". What information should be collected or what should go into a diagram became more and more difficult, as the complexity of the tools and systems to be modeled, increased. Thus one expert mentions, " The ability to hold and track the growing complexity of a set of analytical models as the scope of the system broadens strongly encourages an indefinite extension of the process, leading to the familiar ' paralysis by analysis.' " [p. 3][1].

Complexity has another face. Many complain of the notoriety of CASE tools, many of which enforce a particular design method, thereby increasing the complexity of the implementation task at hand. "Some

automated tools force the user in a certain way, which may not be the most time-efficient"
[p. 12][1]. This may not have decreased with the advances in tools over the years. Further, many users do not understand the complexity of implementation details. ." Thus one CASE designer mentions, " users... found it difficult to understand why things had been modeled in a complex fashion," [1]. The clients were affected; Some organizations needed changes in structures. So increased complexity affected negatively the adoption process in later years.

Compatibility deals with consistency with existing values, past experiences etc. CASE with its initial appearance provided a consistency with existing values. Thus one expert notes, " The s/w development process has been gaining tremendous attention in the literature in the last few years with emphasis on modeling the process, developing the steps with the software development life cycle, creating standard and metrics for the process and increasing productivity."[2] The CASE technology provided consistency with these values in the initial stages by providing support for these facilities. Later on, when the OO-paradigm and AI-based techniques and open system concepts were introduced., the technology failed to catch on to these techniques in a timely fashion thus affecting compatibility. Thus Word notes, " Although a few current generation CASE tools provide OO design notations, there is little support for more abstract OO models." or as Church et al remark on the evaluation result of 14 OO-based tools, "most of the tools have poor code generation ability..None of the tools have good documentation generation ability...and most of them have user interfaces that we would describe as unpleasant to use.."[21, p.5] or as Stobart et al., in [21 p. 85] mention, " tools in all countries seem to be considered immature."

Many CASE tools are incompatible with the methodology of a given organization. In such cases, use of multiple tools or a change in the methodology or suitable adjustments are needed to use a tool. Some companies were forced to postpone buying of a tool or even went for a complete abandoning , because the use of the tool became impossible as it did not support their methodology. Consistency with past experiences was absent in late nineties. Thus although authors in early nineties mentioned the necessity of better tool integration, method support or multi-user development facilities, the problem still remained in late nineties. "Poor tool integration, lack of multi-user development facilities and poor method support were common problems ..." [31, p. 85]. Compatibility of various CASE products have not shown any improvement in later years, because of a lack of standard. So compatibility declined in later years.

So it is reasonable to assume that both complexity and compatibility factors contributed in a manner so that the diffusion process was more rapid in the beginning and then declined in later stages. The exponential growth assumption may not be realistic , as the growth rate (as discussed above) may not be constantly proportional one in nature, as required for exponential growths . The growth rate may not also be linear, because of the possible decline in later stages. This leads us to the possibility that the diffusion curve could not be linear or exponential in nature. The growth rate may not be pure external in nature, as the model does not allow any diffusion due to interaction between prior and potential adopters, which will be unrealistic in the present case. Therefore, an S-curve , with a rate of growth like internal (Gompartz or Logistic) or mixed (with high internal influence factor) models may be more appropriate.

The first research question of this study is described next. It is concerned with the diffusion pattern of CASE over time, *when the IT product is considered in isolation*, ignoring other such products, which is described below.

Research Question 1. Which diffusion model/models can be used to study the market-adoption of CASE?

From the discussions above, it appears that the rate of adoption may have slowed down in recent years. Thus it was observed that CASE started with an initial promise; Researchers and experts were highly optimistic about this new IT product. Factors like 30-300% productivity gains , definite quality gains were reported in earlier studies. Later on, conflicting claims have appeared regarding the adoption and usage of CASE in literature [3,19]. A recent study reports about 39% of CASE tool buying organizations deserting the CASE technology or trying to adopt a newer one, [2]. The CASE failures resulted from no plans, no pilot projects , no involvement of end-users, little or no training. No productivity gains or no support for current methodology were cited for looking for a new CASE tool. Another later-year study reports some 51% of IT users had either dismissed it (with or without evaluation) or were uncertain of the technology.[2]

Therefore, our next question can be stated as :

Research Question 2: How CASE has been adopted in the IT market over a period of time?

Another interesting research question is related to the type of CASE tools. As already mentioned , CASE tools exist at different levels of system life cycle. Prices vary greatly , depending on the complexities of such tools. Companies using CASE tools may require these for complete life-cycle support. There are two ways of doing that. One is packaging : buying tools from more than one vendors, developing in-house and integrating them into a coherent design environment or buying a single ICASE tool and adjusting it if needed, to do the same job. Integrating different tools from more than one vendors may not be an easy task , because of the absence of compatibility resulting from a lack of any rigorous standard development effort in this part of IT segment. Building in-house or a complete customized solution may not be cost-effective, especially for small-sized companies. A few matured ICASE tools have appeared recently that provide full life-cycle design support and these are customizable , especially tools from late nineties. These tools are natural candidates of adoption by the firms. Thus the next hypothesis is formulated:

Research Question 3. Among all the CASE products, does the life-cycle tools or ICASE tools occupy the major segment of the CASE tool market in recent years?

Sometimes a single CASE tool maintains a dominant position in the market, like for example SDW in Holland or POSE in Malaysia. Sometimes, it does not seem that any single tool dominates the market, like for example, in Norway [21,31] . In U.S., no uniform standard was available from the beginning, with the result that the initial CASE market developed in more than two schools based on different design philosophies. Compatibility of these product/technologies was not discernible. A plenty of vendors have announced their tools for the US market. Thus it is possible that in US job-market at least, the pattern of demand could be that of a combination of a number of tools. Since a quite few mature CASE tools have appeared in the market of US that can be easily adapted or suitably adjusted , the following hypothesis is formed:

Research Question 4. Does a collection of a few CASE tools rather than a single tool dominates the US CASE job- market?

13.5. THE DATA COLLECTION METHOD

The study is based on job-market data, collected from samples of job-advertisements from one of the most popular and representative IS magazines, the ComputerWorld. The method adopted in the present work is based on content-analysis scheme and is a similar one as described in [13]. Job-ads are examined for possible reference to CASE tools, which are then recorded as data. It may be mentioned here that ComputerWorld is one of the standard outlets for IS job-ads in recent years. The job ads are surveyed for a 10-year period, starting from 1986. 1986 can be considered as the year when CASE became commercially available, as Parkinson mentions, in [1, page 214] : "Most current (CASE) tools did not become commercially available until 1986 or later..." . The selected data set is based on half-yearly data. The first issues of the months April and October are reviewed for each of the selected years resulting in 20 data points. This set carries about 4% of total job ads from 1986-1995. The number of job-ads that ask for CASE skills are counted. For example, if a job-ad required skills in IEF and/or ADW, it is counted as a job-ad for CASE skills. Job-ads with no specific requirements were discarded as also some other vague job-ads. It is not practical to gather all data from ComputerWorld, because of the sheer volume of data. This kind of data gathering in small but representative samples is fairly common in IS research.[13,14]

The set of CASE tools sampled consisted of products like IEW/IEF, Foresight/ADW, Telon/Synon, Packbase, Teamwork, Mestro, Design-aid,

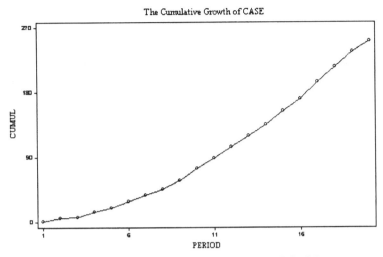

Figure 13.1. The Cumulative Growth of CASE

Year	No. of CASE job-ads	Cumulative No. of CASE job-ads	Total Job-ads	CASE job-ads as fraction of total
April, 1986	1	1	83	0.01
Oct., 1986	5	6	90	0.06
April, 1987	1	7	69	0.01
Oct., 1987	8	15	108	0.07
April, 1988	5	20	68	0.07
Oct., 1988	9	29	84	0.11
April, 1989	9	38	70	0.13
Oct., 1989	8	46	79	0.1
April, 1990	12	58	68	0.18
Oct., 1990	16	74	69	0.23
April, 1991	15	89	57	0.26
Oct. 1991	15	104	58	0.26
April, 1992	16	120	52	0.31
Oct., 1992	16	136	50	0.32
April, 1993	18	154	57	0.32
Oct., 1993	17	171	54	0.315
April, 1994	24	195	77	0.311
Oct. 1994	21	216	75	0.28
April, 1995	21	237	77	0.27
Oct., 1995	14	251	79	0.18

Table 13.1. The CASE Job-ad Breakdown

Foundation, Excelerator, APS/HPS,   Prism, Easel, Oracle CASE, Bachman, Delphi, Erwin, TIP, DEC MMS/CMS/Rally, Natural Construct, Unisys Ally/Mapper/Linc, Cradle, Analyst/Design Tool Kit, MicroFocus Workbench etc. Some of these have been in the market for a long time. Others have recently emerged with many attractive facilities and can be called as the newest generation of products. A few others are cited by books/journals/trade magazines as among the standard available CASE tools [2, 32-33]. This set can be considered as fairly representative as far as the US job-market is concerned.

13.6. THE ANALYSIS

13.6.1. The Adoption Pattern of the CASE Technology

The evolution of CASE technology, independent of how the total IT job-market evolved is considered here. It is shown in figure 13.1, studied over a period of 10 years, from 1986-1995.

Period	Actual	Gompertz	Linear	Logistic	Exp
1	1	4	-31	9	6
2	6	7	-18	11	7
3	7	10	-4	14	9
4	15	15	10	18	12
5	20	21	23	23	15
6	29	28	37	29	19
7	38	36	51	37	24
8	46	47	64	46	30
9	58	59	78	56	37
10	74	72	92	69	47
11	89	87	105	83	59
12	104	103	119	100	74
13	120	120	132	118	94
14	136	138	146	137	118
15	154	156	160	158	149
16	171	175	173	178	187
17	195	195	187	198	236
18	216	214	201	216	297
19	237	234	214	234	374
20	251	253	228	249	471

Table 13.2. Some Fit Values from Various Models

The *cumulative* number of such growths is plotted against time and the data is depicted in Table 13.1.

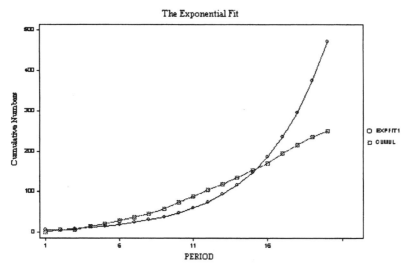

Figure 13.2. The Exponential Fit

Model Type	R^2	Adjusted R^2	T-statistic	Other Parameters
Linear	.96	.958	20.83	a=-44.92, b=13.64
Exponential	.86	.856	10.70	a=1.545, b=.2305
Gompertz (Internal)	.9997	.99		K= 553, A=.00493, B=.90873
External	.663	.65		K=500, p=.025674
Mixed	.975	.96		K=400, p=.00766 q=.181916
Logistic (Internal)	.9989	.99		K=.00308, A=.14066, b= .77799

Table 13.3. The Statistical Test Results

Two statistical packages have been used to run the simulation. These are

Statistix [26] and SAS [27]. Statistix has a PC version that is very easy to use in many statistical calculations. For non-linear regressions, SAS has a module called NONLIN which is used in the present study.

First, the hypothesis that the adoption pattern of CASE technology can be modeled as an S -curve is tested against the alternative hypothesis that the rate of growth follows an exponential pattern.

To start with , the pattern of growth from the figure indicates that the growth rate can not be approximated by a straight line, which is verified by a linear regression . Refer to Table 13.2 . The regression equation is given by:

$$Y=-44.92+13.64*Period$$

The results show that the line is not a good fit to the data. However, the curve of growth-rate is not obvious from figure 13.1 and so detailed statistical analyses need to be conducted.[24,25]

Next, the exponential growth model is tested. The parameters of this equation are estimated by using linear least square regression of log of the estimated parameter and the variable Period. The results are shown in figure 13.2 and given in tables 13.2 and 13.3.

From table 13.3 one can see that the value of R^2 is high and is equal to 0.86. However, it is clear from the figure that the exponential model overestimates the growth rate in the later years. So it is not at all accurate.

The External model is tried next. The R^2 is not very high (=.663) and the curve is not at all a good fit , as shown in figure 13.5.

Next, the internal logistic model is considered. Non-linear least square estimates of the parameters based on the logistic model of the parameters are shown in figure 13.3 and given in tables 13.2-13.3.

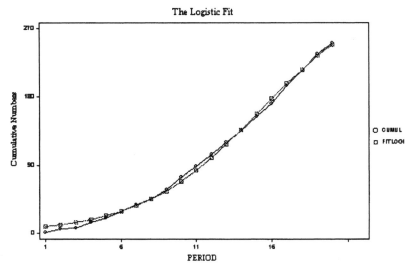

Figure 13.3. The Logistic Fit

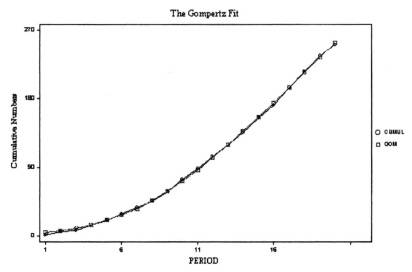

Figure 13.4. The Gompertz Fit

The value of R^2 is quite high (=.99) and the t-statistic values of all the parameters are significant thus indicating a close fit. Fits are better in later years than in earlier ones. From visual inspections also, the close fit is apparent. However, a few points show disagreement and so internal Gompertz model is tried next.

The non-linear least squares method is used again to estimate the parameters of this equation. The results are shown in table 13.2 and in figure 13.4. The value of R^2 is quite high (=.99) and the values of t-statistic for the estimated coefficients are also significant. The data show a close fit. The estimated values are mostly a close fit and a few values differ with the observed values in later years. The upper bound K's estimated value also appear to be realistic.

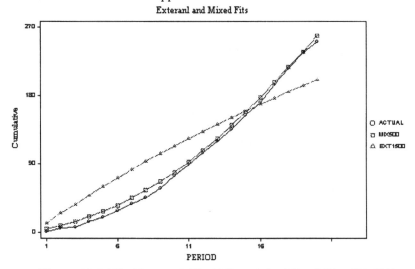

Exteranl and Mixed Fits

Figure 13.5. The External (K=400) and the Mixed Fits (K=500)

Finally the mixed model is tried. Although R^2 (=.97) is not as high as internal Gompertz or logistic, the model cannot be rejected at all and the fit shows quite a close match.

From the above it is reasonable to conclude that the pattern of independent diffusion in case of CASE technology as obtained from the job-market data is consistent with a S- curve (internal or mixed). This answers question 1.

13.6.2. The CASE and the Overall Job-market Data

So far, the analysis does not indicate how CASE has performed relative to the overall IT market. The existing adoption studies on other IT products frequently fail to focus on this aspect, due mainly to the non-availability of data. Thus, for example, the adoption study of BITNET contains research observations that are valid for BITNET alone. Other survey-based studies also frequently fail to capture the performance of an IT product relative to the overall market. One advantage of job-market based data is that the total market data can be gathered and the progress of any given IT product can be noted, with respect to other IT products as well as with the total market. This is studied next. First the adoption pattern as related to the overall job-market is studied. For this the fraction of CASE-related job-ads over the total no. of IT job-ads for each year is observed. This is shown in figure 13.6 and Table 13.1.

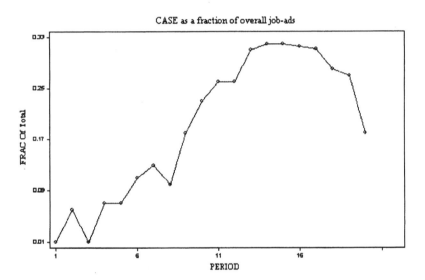

Figure 13.6. The CASE Jobs as a Fraction of Total Job-ads

In figure 13.6, CASE shows an interesting pattern. After showing initial promise of market-acceptance, the adoption of CASE , as measured by the fraction of overall IT job-ads, has been showing a decreasing pattern in recent years. This answers question 2.

The breakup of different CASE tool usage in recent years is next shown in table 13.4.

Year	ADW (1)	IEW/ IEF/IE (2)	Total of (1) + (2)	Total CASE Ads	Fraction
1991	2	7	9	30	.3
1992	5	12	17	32	.53
1993	9	14	23	35	.66
1994	12	19	31	45	.69
1995	10	16	26	35	.74

Table 13.4. The Combined Share of IEF/IEW/ADW

From 1986 to 1990, Pacbase and Telon appeared in 30-50% of all CASE related job-ads. Thus the percentage was 50% in 1986, 44% in 1987, 50% in 1988, 35% in 1989 and 32% in 1990. From the table 13.4 , one can see that a combination of IEF/IEW, ADW dominates the requirements of IT job market in recent years. IEW/IEF, ADW are well known CASE tools that support the design of entire system life-cycle. This answers questions 3 and 4.

13.7. DISCUSSION

First, the mode of such innovation diffusion is discussed . Let us start with the initial stages of adoption. The CASE was hyped as the IT s/w product/technology for improved productivity and quality for the next century ; numerous articles were written and discussion took place in support of this technology. As a result the technology became socially visible. Many IT professionals and managers considered CASE to be the right technology for adoption and thus gain competitive advantage. Some of them thus may have bought CASE products and in some cases hired CASE professionals, without any rigorous plan. A study reports buying of a CASE tool by an organization at the cost of $500, 000 without any rigorous plans and then trying to figure out what to do with it. [p.62] [31.] This was done , no doubt, to gain competitive advantage. Given also that the social system of IT professionals is small , it is more appropriate to assume that the internal influence models (or a mixed model with a higher internal influence coefficient) will show better fit in such cases[34] and this has indeed been the case. Both Gompertz and logistic are internal influence models.

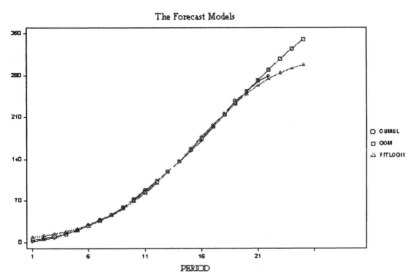

Figure 13.7. The Logistic and Gompertz Forecast Models (through the year 2000)

Next, forecast models of CASE through the year 2000 are developed, based on Gompertz and logistic estimates. This is shown in figure 13.7. This adoption rate is much slower than BITNET , which achieved saturation within eight years of its inception, but comparable to many other non-IT products like household telephones. [28] The forecast models are used to analyze the 1996 data. The actual values of CASE cumulative data for 1996 are 270 and 278. The corresponding predicted values from Gompertz and Logistics are : 271 and 290, 262 and 274 respectively. The maximum forecast error estimates resulting from these models are around 3-4%. Note also that the Gompertz model predicted an increased number of adopters, whereas the logistic estimates are lower.

13.8. CONCLUSIONS

In this exploratory study, a few hypotheses on CASE technology adoption were developed and tested with actual data from job-market. The contribution of this article is in development of modeling the adoption and diffusion of CASE. A number of adoption models were tested to see which one was best suited for the technology. When considered separately from other IT products, the S-curve based models were found to be a more appropriate fit to the job-market data. One future interesting development could be in the directions of model building efforts for adoption, by incorporating other adoption factors. A larger-sized sample may be used for verifying the robustness of the observations made here. Other mixed models, combining both internal and external factors, like the von Bertalanffy model [8] can be used. Dynamic models may be used to verify how the rates of adoption have progressed. Some of these extension works are already in progress. The adoption rate of CASE when observed in the context of total job market data, appeared to be decaying in the later stages, thus showing a market-avoidance or possible rejection of the technology. It is too early to say whether CASE will be ultimately rejected by the market or will exist in a niche segment of the market or even revive market interest with infusion of new ideas. However, job-market data do indicate that the market-interest in CASE technology has recently gone down and the trend is continuing.

ACKNOWLEDGEMENT. I would like to thank Dr. Qing Hu and Prof. Robert Cerveney of Florida Atlantic University for many of their valuable suggestions and comments on the draft of this paper.

REFERENCES

1. K. Spurr and P. Layzell (eds.), CASE on Trial , John Wiley & Sons, 1990.
2. K. Brathwaite, Applications Development Using CASE Tools, Academic Press, 1990.
3. W. Orlikowski, " CASE Tools as Organizational Change...," MISQ, Sept. 1993, pp. 309-340.
4. J. C. Brancheau and J. C. Wetherbe, " The Adoption of Spreadsheet S/W: Testing Innovation Diffusion Theory in the Context of End-User Computing," Information Systems Research, Vol. 1, 1990, pp. 115-143.
5. R. W. Zmud, " Diffusion of Modern S/W Practices, " Management Science, Vol. 28, No. 12, 1982, pp. 1421-1431.
6. V. Gurbaxani, "Diffusion in Computer Networks: The CASE of BITNET," CACM, Dec., 1990, pp. 65-75.
7. L. Loh and N. Venkatraman, " Diffusion of IT Outsourcing: Influence Sources and the Kodak Effect," Information Systems Research, Vol. 3, No. 4, 1992, pp. 334-358.
8 Q. Hu, C. Saunders, M.Gebelt, " Diffusion of IS Outsourcing: A Reevaluation of Influence Sources," To appear, Information Systems Research, 1997.
9. G. C. Chow, " Technological Change and the Demand of Computers," American

Economic Review, Vol. 57, 1967, pp. 1117-1130.

10. V. Mahajan, E. Muller, F. Bass, " New Product Diffusion Models in Marketing: A Review and Directions for Research," J. of Marketing, Vol. 54, January 1990, pp. 1-26.

11. E. Rogers, The Diffusion of Innovation, Free Press, NY 1983.

12 L. W. Kwok and K. P. Arnett, " Organizational Impact of CASE Technology," JSS, March 1993, pp. 24-28.

13. S. Slaughter and S. Ang, " Employment Outsourcing in IS," CACM, July 1996, Vol. 39, No.7, pp. 47-54.

14 P. Todd, J. D. McKeen and R.B. Gallupe," The Evolution of IS Job Skills : A Content Analysis of IS Job Advertisements from 1970 to 1990," MISQ, March, 1995.

15. S. Nilakanta and R. Scamell, " The Effects of Information Sources and Communication Channels on the Diffusion of Innovation in a Data Base Development Environment, Management Science, Vol. 36, No. 1, 1990, pp. 24-40.

16. T Lewis ," The Big Software Chill," IEEE Computer , March 1996, pp. 12-14.

17. K. Swanson et al., " The Application S/W Factory...," MISQ , December 1991, pp. 567-579.

18. I. Vessey, S. Jarvenpaa, N. Tractinsky, " Evaluation of Vendor Products: CASE Tools as Methodology Comparisons," CACM, April 1992, pp. 90-105.

19. C. Necco, N.W. Tsai, K.W. Holgeson, " Current Usage of CASE Software," JSM, Vol. 40, No. 5, May, 1989, pp. 6-11.

20. M. Martin, " The CASE Against CASE," JSM, Jan/Feb. 1995, pp. 54-56.

21. Proceedings of International Workshop on CASE, 1993.

22. P.N. Finlay and A.C. Mitchell, " Perceptions of the Benefits from Introduction of CASE: An Empirical Study," MIS Q, Vol. 18, No. 4, 1984, pp. 353-370.

23. R. J. Norman and J. F. Nunamaker," CASE Productivity Perceptions of Software Engineering Professionals, " CACM, Vol. 32, No. 9, September, 1989, pp. 1102-1108.

24. G. Snedecor and W. Cochran, Statistical Methods, ISU Press, 1989.

25. J. Neter, M. Kutner, C. Nachtsheim, W. Wasserman, Applied Linear Statistical Models, Irwin Publishers, 1996.

26. SAS Users Guide, Version 5, SAS Institute, 1985

27. Statistix for Windows, User's Manual, Analytical Software, 1996.

28. V. Gurbaxani and H. Mendelson, " An Integrative Model of IS Spending Growth", IS Research, Vol. 1, 1990, pp. 23-46.

29. J. Iivari, "Why are CASE Tools not Used," CACM, Vol. 30, No. 10, Oct 1996, pp. 94-103.

30. C. Kemerer, " How the Learning Curve Affects CASE Tool Adoption," IEEE Software, Vol. 9., no. 3, 1992, pp. 23-28.

31.Proceedings of International Workshop on CASE, 1995.

32. ComputerWorld, March 27, 1989.

33. ComputerWorld, June 6, 1988.

34. V. Mahajan and R. Peterson, "Models for Innovation Diffusion," In Quantitative Applications in the Social Sciences, SAGE Publications, pp. 5-87,1995.

Notes on the Contributors

KALLOL BAGCHI received his MSc in Mathematics from Calcutta University and Ph.D. in Computer Science in 1988 from Jadavpur University, Calcutta, India. He has worked in industry in India and in Finland. He taught a course at the University of Oulu, Finland in 1986. He worked as an **Assistant** and **Associate Professor** in Computer Science and Engineering at Aalborg University, Denmark from 1987-1992. In 1993, he visited Stanford University, CA. He also completed a certificate in Computer Networking from Columbia University, NY. His interests are in performance modeling and simulation, parallel systems. He has authored or co-authored over 40 international papers in these areas. He has been an associate editor or member of the editorial board of the International Journal in Computer Simulation for the last few years and have guest-edited several issues of the journal. He was a member of the board of directors of SCS in 1993. He has been cited in World Who's who and in Who's who in Science and Engineering. He is a member of the ACM and IEEECS. He has been associated with the MASCOTS workshop, since its inception. At present, he is **pursuing a second Ph.D. degree** in business (DIS) at Florida Atlantic University.

DOUGLAS M. BLOUGH received the B.S. degree in electrical engineering and the M.S. and Ph.D. degrees in computer science from The Johns Hopkins University, Baltimore, MD, in 1984, 1986, and 1988, respectively. Since 1988, he has been with the Department of Electrical and Computer Engineering, University of California, Irvine, where he is currently **Associate Professor.** Since 1989, he has also held a joint appointment in the Information and Computer Science Department at UC Irvine. His research interests include fault-tolerant computing, computer architecture, and parallel processing. Dr. Blough is a member of Eta Kappa Nu, Tau Beta Pi, Phi Beta Delta, IEEE, and the Association for Computing Machinery.

THOMAS BRÄUNL studied Computer Science at the Univ. Kaiserslautern (Germany) and at the Univ. of Southern California, Los Angeles (on a Fulbright grant), receiving M.S. degrees from both institutions in 1986 and 1987, respectively. He received a **Ph.D.** and the

German habilitation degree from the Univ. Stuttgart (Germany) in 1989 and 1994. Since 1989, Thomas Bräunl is **teaching** Computer Science at the Institute for Parallel and Distributed High Performance Systems at the Univ. Stuttgart. His textbook on *Parallel Programming* was published by Prentice-Hall in 1993. He co-chaired several MASCOTS workshops and was co-editor of the 1994 Autonomous Mobile Systems Proceedings. Currently, he directs two working groups, one in the area of parallel language design and parallel image processing, and one in the area of robotics (cooperation of autonomous vehicles).

DAVID B. CAVITT is a **doctoral student** at Old Dominion University, Norfolk, Virginia. He received a BS degree in Computer Science at Old Dominion University. He has 9 years of experience in the use and development of simulations for military and engineering applications. His research interests include modeling and simulation, performance analysis, and distributed systems. David Cavitt is a member of ACM, and IEEE CS.

WILLIAM P. DAWKINS received a B.S. degree in Electrical Engineering from Oklahoma State University in 1987. He received M.S. and Ph.D. degrees in Computer Engineering from Rice University in 1989 and 1993, respectively. He is currently a **Member of the Technical Staff** at ViaSat, Inc., Carlsbad California. At ViaSat he has been involved in the development of Demand Assigned Multiple Access (DAMA) communication protocols for satellite modems and network controllers. His interests currently center on communication protocols, network analysis, and parallel processing.

MARIOS DIKAIAKOS received a Diploma in Electrical Engineering (with high honors) from the National Technical University of Athens, Greece in 1988 and the M.A. and Ph.D. degrees from Princeton University, in 1991 and 1994 respectively. In 1994 he joined the University of Washington in Seattle as Research Faculty with the Departments of Computer Science-Engineering and Astronomy. Since January 1996 he has been an **Assistant Professor** in the Department of Computer Science at the University of Cyprus in Nicosia. His current research focuses on performance modeling tools for Parallel Computing, Scientific Computing, Parallel Compilers and Hypermedia Systems.

PRADEEP K. DUBEY is a **Research Staff Member** at the IBM T.J. Watson Research Center. Prior to joining IBM in 1991, he worked at Intel Corporation. Both at IBM and Intel, he has worked on design, architecture, and performance modeling issues of various microprocessors. At Intel he was a member of the 80386, 80486, and the Pentium architecture teams. At IBM he is currently working on research issues related to general purpose processors based on multiple speculative control flows and special purpose processors aimed at emerging multimedia applications. He is an adjunct faculty member at New York University. He has published extensively and filed several patents in the area of computer architecture. He is also a Senior Member of IEEE. He received the B.S. degree in Electronics from BIT, Mesra, India in 1982. He received the M.S. degree from University of Massachusetts at Amherst in 1984, and Ph.D. from Purdue University, in 1991, both in Electrical and Computer Engineering.

RICARDO FRICKS is a **Ph.D. student** at Duke University. He received a diploma in Electrical Engineering from the Federal University of Paran'a State in 1982 and a Master Science degree in Computer Science from the Federal University of Rio Grande do Sul State in 1989, both in Brazil. Since 1989 he has been engaged in research on hard real-time computer systems with the Central Laboratory of Electrotecnics and Electronics, which is a joint laboratory mantained by the Federal University of Paran'a State and the Paran'a State Energy Company. His research interests include stochastic modeling of hard real-time systems and communication networks.

JOSÉ A. GIL is an **Assistant Teacher** in the Department of System Engineering, Computers and Automatic of Polytechnical University of Valencia, Spain. He received an MS degree in Computer Science in 1987 and a PhD in Computer Engineering in 1995, both from Polytechnical University of Valencia. His research interest include performance evaluation, simulation techniques, networks and real-time systems. Readers may contact J. A. Gil at Departamento De Ingeniería De Sistemas, Computadores Y Automática Universidad Politécnica De Valencia Cno. de Vera s/n, 46022 Valencia, SPAIN. His e-mail is jagil@aii.upv.es.

ARVIND KRISHNA is at the IBM T.J. Watson Research Center, where he is currently the **Manager of the wireless and mobile networking group**. He joined IBM in 1990 and has worked on high-speed and wireless networks, including network protocols for mobile users, network architectures for wireless data, radio capture, and packet routing. He remains interested in applied probability, algebraic coding, and switch architectures. He received the Ph.D. and M.S. degrees from the

University of Illinois at Urbana-Champaign in 1990 and 1987, respectively, and the B.Tech. degree from IIT, Kanpur in 1985, all in Electrical and Computer Engineering. He is an editor of the IEEE Personal Communications magazine and actively serves on the technical program committee for various conferences. He has been an adjunct faculty member at Columbia University and at the Polytechnic University of Brooklyn. He has published numerous technical papers and filed several patents in the areas of wireless networks and high-speed networks.

ALBERT LLAMOSI received his Industrial Engineering degree from the Polytechnical University of Catalonia, Graduated in History from the Autonomous University of Barcelona and Doctor in Computer Science from the Polytechnical University of Catalonia. He has taught on programming related topics at the Faculty of Computer Science of the Polytechnical University of Catalonia (1978-1989), the University of the Balearic Islands (1989-1993), where he became **Full Professor**, and the University Rovira i Virgili, at Tarragona, where he is currently working. His main research topics have been concurrent programming and real-time system design. In such a domain, he has participated in several projects for the European Space Agency and also in several ESPRIT research projects. He is currently a member of the board of the Ada Europe association.

KURT J. MALY received the Dipl. Ing. degree from the Technical University of Vienna, Austria, and the M.S. and Ph.D. Degrees from the Courant Institute of Mathematical Sciences, New York University, New York, NY. He is **Kaufman Professor and Chair of Computer Science** at Old Dominion University, Norfolk, VA. Before that, he was at the University of Minnesota, both as faculty member and Chair. His research interests include modeling and simulation, very high-performance networks protocols, reliability, interactive multimedia remote instruction, Internet resource access, and software maintenance. His research has been supported by DARPA, NSF, NASA, CIT, ARPA and the U.S. Navy among others. Dr. Maly is a member of the IEEE Computer Society and the Association for Computing Machinery.

MICHAEL OVERSTREET is an **Associate Professor** of Computer Science at Old Dominion University. He is immediate past chair of the Special Interest Group in Simulation (SIGSIM) of the ACM. He received his B.S. from the University of Tennessee in 1966, an M.S. from Idaho State University in 1968, and an M.S. and Ph.D. from Virginia Polytechnic Institute and State University in 1975 and 1982 respectively. He has been a visiting research faculty member at the Kyushu Institute of Technology in Japan. His current research interests include model specification and analysis, distributed simulation, high performance networking, support for interactive instruction, and static code analysis in support of software maintenance tasks. He is currently a principal investigator in tasks funded by ARPA, ICASE at NASA Langley, and the National Science Foundation. Dr. Overstreet is a member of ACM, and IEEE CS.

ANA PONT is an **Assistant Teacher** in the Department of System Engineering, Computers and Automatic of Polytechnical University of Valencia, Spain. Her research interest include multiprocessor architecture, memory hierarchy design and performance evaluation. She received an MS degree in Computer Science in 1987 and a PhD in Computer Engineering in 1995, both from Polytechnical University of Valencia. Readers may contact A. Pont at Departamento De Ingeniería De Sistemas, Computadores Y Automática Universidad Politécnica De Valencia, Cno. de Vera s/n, 46022 Valencia, SPAIN. Her e-mail is apont@aii.upv.es.

RAMON PUIGJANER is a **Full Professor** at the University of Illes Balears, SPAIN and is an well-known expert on real-time system modeling and design. His e-mail address is putxi@ps.uib.es.

ANTONIO PULIAFITO received the electrical engineering degree in 1988 from the University of Catania and the Ph.D. degree in 1993 in computer engineering, from the University of Palermo. Since 1988 he has been engaged in research on parallel and distributed systems with the Institute of Computer Science and Telecommunications of Catania University, where he is currently an **Assistant Professor** of computer engineering. His interests include performance and reliability modeling of parallel and distributed systems, networking and multimedia. During 1994-1995 he spent 12 months as visiting professor at the Department of Electrical Engineering of Duke University, North Carolina, USA, where he was involved in research on advanced analytical modelling techniques. Dr. Puliafito is co-author (with R. Sahner and Kishor S. Trivedi) of the text entitled Performance and Reliability Analysis of Computer Systems: An Example-Based Approach Using the SHARPE Software Package, edited by Kluwer Academic Publishers.

ANNE ROGERS received a Bachelor of Science from Carnegie-Mellon University in 1983 and an M.S. (1987) and Ph.D. (1990) from Cornell

University. She has been an **Assistant Professor** in the the Department of Computer Science at Princeton University since 1990. Her research focuses on compiling for parallel architectures and the interaction between compilers and architectures. In particular, she works on tools for supporting irregular problems, that is, programs that use dynamically allocated data structures.

SEKHAR SARUKKAI obtained his **PhD** in Computer Science from Indiana University in December 1992. He was employed at NASA Ames Research center for about 3 years before moving to **HP labs** in November 1995. His research work has focused on developing techniques and tools for enabling efficient mapping of applications to parallel systems. Currently he is working on characterizing, analyzing, and modeling the effect of parallel system design choices on end-user application performance.

FADI N. SIBAI is currently a **Senior System Engineer** with Intel Corporation, Santa Clara, California. His technical interests are in computer architecture, operating systems, processor validation, parallel and distributed computing, fault tolerance and testability, and networks and routing. He has published extensively in these areas. In the past two years, he served on the program committee of the international conference on parallel and distributed computing systems. He also serves as a reviewer to numerous journals and international conferences. Dr. Sibai received the Ph.D. and M.S. degrees from Texas A&M University and the BS degree from the University of Texas at Austin, all in Electrical Engineering. He is a member of IEEE's Computer Society and Eta Kappa Nu.

JAMES P. (BART) SINCLAIR received his BSEE, MEE, and Ph.D. degrees from Rice University. He is currently an **Associate Professor** in the Department of Electrical and Computer Engineering at Rice. His research interests include parallel computers, performance analysis and simulation of computer systems, and high performance I/O systems. He is a member of the ACM and a senior member of the IEEE.

YONGSHENG SONG is a **Visiting Scholar** at the High Performance Computing and Software Laboratory at the University of Texas at San Antonio.He is a senior research engineer in the Jiangnan Research Institute, China. Song received his B.S. and M.S. degrees in Computer Science from the Changsha Institute of Technology, China, in 1977 and in 1991 respectively. His research interests are in the area of parallel compilers.

MARK S. SQUILLANTE received the Ph.D. degree in computer science from the University of Washington, Seattle, WA, in 1990. He has been a **Research Staff Member** at the IBM Thomas J. Watson Research Center, Yorktown Heights, NY, since 1990, and an adjunct faculty member of the Department of Computer Science at Columbia University, New York, NY, since 1991. The summers of 1988 and 1989 were also spent at the T. J. Watson Research Center. From 1982 to 1985 he was a Member of the Technical Staff at Bell Telephone Laboratories, Murray Hill, NJ. His research interests concern the theory, analysis and design of computer systems, including mathematical modeling/analysis, scheduling, algorithms, and distributed and parallel systems. He is a member of ACM, IEEE, INFORMS and SIAM.

KENNETH STEIGLITZ received the B.E.E. (magna cum laude), M.E.E., and Eng.Sc.D. degrees from New York University, in 1959, 1960, and 1963, respectively. Since September 1963 he has been at Princeton University, where he is now **Professor** in the computer science department. His current research interests are computing with particles, economic simulation, and computer music. He is the author of *Introduction to Discrete Systems* (Wiley, 1974); coauthor, with C. H. Papadimitriou, of *Combinatorial Optimization* (Prentice-Hall, 1982); and author of *A DSP Primer* (Addison-Wesley, 1996).

A member of Eta Kappa Nu, Tau Beta Pi, and Sigma Xi, he was elected Fellow of the IEEE in 1981, received the Technical Achievement Award of the Signal Processing Society in 1981, their Society Award in 1986, and the IEEE Centennial Medal in 1984.

MIKLÓS TELEK was graduated at the Faculty of Electrical Engineering, Technical University of Budapest in 1987 and he received the candidate of science degree from the Hungarian Academy of Science in 1995. Since 1990 he has been with the Department of Communications, Technical University of Budapest, where he is **Assistant Professor** currently. In 1993 and 1994 he took part of the PHARE-ACCORD H-9112-353 European research project, in which he was working on modeling and analysis problems of B-ISDN/ATM communication network. In 1991 and 1993 he visited Andrea Bobbio at the University of Brescia and in 1995 he spent a semester at the University of North Carolina at Chapel Hill. His current research interests are in stochastic performance modeling and analysis of computer and communication systems.

MENG-LAI YIN received the M.S. degree in electrical engineering from National Cheng-Kung University in Taiwan, and the M.S. and **Ph.D.** degrees in computer science from The University of California, Irvine in 1983, 1989, and 1995, respectively. Since 1990, she has been with the **Hughes Aircraft Company** at Fullerton, where she is currently responsible for evaluation of the safety aspects of the Oceanic System Development and Support project. Her research interests include fault-tolerant computing, performability modeling, reliability modeling, and safety process.

GEORGE W. ZOBRIST received his BS and PhD in Electrical Engineering from the University of Missouri-Columbia in 1958 and 1965, respectively and his MSEE from the University of Wichita in 1961.

He has been employed by industry, government laboratories and various Universities during his career. He is presently **Chairman/Professor** of Computer Science at the University of Missouri-Rolla.

His current research interests include: Simulation, Computer Aided Analysis and Design, Software Engineering and Local Area Network Design. He is presently Editor of IEEE Potentials Magazine, VLSI Design and International Journal in Computer Simulation.

XIAODONG ZHANG is an **Associate Professor** of computer science and director of the High Performance and Computing and Software Laboratory at the University of Texas at San Antonio. His research interests are parallel and distributed computation, parallel architecture and system performance evaluation, and scientific computing. Zhang received his Ph.D. degree in Computer Science from the University of Colorado at Boulder in 1989. He is a senior member of the IEEE, and the current Chair of the Technical Committee on Supercomputing Applications, IEEE Computer Society.

Author Index

Subject Index